From **The Best of Bridge Cookbooks**

The Best
of The Best
and more

Written by The Best of Bridge Publishing Ltd.

Robert
ROSE

The Best of The Best and More
Recipes from The Best of Bridge Cookbooks

Disclaimer

The recipes in this book have been carefully tested by our kitchen and our tasters. To the best of our knowledge, they are safe and nutritious for ordinary use and users. For those people with food or other allergies, or who have special food requirements or health issues, please read the suggested contents of each recipe carefully and determine whether or not they may create a problem for you. All recipes are used at the risk of the consumer.

We cannot be responsible for any hazards, loss or damage that may occur as a result of any recipe use.

For those with special needs, allergies, requirements or health problems, in the event of any doubt, please contact your medical adviser prior to the use of any recipe.

Library and Archives Canada Cataloguing in Publication

The best of the best and more : from the Best of Bridge cookbooks / written by the Best of Bridge Publishing Ltd.

Includes index.
ISBN 978-0-7788-0299-0

1. Cooking. 2. Cookbooks. I. Best of Bridge Publishing Ltd

TX715.6.B48 2012   641.5   C2011-907192-4

Cover design by: KARO, Calgary, Alberta
Production by: PageWave Graphics Inc.

Photography by: Lisa Preston
Bilodeau Preston Photography
Calgary, Alberta

Published by Robert Rose Inc.
120 Eglinton Avenue East, Suite 800, Toronto, Ontario, Canada M4P 1E2
Tel: (416) 322-6552 Fax: (416) 322-6936
www.robertrose.ca

Printed in China

01 02 03 04 05 06 07 08 09 PPLS 20 19 18 17 16 15 14 13 12

FOREWARNING

ONCE UPON A TIME, A SENIOR BOOK EDITOR LOOKED AT "THE BEST OF BRIDGE", OUR FIRST COOKBOOK, AND SAID "THIS BOOK WILL HAVE A LIFE OF TWO DECADES". UNBELIEVABLE! SHE WAS RIGHT!! "THE BEST OF BRIDGE" (COMMONLY REFERRED TO AS "THE RED ONE") IS NOW 22 YEARS OLD AND HAS SOLD NEARLY 1,000,000 COPIES.

TODAY, ALL THE KIDS WHO WERE RAISED ON BEST OF BRIDGE RECIPES ARE COOKING FOR THEMSELVES AND ASKING FOR A COLLECTION OF THEIR FAVORITES. SO ARE THEIR PARENTS. OUR NEW CUSTOMERS WANT TO KNOW "WHICH BOOK DO I BUY FIRST?"

YOU'RE HOLDING THE ANSWER – A COLLECTION OF YOUR FAVORITE RECIPES FROM ALL SIX BEST OF BRIDGE COOKBOOKS. WE'VE UPDATED LOTS OF THE RECIPES TO INCLUDE MORE FRESH INGREDIENTS AND LOW-FAT SUBSTITUTIONS AND INCLUDED MORE OF OUR NEW FAVORITES COLLECTED OVER THE PAST 3 YEARS. THE JOKES ARE NEW AND THE RECIPES WORK!

"THE LADIES OF THE BRIDGE" PROMISE YOU SIMPLE RECIPES WITH GOURMET RESULTS. WE KNOW YOU'LL HAVE FUN IN THE KITCHEN WITH "THE BEST OF THE BEST AND MORE"!

TABLE OF CONTENTS

FRONT COVER RECIPE

ASPARAGUS VINAIGRETTE (PAGE 151)

MUFFINS

Jalapeño Corn Muffins
Phantom Rhubarb Muffins
Sunshine Muffins
Super Blueberry Lemon Muffins
Apple Bran Muffins
Banana Muffins
Cheddar Apple Muffins

BREADS

Best-Ever Banana Bread
"Land of Nod" Cinnamon Buns
Cranberry Scones
Flaky Freezer Biscuits
Yorkshire Pudding
Pita Toasts
Baguette Sticks

BRUNCHES

Relatively Low-Fat Granola
Swiss Apple Quiche
French Toast Raphael
Mediterranean Pie
Christmas Morning Wife Saver
Southwest Brunch Bake
Huevos Rancheros
Eggs Olé!
Weekend Spouse Saver
Stampede Casserole
Mexican Strata
Scotty's Nest Eggs
Vegetable Frittata

JALAPEÑO CORN MUFFINS

½ CUP	FLOUR	125 ML
1 TBSP.	BAKING POWDER	15 ML
½ TSP.	SALT	2 ML
1½ CUPS	YELLOW CORNMEAL	375 ML
2	EGGS	2
1 CUP	FAT-FREE SOUR CREAM	250 ML
1 CUP	GRATED LIGHT CHEDDAR CHEESE	250 ML
10 OZ.	CAN CREAMED CORN	284 G
¼ CUP	SEEDED & CHOPPED JALAPEÑO PEPPERS	60 ML
½ CUP	BUTTER OR MARGARINE, MELTED	125 ML

SIFT FLOUR, BAKING POWDER AND SALT TOGETHER.
ADD CORNMEAL, EGGS, SOUR CREAM, CHEESE, CREAMED
CORN, JALAPEÑO PEPPERS AND BUTTER; MIX WELL.
SPRAY MEDIUM MUFFIN TINS OR USE PAPER LINERS
AND FILL WITH MIXTURE. BAKE AT 450°F (230°F) FOR
15-20 MINUTES. MAKES ABOUT 18 MEDIUM MUFFINS.

HOW DO YOU EXPLAIN COUNTERCLOCKWISE TO A CHILD
WITH A DIGITAL WATCH?

PHANTOM RHUBARB MUFFINS

WHAT DO YOU MEAN THEY'RE GONE? – AGAIN?

RHUBARB MUFFINS

1/2 CUP	FAT-FREE SOUR CREAM	125 ML
1/4 CUP	VEGETABLE OIL	60 ML
1	LARGE EGG	1
1 1/3 CUPS	FLOUR	325 ML
1 CUP	DICED RHUBARB	250 ML
2/3 CUP	BROWN SUGAR	150 ML
1/2 TSP.	BAKING SODA	2 ML
1/4 TSP.	SALT	1 ML

BROWN SUGAR CINNAMON TOPPING

1/4 CUP	BROWN SUGAR	60 ML
1/4 CUP	CHOPPED PECANS	60 ML
1/2 TSP.	CINNAMON	2 ML
2 TSP.	MELTED BUTTER	10 ML

TO MAKE MUFFINS: BLEND TOGETHER SOUR CREAM, OIL AND EGG. SET ASIDE. IN ANOTHER BOWL, STIR REMAINING INGREDIENTS TOGETHER AND COMBINE WITH SOUR CREAM MIXTURE. MIX JUST UNTIL MOISTENED. FILL 12 LARGE MUFFIN CUPS 2/3 FULL.

TO MAKE TOPPING: COMBINE ALL INGREDIENTS AND SPOON ONTO EACH MUFFIN. BAKE AT 350°F (180°C) FOR 25-30 MINUTES.

IF YOU THINK YOU'RE TOO SMALL TO HAVE AN IMPACT, TRY GOING TO SLEEP WITH A MOSQUITO IN THE ROOM.

SUNSHINE MUFFINS

SO QUICK YOU WON'T BELIEVE IT!!

1	ORANGE	1
1/2 CUP	ORANGE JUICE	125 ML
1	EGG	1
1/4 CUP	OIL	60 ML
1 1/2 CUPS	FLOUR	375 ML
3/4 CUP	SUGAR	175 ML
1 TSP.	BAKING POWDER	5 ML
1 TSP.	BAKING SODA	5 ML
1 TSP.	SALT	5 ML
1/2 CUP	RAISINS (OPTIONAL)	125 ML
1/2 CUP	CHOPPED NUTS (OPTIONAL)	125 ML

CUT ORANGE INTO 8 PIECES. PUT CUT-UP ORANGE (THAT'S RIGHT - THE WHOLE ORANGE), ORANGE JUICE, EGG AND OIL IN BLENDER. BLEND UNTIL SMOOTH. ADD FLOUR, SUGAR, BAKING POWDER, BAKING SODA AND SALT. BLEND. ADD RAISINS AND NUTS. BLEND JUST UNTIL MIXED. POUR MIXTURE INTO MUFFIN TINS AND BAKE AT 375°F (190°C) FOR 15-20 MINUTES. MAKES 16 MEDIUM MUFFINS.

UPDATE: TRY THIS RECIPE WITH DRIED CRANBERRIES.

DID YOU HEAR ABOUT THE NEW GARLIC DIET? YOU DON'T ACTUALLY LOSE ANY WEIGHT, BUT YOU LOOK THINNER FROM A DISTANCE.

SUPER BLUEBERRY LEMON MUFFINS

THESE WILL DISAPPEAR AS QUICKLY AS YOU MAKE THEM!

BLUEBERRY LEMON MUFFINS

2 CUPS	FLOUR	500 ML
1/2 CUP	SUGAR	125 ML
1 TBSP.	BAKING POWDER	15 ML
1/2 TSP.	SALT	2 ML
	RIND OF 1 LEMON	
1	EGG	1
1 CUP	MILK	250 ML
1/2 CUP	BUTTER, MELTED	125 ML
1 CUP	FRESH OR FROZEN BLUEBERRIES	250 ML

LEMON BUTTER TOPPING

1/4 CUP	MELTED BUTTER	60 ML
2 TBSP.	LEMON JUICE	30 ML
1/2 CUP	SUGAR	125 ML

TO MAKE MUFFINS: MIX FLOUR, SUGAR, BAKING POWDER, SALT AND LEMON RIND IN LARGE BOWL. BEAT EGG IN MEDIUM BOWL; ADD MILK AND BUTTER. ADD EGG MIXTURE TO DRY INGREDIENTS. STIR UNTIL JUST MIXED (BATTER WILL BE LUMPY). STIR IN BLUEBERRIES. FILL MUFFIN PANS 2/3 FULL; BAKE AT 375°F (190°C) FOR 20 MINUTES.

TO MAKE TOPPING: COMBINE MELTED BUTTER AND LEMON JUICE. MEASURE SUGAR IN SEPARATE DISH. DUNK TOPS OF SLIGHTLY COOLED MUFFINS INTO LEMON BUTTER AND THEN SUGAR. MAKES 16 MEDIUM MUFFINS.

APPLE BRAN MUFFINS

A SPICY VARIATION OF AN OLD FAVORITE. KEEP THE BATTER IN THE REFRIGERATOR SO YOU CAN BAKE FRESH MUFFINS DURING THE WEEK.

4 CUPS	FLOUR	1 L
3 CUPS	NATURAL BRAN	750 ML
2 TSP.	BAKING POWDER	10 ML
2 TSP.	BAKING SODA	10 ML
2 TSP.	CINNAMON	10 ML
1 TSP.	SALT	5 ML
1/4-1/2 TSP.	NUTMEG	1-2 ML
1 CUP	PACKED BROWN SUGAR	250 ML
3/4 CUP	MARGARINE, ROOM TEMPERATURE	175 ML
3	EGGS	3
14 OZ.	JAR UNSWEETENED APPLESAUCE	398 ML
1 1/2 CUPS	BUTTERMILK	375 ML
1/2 CUP	MOLASSES	125 ML
1 CUP	RAISINS	250 ML
1	MEDIUM APPLE, PEELED, CORED & CHOPPED	1

STIR TOGETHER FLOUR, BRAN, BAKING POWDER, BAKING SODA, CINNAMON, SALT AND NUTMEG. IN SEPARATE BOWL, CREAM TOGETHER SUGAR AND MARGARINE. BEAT IN EGGS 1 AT A TIME UNTIL FLUFFY. STIR IN APPLESAUCE, BUTTERMILK, MOLASSES, RAISINS AND APPLE. ADD TO FLOUR MIXTURE AND STIR JUST UNTIL DRY INGREDIENTS ARE MOISTENED (BATTER SHOULD STILL BE LUMPY). STORE IN COVERED CONTAINER IN THE REFRIGERATOR FOR UP TO 5 DAYS. TO BAKE, PREHEAT OVEN TO 375°F (190°C) SPOON BATTER

APPLE BRAN MUFFINS

CONTINUED FROM PAGE 12.

INTO GREASED OR PAPER-LINED MUFFIN CUPS. BAKE 15-20 MINUTES, UNTIL TOOTHPICK INSERTED INTO CENTER OF MUFFIN COMES OUT CLEAN. MAKES 30 LARGE MUFFINS.

BANANA MUFFINS

ANOTHER RECIPE FOR ALL THOSE OVERRIPE BANANAS. VERY MOIST. GREAT FOR THE LUNCH BOX!

1/2 CUP	BUTTER OR MARGARINE	125 ML
1 CUP	SUGAR	250 ML
2	EGGS	2
1 CUP	MASHED RIPE BANANAS	250 ML
1 1/2 CUPS	FLOUR	375 ML
1 TSP.	NUTMEG	5 ML
1 TSP.	BAKING SODA	5 ML
2 TSP.	HOT WATER	10 ML
1 TSP.	VANILLA	5 ML

CREAM BUTTER AND SUGAR. ADD EGGS AND BANANAS. MIX WELL. STIR IN FLOUR AND NUTMEG. DISSOLVE SODA IN HOT WATER, ADD TO BANANA MIXTURE. STIR IN VANILLA. FILL GREASED MUFFIN TINS 1/2 FULL. BAKE AT 350°F (180°C) FOR ABOUT 20 MINUTES, OR UNTIL GOLDEN BROWN. MAKES 24 MEDIUM MUFFINS.

CHEDDAR APPLE MUFFINS

AN AWARD WINNER!

3 CUPS	FLOUR	750 ML
2/3 CUP	SUGAR	150 ML
4 TSP.	BAKING POWDER	20 ML
1 TSP.	SALT	5 ML
1 TSP.	CINNAMON	5 ML
2 CUPS	GRATED CHEDDAR CHEESE	500 ML
2	EGGS	2
1 CUP	APPLE JUICE	250 ML
1/2 CUP	BUTTER OR MARGARINE, MELTED	125 ML
2 CUPS	PEELED, FINELY CHOPPED APPLES	500 ML

PREHEAT OVEN TO 375°F (190°C). COMBINE FLOUR, SUGAR, BAKING POWDER, SALT AND CINNAMON IN LARGE BOWL. MIX IN CHEESE. BEAT EGGS IN MEDIUM BOWL. ADD APPLE JUICE; STIR IN BUTTER AND APPLE. ADD ALL AT ONCE TO FLOUR MIXTURE. STIR JUST UNTIL MOISTENED. FILL GREASED MUFFIN TINS. BAKE FOR 25-30 MINUTES. MAKES 2 DOZEN MEDIUM MUFFINS.

THE ONLY THING WRONG WITH DOING NOTHING IS THAT YOU NEVER KNOW WHEN YOU'RE FINISHED.

BEST-EVER BANANA BREAD

1 CUP	BUTTER	250 ML
2 CUPS	SUGAR	500 ML
2½ CUPS	MASHED RIPE BANANAS	625 ML
	(5 BANANAS)	
4	EGGS, WELL BEATEN	4
2½ CUPS	FLOUR	625 ML
2 TSP.	BAKING SODA	10 ML
1 TSP.	SALT	5 ML
1 TSP.	NUTMEG	5 ML

PREHEAT OVEN TO 350°F (180°C). CREAM BUTTER AND SUGAR UNTIL LIGHT AND FLUFFY. ADD BANANAS AND EGGS AND BEAT UNTIL WELL MIXED. MIX DRY INGREDIENTS AND BLEND WITH BANANA MIXTURE, BUT DO NOT OVERMIX. POUR INTO 2 LIGHTLY GREASED LOAF PANS OR A BUNDT PAN. BAKE 55 MINUTES TO 1 HOUR; TEST FOR DONENESS (TOOTHPICK INSERTED IN MIDDLE COMES OUT CLEAN) AND COOL ON RACK FOR 10 MINUTES BEFORE REMOVING FROM PANS. FREEZES BEAUTIFULLY.

HINT: FREEZE OVERRIPE BANANAS IN THEIR SKINS IN A PLASTIC BAG.

THE DIFFERENCE BETWEEN A TAX COLLECTOR AND A TAXIDERMIST IS THE TAXIDERMIST LEAVES THE HIDE.

"LAND OF NOD" CINNAMON BUNS

WHO WOULD THINK YOU COULD BE THIS ORGANIZED SO EARLY IN THE A.M.!!

20	FROZEN DOUGH ROLLS	20
1 CUP	BROWN SUGAR	250 ML
1/4 CUP	VANILLA INSTANT PUDDING	60 ML
1-2 TBSP.	CINNAMON	15-30 ML
3/4 CUP	RAISINS (OPTIONAL)	175 ML
1/4-1/2 CUP	MELTED BUTTER	60-125 ML

BEFORE YOU PUT THE CAT OUT AND TURN OFF THE LIGHTS, GREASE A 10" (25 CM) BUNDT PAN AND ADD FROZEN ROLLS. SPRINKLE WITH BROWN SUGAR, PUDDING POWDER, CINNAMON AND RAISINS. POUR MELTED BUTTER OVER ALL. COVER WITH A CLEAN, DAMP CLOTH. (LEAVE OUT AT ROOM TEMPERATURE) TURN OUT THE LIGHTS AND SAY GOODNIGHT!

IN THE MORNING, PREHEAT OVEN TO 350°F (180°C) AND BAKE FOR 25 MINUTES. LET SIT FOR 5 MINUTES AND THEN TURN OUT ON A SERVING PLATE. NOW, AREN'T YOU CLEVER?

GAS PRICES ARE SO HIGH I ASKED FOR TWO DOLLARS WORTH AND THE ATTENDANT SPRAYED A LITTLE BEHIND MY EAR.

CRANBERRY SCONES

³/₄ CUP	BUTTERMILK OR PLAIN YOGURT	175 ML
I	EGG	I
2³/₄ CUPS	FLOUR	675 ML
4 TSP.	BAKING POWDER	20 ML
¹/₂ TSP.	BAKING SODA	2 ML
¹/₂ TSP.	SALT	2 ML
¹/₂ CUP	BUTTER OR MARGARINE	125 ML
I CUP	COARSELY CHOPPED CRANBERRIES (FRESH OR FROZEN)	250 ML
¹/₂ CUP	SUGAR	125 ML
	RIND OF I ORANGE	
I TBSP.	BUTTER, MELTED	15 ML
¹/₄ CUP	ICING SUGAR	60 ML

PREHEAT OVEN TO 375°F (190°C). BEAT BUTTERMILK AND EGG IN SMALL BOWL AND SET ASIDE. IN LARGE BOWL, MEASURE FLOUR, BAKING POWDER, BAKING SODA AND SALT. CUT IN BUTTER UNTIL MIXTURE RESEMBLES SMALL PEAS. MIX IN CRANBERRIES, SUGAR AND ORANGE RIND. ADD BUTTERMILK MIXTURE AND STIR UNTIL SOFT DOUGH FORMS. USING YOUR HANDS, FORM DOUGH INTO A LARGE BALL AND PLACE ON FLOURED SURFACE. PAT OUT TO I" (2.5 CM) THICKNESS. CUT IN 4" (10 CM) ROUNDS. PLACE ON UNGREASED COOKIE SHEET AND BAKE SCONES FOR 15-20 MINUTES. WHILE STILL WARM, BRUSH WITH BUTTER AND SPRINKLE WITH ICING SUGAR. MAKES 8 LARGE SCONES.

WHY DO WE CALL IT A TV SET WHEN YOU GET ONLY ONE?

FLAKY FREEZER BISCUITS

THESE WONDERFUL BISCUITS CAN BE BAKED IMMEDIATELY OR FROZEN AND BAKED AS NEEDED.

1 TBSP.	YEAST (1 PKG.)	15 ML
2 TBSP.	SUGAR	30 ML
1/4 CUP	WARM WATER	60 ML
5 CUPS	FLOUR	1.25 L
3 TBSP.	SUGAR	45 ML
1 TBSP.	BAKING POWDER	15 ML
1 TSP.	BAKING SODA	5 ML
1 TSP.	SALT	5 ML
1 CUP	BUTTER OR MARGARINE	250 ML
2 CUPS	BUTTERMILK	500 ML

IN A SMALL BOWL COMBINE YEAST AND SUGAR IN WATER. SET ASIDE FOR 10 MINUTES. IN A LARGE BOWL MIX FLOUR, SUGAR, BAKING POWDER, SODA AND SALT. CUT IN BUTTER TO FORM A CRUMBLY MIXTURE. STIR IN YEAST MIXTURE AND BUTTERMILK. MIX JUST ENOUGH TO HOLD DOUGH TOGETHER. ROLL DOUGH 3/4" (2 CM) THICK ON FLOURED SURFACE. CUT OUT BISCUITS WITH THE TOP OF A GLASS OR A CUTTER. PRICK TOPS WITH FORK. FREEZE SEPARATELY ON COOKIE SHEET. AFTER BISCUITS ARE FROZEN, STACK AND WRAP WELL. BEFORE BAKING THAW AND LET RISE UNTIL DOUBLED IN SIZE (ABOUT 30 MINUTES). BAKE AT 425°F (220°C) FOR 10 MINUTES ON A LIGHTLY GREASED COOKIE SHEET. MAKES 3-4 DOZEN.

ALTERNATIVE: GRATED CHEDDAR CHEESE MAY BE ADDED TO SOFT DOUGH FOR FLAKY CHEESE BISCUITS.

YORKSHIRE PUDDING

A FAVORITE WITH ROAST BEEF DINNER! MAKE WHILE ROAST IS RESTING. (WHICH IS MORE THAN YOU GET TO DO!)

1 CUP	FLOUR	250 ML
1/2 TSP.	SALT	2 ML
1/2 CUP	MILK	125 ML
2	EGGS, BEATEN	2
1/2 CUP	WATER	125 ML
	MELTED BUTTER OR OIL	

IN A BLENDER MIX FLOUR, SALT, MILK, EGGS AND WATER. BLEND WELL AND LEAVE AT ROOM TEMPERATURE FOR 1 HOUR. EVERYTIME YOU WALK BY – GIVE IT A WHIRL! WHEN ROAST IS DONE, REMOVE FROM OVEN AND COVER WITH FOIL TO KEEP WARM. PREHEAT OVEN TO 400°F (200°C). POUR 1 TBSP. (15 ML) BEEF DRIPPINGS, MELTED BUTTER OR OIL INTO 8 MEDIUM MUFFIN TINS. PLACE IN OVEN UNTIL BUBBLING HOT. (WATCH CLOSELY BECAUSE YOU DON'T WANT THE BUTTER TO BURN.) REMOVE FROM OVEN AND POUR BATTER INTO HOT BUTTER. BAKE AT 400°F (200°C) FOR 20 MINUTES AND THEN AT 350°F (180°C). FOR 10 MINUTES LONGER. YORKSHIRE WILL PUFF UP AND BE HOLLOW INSIDE. SERVE IMMEDIATELY WITH GRAVY.

THE WAR BETWEEN THE SEXES WILL NEVER BE WON. THERE IS TOO MUCH FRATERNIZING WITH THE ENEMY.

PITA TOASTS

3/4 CUP	BUTTER	175 ML
2 TBSP.	FINELY CHOPPED FRESH PARSLEY	30 ML
1 TBSP.	CHOPPED CHIVES	15 ML
1 TBSP.	LEMON JUICE	15 ML
1	LARGE GARLIC CLOVE, MINCED	1
6	PITA ROUNDS	6

PREHEAT OVEN TO 450°F (230°C). CREAM TOGETHER
FIRST 5 INGREDIENTS, COVER; SET ASIDE FOR AT
LEAST 1 HOUR. CUT PITA ROUNDS INTO 4 WEDGES AND
SEPARATE LAYERS. SPREAD EACH PIECE WITH SOME OF
THE BUTTER MIXTURE. ARRANGE ON A LARGE BAKING
SHEET IN 1 LAYER. BAKE FOR 5 MINUTES, UNTIL
LIGHTLY BROWNED AND CRISP. MAKES 48 TOASTS.
SERVE WITH YOUR FAVORITE DIPS OR IN PLACE
OF GARLIC TOAST OR ROLLS.

BAGUETTE STICKS

GREAT SERVED WITH PASTA OR A STEAMING BOWL
OF SOUP.

1	BAGUETTE	1
1/2 CUP	BUTTER, SOFTENED	125 ML
3 TBSP.	PARMESAN CHEESE	45 ML
2	LARGE GARLIC CLOVES, MINCED	2
1/4 CUP	CHOPPED FRESH PARSLEY	60 ML

CUT BAGUETTE INTO THIRDS. CUT EACH PIECE INTO
4 BREADSTICKS. MIX REMAINING INGREDIENTS AND
SPREAD ON STICKS. BROIL UNTIL BROWNED. MAKES
12 STICKS. PICTURED OPPOSITE PAGE 144.

RELATIVELY LOW-FAT GRANOLA

EXCELLENT SERVED OVER YOGURT - OR JUST FOR NIBBLIES.

4 CUPS	LARGE FLAKE OATMEAL	1 L
1 CUP	SLICED ALMONDS	250 ML
1/2 CUP	SUNFLOWER SEEDS	125 ML
1/2 CUP	WHEAT GERM	125 ML
1/2 TSP.	CINNAMON	2 ML
1/2 CUP	BROWN SUGAR	125 ML
1/3 CUP	HONEY	75 ML
	RIND & JUICE OF 1 LEMON	
	RIND & JUICE OF 1 ORANGE	
2 CUPS	FINELY CHOPPED DRIED FRUIT	500 ML
	(CRANBERRIES, APRICOTS, PEACHES,	
	BANANA CHIPS, APPLES)	

IN A LARGE BOWL, COMBINE OATMEAL, ALMONDS, SUNFLOWER SEEDS, WHEAT GERM AND CINNAMON. IN A SAUCEPAN, COMBINE BROWN SUGAR AND HONEY AND BRING TO BOIL. REMOVE FROM HEAT AND ADD LEMON AND ORANGE RIND AND JUICE. TOSS LIQUID MIXTURE WITH DRY MIXTURE. SPRAY A LARGE, EDGED BAKING SHEET WITH COOKING SPRAY. SPREAD WITH GRANOLA AND BAKE AT 300°F (150°C) FOR 30 MINUTES, STIRRING EVERY 10 MINUTES, UNTIL GOLDEN BROWN. COOL. ADD DRIED FRUIT AND STORE IN AIRTIGHT CONTAINER. MAKES ABOUT 7 CUPS (1.75 L).

A BRAIN IS A WONDERFUL ORGAN; IT STARTS THE MOMENT YOU GET UP AND DOESN'T STOP UNTIL YOU GET TO THE OFFICE.

SWISS APPLE QUICHE

FULL MARKS! YOU CAN TAKE THIS ONE TO THE BANK. MAKES 2 QUICHES.

PASTRY SHELLS

1 CUP	FLOUR	250 ML
1/2 CUP	WHOLE-WHEAT FLOUR	125 ML
1 1/2 TSP.	SUGAR	7 ML
1/2 CUP	BUTTER	125 ML
1	EGG YOLK	1
3 TBSP.	ICE WATER	45 ML

FILLING

3	MEDIUM TART GREEN APPLES, PEELED & FINELY CHOPPED	3
8	GREEN ONIONS, THINLY SLICED	8
1/4 TSP.	NUTMEG	1 ML
1/2 TSP.	CURRY POWDER	2 ML
2 TBSP.	BUTTER	30 ML
4 CUPS	GRATED GRUYÈRE CHEESE	1 L
1 CUP	WHIPPING CREAM	250 ML
4	EGGS LIGHTLY BEATEN	4
1/2 CUP	DRY VERMOUTH OR DRY WHITE WINE	125 ML
1/4 TSP.	COARSELY GROUND PEPPER	1 ML

PASTRY SHELLS: SIFT TOGETHER THE FLOURS AND SUGAR, CUT IN THE BUTTER UNTIL MIXTURE RESEMBLES COARSE MEAL. BEAT EGG YOLK WITH ICE WATER AND STIR INTO FLOUR MIXTURE UNTIL DOUGH IS FORMED, ADDING ADDITIONAL WATER, 1 TSP. (5 ML) AT A TIME, IF NEEDED. FORM DOUGH INTO 2 BALLS AND FLATTEN SLIGHTLY. WRAP IN WAXED PAPER AND CHILL FOR 1 HOUR.

SWISS APPLE QUICHE

CONTINUED FROM PAGE 22.

PREHEAT OVEN TO 425°F (220°C). ROLL OUT DOUGH ON FLOURED SURFACE. PLACE IN 2, 9" (23 CM) PIE PLATES OR QUICHE PANS AND CRIMP EDGES. PRICK BOTTOMS LIGHTLY WITH A FORK AND BAKE ON LOWER RACK OF OVEN FOR 15 MINUTES. CHECK AND COVER EDGES WITH FOIL IF TOO BROWN. RETURN TO OVEN AND BAKE AN ADDITIONAL 5 MINUTES. REMOVE FROM OVEN AND COOL.

FILLING: PREHEAT OVEN TO 375°F (190°C). COMBINE APPLES, GREEN ONIONS, NUTMEG AND CURRY. SAUTÉ IN BUTTER FOR 3-5 MINUTES, OR JUST UNTIL SOFT. COOL. SPOON INTO COOLED PIE SHELLS AND TOP WITH GRATED CHEESE. COMBINE CREAM, EGGS, VERMOUTH AND PEPPER. POUR SLOWLY OVER CHEESE. REDUCE HEAT TO 350°F (180°C). BAKE QUICHES ON MIDDLE RACK FOR 35-45 MINUTES, OR UNTIL FIRM AND GOLDEN. WATCH THAT PASTRY EDGES DON'T GET TOO BROWN. COVER IF NECESSARY. REMOVE FROM OVEN AND COOL ON A RACK FOR 15 MINUTES. EACH QUICHE SERVES 8.

TOO BAD THAT ALL THE PEOPLE WHO KNOW HOW TO RUN THE COUNTRY ARE BUSY DRIVING TAXICABS AND CUTTING HAIR.

FRENCH TOAST RAPHAEL

A GREAT BRUNCH DISH TO BE PREPARED THE NIGHT BEFORE!

6 CUPS	WHITE BREAD, CRUSTS REMOVED CUT INTO 1" (2.5 CM) CUBES	1.5 L
6 OZ.	CREAM CHEESE, CUT INTO SMALL CUBES	170 G
6	EGGS, WELL-BEATEN	6
1 CUP	MILK	250 ML
1/2 TSP.	CINNAMON	2 ML
1/3 CUP	DARK MAPLE SYRUP	75 ML

PLACE HALF THE BREAD IN A GREASED 8" (20 CM) SQUARE PAN. DOT CHEESE ON TOP. COVER WITH REMAINING BREAD. COMBINE REMAINING INGREDIENTS AND POUR OVER ALL. COVER WITH PLASTIC WRAP AND REFRIGERATE OVERNIGHT. IN THE MORNING, REMOVE PLASTIC AND BAKE IN PREHEATED 375°F (190°C) OVEN FOR 45 MINUTES. IT WILL BE PUFFY AND GOLDEN. SERVE IMMEDIATELY WITH EXTRA MAPLE SYRUP AND CRISP BACON. SERVES 6.

IF BANKERS CAN COUNT, WHY DO THEY HAVE EIGHT WINDOWS AND FOUR TELLERS?

MEDITERRANEAN PIE

IMPRESSIVE, EASY TO MAKE & TASTES TERRIFIC!

2	SMALL ONIONS, CHOPPED	2
2	GARLIC CLOVES, MINCED	2
2 TBSP.	BUTTER OR MARGARINE	30 ML
3	10 OZ. (283 G) PKGS. FROZEN SPINACH, THAWED & SQUEEZED DRY	3
2	14 OZ. (397 G) PKGS. FROZEN PUFF PASTRY, ROLLED TO 1/8" (3 MM)	2
3/4 LB.	BLACK FOREST HAM, SLICED	365 G
1 LB.	MOZZARELLA CHEESE, GRATED	500 G
2	RED PEPPERS, SEEDED & DICED	2
8	EGGS, BEATEN	8
1	EGG, BEATEN	1

SAUTÉ ONIONS AND GARLIC IN BUTTER. STIR IN SPINACH. LINE A 10" (25 CM) SPRINGFORM PAN WITH PASTRY, MAKING SURE IT OVERLAPS THE SIDES. LAYER 1/2 THE HAM, 1/2 THE CHEESE, 1/2 THE RED PEPPER, 1/2 THE SPINACH MIXTURE INTO THE PIE SHELL. POUR IN 1/2 THE BEATEN EGGS. REPEAT ALL LAYERS, PAN WILL BE FULL. COVER WITH PASTRY AND PINCH THE EDGES TO SEAL. TRIM EXCESS PASTRY AND SLASH THE TOP TO ALLOW STEAM TO ESCAPE. BRUSH TOP CRUST WITH BEATEN EGG. BAKE AT 400°F (200°C) FOR 15 MINUTES, REDUCE HEAT TO 350°F (180°C) AND BAKE FOR 45 MINUTES. IF THE CRUST BECOMES TOO BROWN, COVER LIGHTLY (DON'T SEAL) WITH FOIL. COOL THE PIE FOR 15 MINUTES AND REMOVE SPRINGFORM. THIS IS A SURE-FIRE HIT! SERVES 10.

CHRISTMAS MORNING WIFE SAVER

A CANADIAN TRADITION - DON'T WAIT FOR CHRISTMAS! MAKE BREAKFAST THE NIGHT BEFORE AND ENJOY YOUR MORNING.

16	SLICES WHITE BREAD, CRUSTS REMOVED	16
	SLICES OF CANADIAN BACK BACON	
	OR HAM	
	SLICES OF SHARP CHEDDAR CHEESE	
6	EGGS	6
1/2 TSP.	PEPPER	2 ML
1/2-1 TSP.	DRY MUSTARD	2-5 ML
1/4 CUP	MINCED ONION	60 ML
1/4 CUP	FINELY CHOPPED GREEN PEPPER	60 ML
1-2 TSP.	WORCESTERSHIRE SAUCE	5-10 ML
3 CUPS	MILK	750 ML
	DASH TABASCO	
1/2 CUP	BUTTER	125 ML
	SPECIAL "K" OR CRUSHED CORNFLAKES	

PUT 8 PIECES OF BREAD IN A 9 X 13" (23 X 33 CM) BUTTERED GLASS BAKING DISH. ADD PIECES TO COVER DISH ENTIRELY. COVER BREAD WITH THINLY SLICED BACON. TOP WITH SLICES OF CHEDDAR CHEESE. COVER WITH SLICES OF BREAD. IN A BOWL, BEAT EGGS AND PEPPER. ADD MUSTARD, ONION, GREEN PEPPER, WORCESTERSHIRE, MILK AND TABASCO. POUR OVER BREAD, COVER AND REFRIGERATE OVERNIGHT. IN THE MORNING, MELT BUTTER AND POUR OVER TOP. COVER WITH CRUSHED SPECIAL "K" OR CORNFLAKES. BAKE AT 350°F (180°C) UNCOVERED, 1 HOUR. LET SIT 10 MINUTES BEFORE SERVING. SERVE WITH FRESH FRUIT AND "LAND OF NOD" CINNAMON BUNS (PAGE 16). SERVES 8.

4 CUPS	FROZEN SHREDDED-STYLE HASH BROWN POTATOES	1 L
15 OZ.	CAN BLACK BEANS, RINSED & DRAINED	425 ML
1 CUP	FROZEN WHOLE KERNEL CORN	250 ML
1	RED PEPPER, CHOPPED	1
1/2 CUP	CHOPPED ONION	125 ML
2 CUPS	SHREDDED MONTEREY JACK CHEESE	500 ML
2 TBSP.	CHOPPED FRESH CILANTRO	30 ML
8	EGGS	8
1 1/4 CUPS	MILK	300 ML
1/2 TSP.	SALT	2 ML
1/4 TSP.	CAYENNE PEPPER	1 ML

SPRAY 7 X 11" (18 X 28 CM) BAKING DISH WITH COOKING SPRAY. MIX POTATOES, BEANS, CORN, RED PEPPER AND ONION IN BAKING DISH. SPRINKLE WITH CHEESE AND CILANTRO. BEAT EGGS, MILK, SALT AND CAYENNE PEPPER UNTIL WELL BLENDED. POUR EVENLY OVER POTATO MIXTURE. COVER AND REFRIGERATE AT LEAST 2 HOURS BUT NO LONGER THAN 24 HOURS. HEAT OVEN TO 350°F (180°C) AND BAKE, UNCOVERED, 55-60 MINUTES, OR UNTIL KNIFE INSERTED IN CENTER COMES OUT CLEAN. LET STAND 5 MINUTES BEFORE CUTTING. SERVES 6-8. SERVE WITH SLICED FRESH TOMATOES OR SALSA AND JALAPEÑO CORN MUFFINS (PAGE 8).

POACHED EGGS - SOUTHWESTERN STYLE

CHILI SAUCE

2 TBSP.	VEGETABLE OIL	30 ML
I CUP	FINELY CHOPPED ONION	250 ML
I CUP	FINELY CHOPPED RED OR ANAHEIM PEPPER	250 ML
2	GARLIC CLOVES, MINCED	2
28 OZ.	CAN CHOPPED TOMATOES	796 ML
I TSP.	SUGAR	5 ML
	SALT & PEPPER TO TASTE	
1/4 TSP.	CRUSHED HOT PEPPER FLAKES (OPTIONAL)	I ML
I CUP	GRATED CHEDDAR CHEESE	250 ML
4	8" (20 CM) FLOUR OR CORN TORTILLAS	4
8	EGGS (FOR POACHING)	8

GARNISH:

SALSA, SOUR CREAM, GRATED CHEDDAR, GUACAMOLE, CANNED BLACK BEANS, RINSED & DRAINED

TO PREPARE SAUCE: IN A DEEP FRYING PAN, HEAT OIL; SAUTÉ ONION, PEPPER AND GARLIC UNTIL SOFT. ADD TOMATOES AND SEASONINGS; SIMMER 20 MINUTES. ADD CHEESE; HEAT AND STIR UNTIL MELTED AND WELL BLENDED.

WRAP TORTILLAS IN FOIL AND HEAT IN OVEN. HEAT BEANS.

TO POACH EGGS: BREAK EGGS INTO BUBBLING SAUCE AND POACH 3-5 MINUTES TO DESIRED DONENESS. PLACE EGGS AND CHILI SAUCE ON TORTILLAS AND PASS THE GARNISHES. SERVES 4.

EGGS OLÉ!

EASY, COLORFUL AND OF COURSE, DELICIOUS!

12	EGGS	12
1/4 CUP	WATER	60 ML
	SALT & PEPPER TO TASTE	
3 TBSP.	BUTTER – AND THEN	45 ML
3 TBSP.	BUTTER	45 ML
1 CUP	SLICED MUSHROOMS	250 ML
1/2 CUP	CHOPPED GREEN ONION	125 ML
1/2 CUP	COARSELY CHOPPED GREEN PEPPER	125 ML
1/2 CUP	COARSELY CHOPPED RED PEPPER (NOTHING'S TOO GOOD FOR YOUR GUESTS)	125 ML
1/2 CUP	COARSELY CHOPPED ZUCCHINI	125 ML
1/2 CUP	COARSELY CHOPPED TOMATOES	125 ML
1/4 CUP	GREEN CHILIES (OPTIONAL)	60 ML
	SALT AND PEPPER TO TASTE (AGAIN)	
1/2 LB.	MONTEREY JACK CHEESE, GRATED	250 G
	SALSA, MILD OR HOT	

BEAT EGGS AND WATER TOGETHER. SEASON WITH SALT AND PEPPER. MELT THE FIRST BUTTER IN FRYING PAN AND ADD EGG MIXTURE. SCRAMBLE JUST UNTIL MOIST. PLACE IN LARGE OVENPROOF DISH; KEEP WARM IN 150°F (65°C) OVEN. MELT THE OTHER BUTTER IN FRYING PAN; SAUTÉ ALL VEGGIES TILL TENDER. SEASON WITH SALT AND PEPPER. SPOON OVER EGGS, SPRINKLE WITH GRATED CHEESE AND BAKE AT 300°F (150°C) OVEN UNTIL CHEESE MELTS. SERVE WITH LOTS OF SALSA. GOOD FOR 6. CARAMBA!

HAVE THE SEÑOR MAKE THIS MEXICAN MARVEL — THE NEXT BRUNCH FAVORITE.

3-4 OZ.	CANS MILD GREEN CHILIES, CHOPPED	3-115 G
6	CORN TORTILLAS, IN 1" (2.5 CM) STRIPS	6
2 LBS.	HOT ITALIAN SAUSAGE, CASING REMOVED, COOKED, DRAINED	1 KG
2½ CUPS	GRATED MONTEREY JACK CHEESE	625 ML
½ CUP	MILK	125 ML
8	EGGS	8
½ TSP.	SALT	2 ML
½ TSP.	GARLIC SALT	2 ML
½ TSP.	ONION SALT	2 ML
½ TSP.	CUMIN	2 ML
½ TSP.	FRESHLY GROUND PEPPER	2 ML
	PAPRIKA TO SPRINKLE	
2	LARGE RIPE TOMATOES, SLICED	2
	SALSA & SOUR CREAM FOR CONDIMENTS	

THE NIGHT BEFORE, GREASE A 9 X 13" (23 X 33 CM) CASSEROLE; LAYER ½ THE CHILIES, ½ THE CORN TORTILLAS, ½ THE COOKED SAUSAGE, AND ½ THE CHEESE. REPEAT LAYERS. IN A MEDIUM BOWL, BEAT MILK, EGGS, SALT, GARLIC SALT, ONION SALT, CUMIN AND PEPPER. POUR OVER CASSEROLE INGREDIENTS. SPRINKLE WITH PAPRIKA. COVER WITH PLASTIC WRAP AND REFRIGERATE OVERNIGHT. HOORAY — IT'S THE FOLLOWING DAY, AND YOU'RE READY! PREHEAT OVEN TO 350°F (180°C). PLACE TOMATOES OVER

WEEKEND SPOUSE SAVER

CONTINUED FROM PAGE 30.

TOP OF CASSEROLE. BAKE 1 HOUR, OR UNTIL SET IN CENTER AND SLIGHTLY BROWNED AT EDGES. LET SIT 5 MINUTES BEFORE SERVING. PASS THE SALSA AND SOUR CREAM. SERVE WITH A TRAY OF SLICED FRESH FRUIT. MAGNIFICO! SERVES 10.

STAMPEDE CASSEROLE

ROUND UP THE COWPOKES - THIS BRUNCH IS A MUST. IT'S EASY TO DO - BUT THEY'LL THINK YOU'VE FUSSED!

1½ LBS.	BULK PORK SAUSAGE	750 G
3-4 OZ.	CANS GREEN CHILIES, DRAINED	3-115 G
1 LB.	CHEDDAR CHEESE, GRATED	500 G
1 LB.	MONTEREY JACK CHEESE, GRATED	500 G
9	EGGS, BEATEN	9
1 CUP	MILK	250 ML
2 TBSP.	FLOUR	30 ML
	PAPRIKA	

BROWN SAUSAGE AND DRAIN WELL. SPLIT CHILIES AND REMOVE SEEDS. SAVE 1/3 OF THE CHILIES AND CUT IN THIN STRIPS. LAYER SAUSAGE WITH CHEESES AND REMAINING 2/3 OF CHILIES IN A GREASED 9 X 13" (23 X 33 CM) GLASS BAKING DISH. BEAT EGGS, MILK AND FLOUR TOGETHER UNTIL WELL-BLENDED. POUR OVER LAYERED MIXTURE. DECORATE TOP WITH STRIPS OF CHILIES IN A LATTICE-WORK PATTERN. SPRINKLE WITH PAPRIKA AND BAKE AT 350°F (180°C) FOR 45 MINUTES. SERVES 12.

OLÉ! – ANOTHER WIFE-SAVER AND A GREAT
MAKE AHEAD!

16	SLICES WHITE BREAD, TRIMMED	16
4	LARGE RIPE TOMATOES, SLICED	4
1	MEDIUM ONION, SLICED & SEPARATED	1
2-4 OZ.	CANS CHOPPED GREEN CHILIES, DRAINED	2-113 G
1½ CUPS	GRATED CHEDDAR OR MONTEREY JACK CHEESE	375 ML
7	EGGS	7
3½ CUPS	MILK	875 ML
½ TSP.	SALT	2 ML
½ TSP.	GARLIC SALT	2 ML
½ TSP.	GROUND CUMIN	2 ML
½ TSP.	CHILI POWDER	2 ML

PLACE 8 SLICES OF BREAD IN BOTTOM OF BUTTERED
9 X 13" (23 X 33 CM) PAN. ARRANGE TOMATO SLICES,
ONION RINGS AND GREEN CHILIES OVER BREAD.
SPRINKLE 2/3 OF THE CHEESE OVER ALL. TOP WITH
REMAINING SLICES OF BREAD. BEAT EGGS, MILK
AND SEASONINGS, POUR OVER BREAD (LIQUID SHOULD
COME TO TOP OF PAN). IF MORE LIQUID IS NEEDED,
ADD MIXTURE OF 1 EGG AND ½ CUP (125 ML) MILK.
SPRINKLE REMAINING CHEESE OVER TOP. COVER
WITH FOIL AND REFRIGERATE OVERNIGHT. REMOVE
FROM REFRIGERATOR 1 HOUR BEFORE BAKING FOR
A LIGHTER AND FLUFFIER DISH. PREHEAT OVEN
TO 350°F (180°C). BAKE, UNCOVERED, FOR 1 TO
1½ HOURS, OR UNTIL KNIFE INSERTED IN CENTER

MEXICAN STRATA

CONTINUED FROM PAGE 32.

COMES OUT CLEAN. ALLOW TO STAND 5 MINUTES BEFORE SERVING. SERVE WITH PICANTE SALSA OR PICALILLI. SERVES 8.

WHY DO PSYCHICS HAVE TO ASK YOUR NAME?

SCOTTY'S NEST EGGS

ONE OF OUR FAVORITE BACHELORS LOVES TO WHIP THIS UP. - UPDATE - SCOTTY IS NOW MARRIED AND WE THINK THIS RECIPE DID IT!

EACH NEST

2-3	THIN SLICES BLACK FOREST HAM	2-3
1	EGG	1
1 TBSP.	CREAM	15 ML
1 HEAPING TBSP.	GRATED SWISS CHEESE	25 ML
	SPRINKLE OF DRIED BASIL	
	ENGLISH MUFFIN	

PREHEAT OVEN TO 350°F (180°C). GREASE LARGE MUFFIN TINS. LINE WITH HAM AND BREAK EGG OVER TOP. ADD CREAM AND SPRINKLE WITH CHEESE AND BASIL. BAKE 12-15 MINUTES. SERVE ON HALF A TOASTED ENGLISH MUFFIN. (PLACE WATER IN ANY UNUSED MUFFIN CUPS TO PREVENT DAMAGE.)

VEGETABLE FRITTATA

1 TBSP.	VEGETABLE OIL	15 ML
1 CUP	BROCCOLI FLORETS, CUT INTO BITE-SIZED PIECES	250 ML
1/2 CUP	SHREDDED CARROT	125 ML
1/2 CUP	CHOPPED ONION	125 ML
1/2	RED PEPPER, CHOPPED	1/2
4	EGGS	4
1/4 CUP	MILK	60 ML
1 TBSP.	CHOPPED FRESH PARSLEY	15 ML
1/4 TSP.	SALT	1 ML
1/4 TSP.	TABASCO	1 ML
3/4 CUP	GRATED CHEDDAR CHEESE	175 ML
1 TBSP.	GRATED PARMESAN CHEESE	15 ML

HEAT OIL IN A MEDIUM-SIZED FRYING PAN. COOK
BROCCOLI, CARROT AND ONION ABOUT 5 MINUTES,
STIRRING FREQUENTLY, UNTIL BROCCOLI IS TENDER-CRISP.
ADD RED PEPPER AND STIR. BEAT EGGS, MILK, PARSLEY,
SALT AND TABASCO UNTIL BLENDED. POUR MIXTURE
OVER VEGETABLES. SPRINKLE WITH CHEESES AND
REDUCE HEAT TO LOW. COVER AND COOK UNTIL EGGS
ARE SET IN THE MIDDLE, 5-10 MINUTES. CUT INTO
WEDGES. SERVES 4. (PICTURED OPPOSITE PAGE 127.)

ONE OF THE ADVANTAGES OF GETTING OLD IS THAT YOU
CAN SING IN THE BATHROOM WHILE YOU ARE BRUSHING
YOUR TEETH.

BEVERAGES

Eggnog Supreme
Winter Punch
Marguaritas Mucho Grande

OTHER GOOD THINGS

Never-Fail Blender Hollandaise
Roasted Orange Pepper and Corn Salsa
Papaya Salsa
Kiwi Salsa
Pickled Onions
Cranberry Pear Chutney
Green Tomato Relish
B.L.'s Best Mustard Pickles

EGGNOG SUPREME

THIS IS A BEST OF BRIDGE CHRISTMAS TRADITION.

12	EGG YOLKS	12
1 CUP	SUGAR	250 ML
7/8 CUP	BRANDY (OKAY! USE THE WHOLE CUP)	205 ML
1 1/3 CUPS	RYE OR RUM	325 ML
2 CUPS	HALF & HALF CREAM	500 ML
12	EGG WHITES	12
3 CUPS	WHIPPING CREAM	750 ML
	NUTMEG FOR GARNISH	

IN A LARGE BOWL, BEAT EGG YOLKS AND SUGAR TOGETHER UNTIL LEMON COLORED AND THICK. ADD BRANDY, RYE OR RUM AND CREAM. BLEND WELL. CHILL FOR SEVERAL HOURS. BEAT EGG WHITES UNTIL STIFF. BEAT WHIPPING CREAM IN LARGE BOWL AND FOLD IN EGG WHITES. FOLD INTO EGG YOLK MIXTURE. POUR INTO A LARGE PUNCH BOWL. SPRINKLE WITH GRATED NUTMEG. ENJOY! SERVES A CROWD!

THE REAL REASON THAT MOUNTAIN CLIMBERS TIE THEMSELVES TOGETHER IS TO KEEP THE SENSIBLE ONE FROM GOING HOME.

Samosas in Phyllo, page 64

Shrimp 'n' Beer, page 70

WINTER PUNCH

A HOT TODDY FOR: AFTER SKATING, AFTER SKIING, AFTER SNOWBOARDING, AFTER TREE CHOPPING OR WHILST SAP GATHERING.

2	CINNAMON STICKS	2
16	WHOLE CLOVES	16
6 CUPS	APPLE JUICE	1.5 L
2 CUPS	CRANBERRY COCKTAIL	500 ML
4 OZ.	CINNAMON HEARTS (RED HOTS)	125 G
1 TSP.	ANGOSTURA BITTERS	5 ML
1 CUP	RUM	250 ML

TIE CINNAMON STICKS AND CLOVES IN CHEESE-CLOTH. IN A LARGE POT COMBINE REMAINING INGREDIENTS, EXCEPT RUM. PLACE CHEESECLOTH BAG IN MIXTURE AND SIMMER FOR 45 MINUTES. ADD RUM. SERVES 8.

MARGUARITAS MUCHO GRANDE

OVER THE RIDGE WITH THE BEST OF BRIDGE.

3/4 CUP	FROZEN LIMEADE	175 ML
3/4 CUP	WATER	175 ML
3/4 CUP	TEQUILA	175 ML
1/3 CUP	TRIPLE SEC	75 ML
	ICE TO FILL BLENDER	

POUR ABOVE INGREDIENTS INTO BLENDER AND BLEND UNTIL FROTHY. MAKES 6 DRINKS. OLÉ!

NEVER-FAIL BLENDER HOLLANDAISE

1 CUP	BUTTER	250 ML
4	EGG YOLKS	4
1/4 TSP.	EACH: SALT, SUGAR, TABASCO & DRY MUSTARD	1 ML
2 TBSP.	FRESH LEMON JUICE	30 ML

HEAT BUTTER TO A FULL BOIL, BEING CAREFUL NOT TO BROWN. COMBINE ALL OTHER INGREDIENTS. WITH BLENDER TURNED ON HIGH, SLOWLY POUR BUTTER INTO YOLK MIXTURE IN A THIN STREAM UNTIL ALL IS ADDED. KEEPS WELL IN REFRIGERATOR FOR SEVERAL DAYS. WHEN REHEATING, HEAT OVER HOT (NOT BOILING) WATER IN TOP OF DOUBLE BOILER. MAKES ABOUT 1¼ CUPS (300 ML) OF SAUCE.

THE ONLY SUBSTITUTE FOR GOOD MANNERS IS FAST REFLEXES.

ROASTED ORANGE PEPPER AND CORN SALSA

GOOD ON TACOS AND FAJITAS.

3	YELLOW PEPPERS, HALVED AND SEEDED	3
1/2 CUP	CHICKEN BROTH	125 ML
1/2 TSP.	CUMIN	2 ML
	SALT AND PEPPER TO TASTE	
19 OZ.	CAN KERNEL CORN	540 ML
1/4-1/2 TSP.	HOT RED PEPPER FLAKES	1-2 ML

PLACE PEPPER HALVES CUT-SIDE DOWN ON A COOKIE SHEET. BROIL UNTIL SKINS ARE BLACKENED AND PUFFED. LEAVE SKINS ON AND PLACE PEPPERS IN SAUCEPAN, ADD CHICKEN BROTH AND COOK, UNCOVERED, 10 MINUTES. PURÉE WITH CUMIN, SALT AND PEPPER. ADD CORN AND PEPPER FLAKES. STORE IN REFRIGERATOR. MAKES 2 CUPS (500 ML).

PAPAYA SALSA

GREAT WITH GRILLED PORK CHOPS OR CHICKEN.

1	RIPE PAPAYA, SEEDED & DICED	1
1/4 CUP	CHOPPED RED ONION	60 ML
1 TBSP.	FINELY CHOPPED JALAPEÑO PEPPER	15 ML
1 TBSP.	CHOPPED FRESH CILANTRO	15 ML
	JUICE OF 1 LIME	
1 TSP.	LIQUID HONEY	5 ML
	SALT & PEPPER TO TASTE	

COMBINE ALL INGREDIENTS AND CHILL. SERVES 4.

KIWI SALSA

REFRESHING! SERVE WITH GRILLED CHICKEN OR FISH.

2 TBSP.	LIME JUICE	30 ML
I TBSP.	OLIVE OIL	I5 ML
I	JALAPEÑO PEPPER, SEEDED & MINCED	I
I TSP.	HONEY	5 ML
I	GARLIC CLOVE, MINCED	I
I TSP.	CURRY	5 ML
I TSP.	CUMIN	5 ML
¼ TSP.	HOT RED PEPPER FLAKES	I ML
6	KIWI FRUIT, PEELED & DICED	6
I	SMALL ONION, PEELED & DICED	I

MIX MARINADE INGREDIENTS IN SMALL BOWL. ADD KIWI AND ONION. STIR AND LET STAND AT ROOM TEMPERATURE FOR AT LEAST I HOUR. REFRIGERATE UNTIL READY TO SERVE. MAKES 2 CUPS (500 ML).

REMEMBER THE GOOD OLD DAYS WHEN IT COST MORE TO RUN A CAR THAN TO PARK IT?

GREAT WITH ROAST BEEF SANDWICHES. SERVES A CROWD.

4	LARGE YELLOW ONIONS, THINLY SLICED	4
1½ CUPS	WHITE VINEGAR	375 ML
1½ CUPS	WATER	375 ML
1 CUP	WHITE SUGAR	250 ML
¼ CUP	FRESH LEMON JUICE	60 ML
¼ TSP.	TABASCO SAUCE	1 ML
1 TSP.	SALT	5 ML
½ TSP.	SEASONED PEPPER	2 ML
2	GARLIC CLOVES, MINCED	2
1 CUP	SOUR CREAM (FAT-FREE IS OKAY)	250 ML
1 TSP.	CELERY SEED	5 ML

COMBINE ALL INGREDIENTS, EXCEPT SOUR CREAM AND CELERY SEED. MARINATE OVERNIGHT. BEFORE SERVING, DRAIN AND STIR IN SOUR CREAM AND CELERY SEED. PLACE IN A PRETTY BOWL - THERE'S NOTHING BEAUTIFUL ABOUT AN ONION!

IF CONVENIENCE STORES ARE OPEN 7 DAYS A WEEK, 365 DAYS A YEAR, WHY ARE THERE LOCKS ON THE DOORS?

CRANBERRY PEAR CHUTNEY

THIS CHUTNEY IS PACKED WITH WONDERFUL FLAVORS.

2 CUPS	WATER	500 ML
I CUP	RAISINS	250 ML
2 CUPS	SUGAR	500 ML
2 TBSP.	WHITE WINE VINEGAR	30 ML
I CUP	ORANGE JUICE	250 ML
2 TBSP.	GRATED ORANGE ZEST	30 ML
2 TBSP.	SLIVERED FRESH GINGER	30 ML
6 CUPS	CRANBERRIES, FRESH OR FROZEN	1.5 L
2	PEARS, PEELED, CORED, CHOPPED	2
I CUP	TOASTED SLIVERED ALMONDS	250 ML

BOIL WATER AND ADD RAISINS. REMOVE FROM HEAT AND LET STAND 20 MINUTES. DRAIN, RESERVING 1/2 CUP (125 ML) LIQUID. ADD SUGAR AND VINEGAR TO RAISIN WATER. HEAT IN SAUCEPAN UNTIL SUGAR DISSOLVES. INCREASE HEAT AND BOIL, WITHOUT STIRRING, UNTIL SYRUP TURNS GOLDEN BROWN, ABOUT 15 MINUTES. ADD ORANGE JUICE, ZEST, GINGER AND CRANBERRIES AND COOK ABOUT 10 MINUTES. STIR IN RAISINS, PEARS AND ALMONDS. POUR INTO STERILIZED JARS AND KEEP REFRIGERATED. MAKES ABOUT 6 CUPS (1.5 L).

IF ALL THE WORLD IS A STAGE,
WHERE DOES THE AUDIENCE SIT?

GREEN TOMATO RELISH

YOU MADE IT YOURSELF? - AREN'T YOU WONDERFUL DEAR!

7½ LBS.	GREEN TOMATOES, THINLY SLICED	3.25 KG
5	GREEN PEPPERS, QUARTERED, SEEDED & SLICED	5
4	RED PEPPERS, QUARTERED, SEEDED & SLICED	4
4	LARGE ONIONS, HALVED & SLICED	4
1 CUP	SALT	250 ML
4 CUPS	VINEGAR	1 L
6 CUPS	SUGAR	1.5 KG
1 TSP.	CINNAMON	5 ML
1 TSP.	GROUND CLOVES	5 ML
1 TBSP.	TURMERIC	15 ML
2 TBSP.	MIXED PICKLING SPICES	30 ML

PLACE SLICED TOMATOES, PEPPERS AND ONIONS IN A LARGE POT. COVER WITH SALT AND LET STAND OVERNIGHT. DRAIN AND RINSE WELL. RETURN TO POT AND ADD REMAINING INGREDIENTS. BRING TO A BOIL, REDUCE TO SIMMER AND COOK UNTIL DESIRED CONSISTENCY, APPROXIMATELY 30 MINUTES. PUT IN STERILIZED PINT (500 ML) JARS AND SEAL. DELICIOUS SERVED WITH EVERYTHING! MAKES APPROXIMATELY 12 PINT (500 ML) JARS.

WHAT WAS THE BEST THING BEFORE SLICED BREAD?

B.L.'S BEST MUSTARD PICKLES

2	BUNCHES CELERY	2
3	LARGE CUCUMBERS	3
6	LARGE ONIONS	6
1	LARGE CAULIFLOWER	1
12	MEDIUM GREEN TOMATOES	12
2	RED PEPPERS	2
1/2 CUP	PICKLING SALT	125 ML

MUSTARD DRESSING

8 CUPS	WHITE SUGAR	2 L
2/3 CUP	DRY MUSTARD	150 ML
1 TBSP.	TURMERIC	15 ML
2 TBSP.	CELERY SALT	30 ML
2 TBSP.	CURRY POWDER	30 ML
1 CUP	FLOUR	250 ML
2 CUPS	MALT VINEGAR	500 ML
4 CUPS	WHITE VINEGAR	1 L

CHOP ALL VEGETABLES AND MIX IN A LARGE POT OR
ROASTER. COVER WITH PICKLING SALT AND LET STAND
1 HOUR. DRAIN OFF 2 CUPS (500 ML) OF LIQUID. MIX
DRY INGREDIENTS TOGETHER IN A SAUCEPAN. ADD
VINEGARS AND BOIL GENTLY UNTIL THICKENED. POUR
OVER VEGETABLES. COOK FOR 10 MINUTES. COOL
ANOTHER 10 MINUTES. POUR INTO STERILIZED JARS.
MAKES APPROXIMATELY 10-12 PINT (500 ML) JARS.

THE TROUBLE WITH CLASS REUNIONS IS THAT OLD
FLAMES HAVE BECOME EVEN OLDER.

APPETIZERS

Antipasto
Year-Round Spinach Dip
Sun-Dried Tomato Dip
Hummus
Pesto Torte
Charred Pepper & Feta Dip
Layered Crab Dip
Mexicana Antipasto
Zippy Crab and Artichoke Dip
Brandy Cheese Spread
Ruth's Chokes
Hot Artichoke Dip
Artichoke Nibblers
Hot Cheese Spread
Brandy-Nut Brie
Brie with Sun-Dried Tomatoes
Cocktail Crisps
Asparagus Roll-Ups
French Blankets
Pasadena Pinwheels
Smoked Salmon Quesadillas
Stacked Pizza
Curried Chicken Triangles
Samosas in Phyllo
Chicken Satay with Spicy Peanut Dipping Sauce
Buffalo Chicken Wings
Hot 'N' Spicy Wings
Jelly Balls
Shrimp 'N' Beer

A DELICIOUS APPETIZER TO SERVE DURING THE FESTIVE SEASON. A GREAT GIFT TO ADD TO A CHRISTMAS BASKET. IT'S A LOT OF CHOPPING BUT DON'T USE A FOOD PROCESSOR!!

1 CUP	OLIVE OIL	250 ML
1	LARGE CAULIFLOWER, CUT INTO BITE-SIZED PIECES	1
2	LARGE GREEN PEPPERS, CHOPPED	2
2	10 1/2 OZ. (294 ML) CANS SLICED RIPE OLIVES, CHOPPED	2
16 OZ.	JAR GREEN OLIVES WITH PIMIENTO, CHOPPED	500 ML
2-13 OZ.	JARS PICKLED ONIONS, CHOPPED	2-375 ML
2-10 OZ.	CANS MUSHROOM STEMS & PIECES	2-284 ML
48 OZ.	JAR MIXED PICKLES, CHOPPED	1.5 L
2-48 OZ.	BOTTLES KETCHUP	2-1.5 L
15 OZ.	BOTTLE HOT KETCHUP	450 ML
2-2 OZ.	CANS ANCHOVIES, CHOPPED (OPTIONAL)	2-55 G
3-4 1/2 OZ.	CANS SOLID TUNA, CHOPPED	3-113 G
3-4 OZ.	CANS SMALL SHRIMP	3-113 G

DRAIN ALL JARS AND CANS. PUT ALL INGREDIENTS, EXCEPT THE FISH, INTO A LARGE DUTCH OVEN. BRING TO A BOIL THEN SIMMER FOR 20 MINUTES, STIRRING OFTEN. POUR BOILING WATER OVER ALL THE FISH TO RINSE. DRAIN AND ADD TO MIXTURE. GENTLY STIR AND SIMMER FOR ANOTHER 10 MINUTES. POUR INTO

ANTIPASTO

CONTINUED FROM PAGE 46.

STERILIZED JARS USING NEW LIDS. PROCESS. SERVE WITH CRACKERS.

TO PROCESS: PLACE JARS ON RACK IN LARGE, DEEP POT. ADD WATER THREE QUARTERS OF THE WAY UP THE JARS. COVER AND BRING WATER TO BOIL. SIMMER FOR AT LEAST 20 MINUTES. LET COOL. LIDS WILL POP AS THEY COOL. TIGHTEN LIDS AND STORE IN COOL PLACE. MAKES 16-18, 8 OZ. (250 ML) JARS OF ANTIPASTO.

YEAR-ROUND SPINACH DIP

1 CUP	MAYONNAISE	250 ML
1 CUP	SOUR CREAM	250 ML
10 OZ.	PKG. FROZEN CHOPPED SPINACH (WELL SQUEEZED!)	283 G
8 OZ.	CAN WATER CHESTNUTS, CHOPPED	236 ML
1½ OZ.	KNORRS VEGETABLE SOUP MIX (1 PKG.)	40 G
½ CUP	CHOPPED GREEN ONION	125 ML
1	ROUND LOAF OF BREAD, RYE, PUMPERNICKEL OR WHITE	1

COMBINE ALL INGREDIENTS, EXCEPT BREAD AND MIX WELL. CHILL SEVERAL HOURS OR OVERNIGHT. SERVE IN A HOLLOWED-OUT ROUND LOAF OF BREAD. CUT SCOOPED OUT BREAD INTO CUBES AND SERVE WITH DIP. YOU'LL NEED SOME CRACKERS TOO!

SUN-DRIED TOMATO DIP

KEEP THESE INGREDIENTS ON HAND AND PRESTO - AN INSTANT APPETIZER!

8 OZ.	LIGHT SPREADABLE CREAM CHEESE	250 G
2 TBSP.	MAYONNAISE	30 ML
1 TSP.	LEMON JUICE	5 ML
1/4 CUP	FINELY CHOPPED SUN-DRIED TOMATOES (RECONSTITUTED IF DRIED)	60 ML
1/4 CUP	FRESH BASIL, CHOPPED	60 ML
2	GARLIC CLOVES, MINCED	2

MIX CREAM CHEESE, MAYONNAISE AND LEMON JUICE TOGETHER IN A BOWL. ADD TOMATOES, BASIL AND GARLIC AND MIX WELL. LET SIT FOR AT LEAST 1 HOUR BEFORE SERVING. SERVE WITH CRACKERS OR BAGEL CHIPS.

LOGIC IS WHEN YOU COME TO THE CONCLUSION THAT EITHER YOU'RE GAINING WEIGHT OR THE HOLES IN YOUR BELT ARE HEALING UP.

HUMMUS

A MIDDLE EASTERN DIP - YUMMUS MAKE.

3	GARLIC CLOVES, MINCED	3
19 OZ.	CAN CHICK-PEAS (GARBANZO BEANS) DRAINED	540 ML
1/4 CUP	TAHINI (SESAME SEED PASTE)*	60 ML
3 TBSP.	LEMON JUICE	45 ML
1 TBSP.	VEGETABLE OIL	15 ML
2 TBSP.	WATER OR CHICK-PEA LIQUID	30 ML
1 TSP.	CUMIN	5 ML
1/2 TSP.	SALT	2 ML

IN FOOD PROCESSOR (OR BLENDER) MINCE GARLIC. ADD CHICK-PEAS, TAHINI, LEMON JUICE, OIL, WATER, CUMIN AND SALT; PROCESS UNTIL SMOOTH. TASTE AND ADJUST SEASONING IF NECESSARY. TRANSFER TO SERVING BOWL. MAKES ABOUT 1 1/2 CUPS (375 ML). SERVE WITH WARM PITA BREAD FOR DIPPING.

* IF YOU'RE OUT OF TAHINI - PEANUT BUTTER MAKES A GOOD SUBSTITUTE.

FOOD IS AN IMPORTANT PART OF A BALANCED DIET.

PESTO TORTE

A GREAT MAKE-AHEAD FOR A CROWD!

12 OZ.	CREAM CHEESE, ROOM TEMPERATURE	340 G
3 OZ.	CHÈVRE (GOAT CHEESE)	85 G
1/2 CUP	PESTO	125 ML
10	SUN-DRIED TOMATOES IN OIL, DRAINED & SLIVERED	10
1/4 CUP	PINE NUTS	60 ML
	FRESH BASIL FOR GARNISH	

LINE A SMALL BOWL WITH PLASTIC WRAP, LEAVING SOME OVERLAPPING THE EDGES. SET ASIDE. IN ANOTHER BOWL, BEAT CHEESES TOGETHER UNTIL VERY SMOOTH. SPREAD A LAYER OF CREAMED MIXTURE IN BOTTOM OF BOWL. TOP WITH A LAYER OF PESTO. SPREAD THIS WITH ANOTHER LAYER OF CHEESE MIXTURE, THEN TOP WITH SOME SUN-DRIED TOMATOES AND A SPRINKLING OF PINE NUTS. REPEAT LAYERS ENDING WITH CHEESE MIXTURE AND A FEW PINE NUTS. FOLD UP PLASTIC WRAP AROUND TORTE AND GENTLY PRESS TO COMPRESS LAYERS. REFRIGERATE UNTIL READY TO SERVE. UNWRAP TOP OF MOLD, LIFT OUT OF BOWL AND INVERT ONTO A PLATE. GARNISH WITH PINE NUTS AND FRESH BASIL. SERVE WITH CRACKERS OR BAGUETTE SLICES.

THE NICE THING ABOUT EGOTISTS IS THAT THEY DON'T TALK ABOUT OTHER PEOPLE.

CHARRED PEPPER & FETA DIP

MAKE THIS THE DAY BEFORE YOU NEED IT!

3	LARGE RED PEPPERS	3
6 OZ.	FETA CHEESE	170 G
2 TBSP.	PINE NUTS	30 ML
I TBSP.	OLIVE OIL	15 ML

TO CHAR PEPPERS: CUT PEPPERS IN THIRDS AND REMOVE SEEDS. PLACE CUT-SIDE DOWN ON COOKIE SHEET. BROIL UNTIL SKINS ARE BLACKENED AND PUFFED. PUT PEPPERS IN A COVERED CASSEROLE AND LET STAND FOR 10 MINUTES TO STEAM. REMOVE AND PEEL. PLACE ALL INGREDIENTS IN FOOD PROCESSOR AND BLEND. REFRIGERATE UNTIL READY TO SERVE. SERVE WITH CRACKERS OR FRESH VEGETABLES.

LAYERED CRAB DIP

LAST MINUTE COMPANY? NO PROBLEM!

8 OZ.	CREAM CHEESE, SOFTENED	250 G
I TBSP.	GRATED ONION	15 ML
I TBSP.	WORCESTERSHIRE SAUCE	15 ML
I 1/2 TSP.	LEMON JUICE	7 ML
1/2 CUP	CHILI OR COCKTAIL SAUCE	125 ML
7 OZ.	CAN CRAB MEAT	198 G
2 TBSP.	CHOPPED PARSLEY	30 ML

MIX CHEESE, ONION, WORCESTERSHIRE SAUCE AND LEMON JUICE TOGETHER. SPREAD IN A SHALLOW SERVING DISH. SPREAD CHILI SAUCE OVER TOP. DRAIN AND RINSE CRAB AND SPREAD OVER CHILI SAUCE. SPRINKLE WITH PARSLEY. SERVE WITH ASSORTED CRACKERS.

MEXICANA ANTIPASTO

BANDITOS STEAL FOR THIS!

8 OZ.	CREAM CHEESE	250 G
	DASH GARLIC POWDER	
½ CUP	SOUR CREAM (FAT-FREE IS FINE)	125 ML
1	LARGE AVOCADO, MASHED	1
¼ TSP.	LEMON JUICE	1 ML
1	TOMATO, FINELY CHOPPED	1
4 OZ.	CAN GREEN CHILIES	114 ML
5	SLICES BACON, COOKED CRISP & DICED	5
3-4	GREEN ONIONS, CHOPPED	3-4
¼ CUP	SLICED RIPE OLIVES	60 ML
¼ CUP	SLICED STUFFED GREEN OLIVES	60 ML
8 OZ.	BOTTLE TACO SAUCE (HOT)	250 ML
1 CUP	GRATED CHEDDAR CHEESE	250 ML

COMBINE CHEESE, GARLIC AND SOUR CREAM AND USE
AS THE FIRST LAYER IN A 9" (23 CM) PIE PLATE.
COMBINE AVOCADO, LEMON JUICE, TOMATO AND GREEN
CHILIES FOR THE SECOND LAYER. SPRINKLE ON
BACON, GREEN ONION AND OLIVES. SPREAD TACO
SAUCE OVER ALL AND SPRINKLE WITH GRATED
CHEDDAR. REFRIGERATE. SERVE WITH CORN CHIPS
OR TACO CHIPS. SERVES 10-12 - HOPEFULLY.

PATIENCE IS THE ABILITY TO LET YOUR LIGHT SHINE
AFTER YOUR FUSE HAS BLOWN.

ZIPPY CRAB AND ARTICHOKE DIP

8 OZ.	CREAM CHEESE, ROOM TEMPERATURE	250 G
1/2 CUP	MAYONNAISE	125 ML
	SALT & PEPPER TO TASTE	
7 OZ.	CAN CRABMEAT, WELL DRAINED	198 G
6 OZ.	JAR MARINATED ARTICHOKE HEARTS, DRAINED & CHOPPED	170 G
1/4 CUP	SLICED GREEN ONION	60 ML
1/2 CUP	DICED RED PEPPER	125 ML
1/2 CUP	DICED CELERY	125 ML
1/4 CUP	FINELY CHOPPED PARSLEY	60 ML
1 TSP.	LEMON JUICE	5 ML
1 TSP.	TABASCO	5 ML

BEAT CREAM CHEESE IN LARGE BOWL UNTIL SMOOTH. ADD MAYONNAISE, BEAT UNTIL WELL BLENDED. FOLD IN ALL REMAINING INGREDIENTS. SERVE WITH CRACKERS OR TOASTED BAGUETTE SLICES.

BRANDY CHEESE SPREAD

THE LONGER STORED - THE BETTER TASTING!

1/2 CUP	BUTTER, SOFTENED	125 ML
3 CUPS	GRATED CHEDDAR CHEESE	750 ML
1 TBSP.	SESAME SEEDS	15 ML
2 TBSP.	BRANDY	30 ML

BLEND TOGETHER, COVER AND REFRIGERATE UNTIL 1/2 HOUR BEFORE SERVING. YUMMY ON CRACKERS! MAKES 2 CUPS (500 ML).

RUTH'S CHOKES

QUICK AND EASY.

14 OZ.	CAN ARTICHOKE HEARTS	398 ML
1/2 CUP	MAYONNAISE	125 ML
1/2 CUP	GRATED PARMESAN CHEESE	125 ML

PLACE ARTICHOKE HEARTS ON COOKIE SHEET. YOU MAY HAVE TO TRIM THEM SO THEY WILL STAND UP. MIX PARMESAN CHEESE IN MAYONNAISE AND TOP EACH ARTICHOKE WITH 1 TSP. (5 ML) OF MIXTURE. PUT UNDER BROILER FOR ABOUT 2 MINUTES, OR UNTIL TOP IS BROWNED. WATCH CONSTANTLY. SERVES 4-6.

NOTE: IF LARGE ARTICHOKES ARE USED, CUT IN HALF AND REST ON SIDES TO BROIL.

HOT ARTICHOKE DIP

IF YOU LOVE IT - SERVES 1! OTHERWISE SERVES 6.

14 OZ.	CAN ARTICHOKE HEARTS, DRAINED & CHOPPED	398 ML
1/2 CUP	FRESHLY GRATED PARMESAN CHEESE	125 ML
1 CUP	MAYONNAISE	250 ML
1	GARLIC CLOVE, MINCED	1
	DASH LEMON JUICE	

MIX ALL INGREDIENTS. BAKE AT 350°F (180°C) FOR 10 MINUTES. SERVE WITH CRACKERS.

Orzo with Veggies, page 90

Papaya Avocado Salad, page 74

ARTICHOKE NIBBLERS

2	6 OZ. (170 G) JARS MARINATED ARTICHOKE HEARTS	2
1	SMALL ONION, FINELY CHOPPED	1
1	GARLIC CLOVE, MINCED	1
4	EGGS, BEATEN	4
1/4 CUP	FINE DRY BREAD CRUMBS	60 ML
1/4 TSP.	SALT	1 ML
1/4 TSP.	EACH PEPPER, OREGANO & TABASCO SAUCE	1 ML
2 CUPS	GRATED SHARP CHEDDAR CHEESE	500 ML
4 OZ.	JAR PIMIENTO	115 G
2 TBSP.	SNIPPED PARSLEY	30 ML

DRAIN LIQUID FROM 1 JAR OF ARTICHOKE HEARTS AND DISCARD. DRAIN LIQUID FROM THE OTHER JAR INTO FRYING PAN. ADD ONION AND GARLIC AND SAUTÉ. CHOP ARTICHOKES INTO QUARTERS. COMBINE EGGS, CRUMBS, SALT, PEPPER, OREGANO AND TABASCO. STIR IN CHEESE, PIMIENTO AND ARTICHOKES. ADD ONION MIXTURE. POUR INTO 9" (23 CM) SQUARE BUTTERED BAKING DISH. SPRINKLE WITH PARSLEY AND BAKE AT 325°F (160°C) FOR 30 MINUTES, OR UNTIL LIGHTLY SET. CUT IN 1" (2.5 CM) SQUARES.

I'M APPROACHING THE AGE OF 40 FROM A LOT OF DIFFERENT DIRECTIONS - ESPECIALLY FROM THE MIDDLE AND THE BACK SIDE.

HOT CHEESE SPREAD

3 CUPS	GRATED SHARP CHEESE	750 ML
1/2 CUP	CHOPPED RIPE OLIVES	125 ML
1	MEDIUM ONION, CHOPPED	1
1 CUP	MAYONNAISE	250 ML
1/2 TSP.	CURRY POWDER	2 ML
1	SMALL GARLIC CLOVE, MINCED	1
	DASH OF PAPRIKA	

MIX CHEESE, OLIVES AND ONION TOGETHER. ADD
MAYONNAISE, CURRY POWDER, GARLIC AND PAPRIKA.
SPOON INTO A JAR AND STORE IN REFRIGERATOR. TO
SERVE, SPREAD ON SMALL RYE BREAD OR CRACKERS.
HEAT UNDER BROILER UNTIL CHEESE MELTS.

BRANDY-NUT BRIE

WHAT COULD BE EASIER?

1/4 CUP	BROWN SUGAR	60 ML
1/4 CUP	PECANS OR CASHEWS, CHOPPED	60 ML
1 TBSP.	BRANDY OR WHISKY	15 ML
7 1/2 OZ.	ROUND BRIE CHEESE	235 G
	CRACKERS	

GET READY . . . STIR TOGETHER SUGAR, NUTS AND
BRANDY. SCORE THE TOP OF THE CHEESE AND PLACE
ON AN OVENPROOF PLATTER. BAKE AT 400°F (200°C)
FOR 4-5 MINUTES, UNTIL CHEESE IS SOFTENED.
MOUND SUGAR MIXTURE OVER CHEESE AND BAKE
2-3 MINUTES MORE UNTIL SUGAR IS MELTED. SERVE
WARM WITH CRACKERS.

BRIE WITH SUN-DRIED TOMATOES

YOU CAN USE ANY SIZE ROUND OF BRIE – ADJUST THE INGREDIENTS TO FIT THE "ROUND".

7½ OZ.	ROUND BRIE CHEESE	235 G
4 OZ.	SUN-DRIED TOMATOES IN OIL, DRAINED & FINELY CHOPPED	115 G
2-3	GARLIC CLOVES, MINCED	2-3
2 TBSP.	CHOPPED FRESH PARSLEY	30 ML

SCORE THE TOP OF THE CHEESE. MIX TOMATOES AND GARLIC; PILE GENEROUSLY ON CHEESE. SPRINKLE WITH PARSLEY. (IT'S NOT NECESSARY TO REMOVE RIND FROM CHEESE.) HEAT IN A 350°F (180°C) OVEN UNTIL CHEESE BEGINS TO MELT. SERVE WITH BAGEL CHIPS OR CRACKERS.

COCKTAIL CRISPS

OUR FAVORITE COCKTAIL COOKIE – FREEZES WELL.

1 CUP	BUTTER	250 ML
8 OZ.	PKG. IMPERIAL CHEESE (SHARP COLD PACK CHEDDAR CHEESE)	250 G
	DASH OF SALT	
¼ TSP.	CAYENNE PEPPER OR TABASCO	1 ML
¼ TSP.	WORCESTERSHIRE SAUCE	1 ML
1½ CUPS	FLOUR	375 ML
4 CUPS	RICE KRISPIES	1 L

CREAM BUTTER AND CHEESE TOGETHER. ADD SEASONINGS. BEAT IN FLOUR THEN ADD RICE KRISPIES. MIX WELL. SHAPE INTO BALLS. PRESS DOWN WITH A FORK WHICH HAS BEEN DIPPED IN COLD WATER. BAKE AT 350°F (180°C) FOR 15-20 MINUTES, UNTIL LIGHTLY BROWNED. MAKES ABOUT 4 DOZEN.

ASPARAGUS ROLL-UPS

A GREAT APPETIZER TO MAKE AHEAD AND FREEZE.

2	LOAVES OF WHITE BREAD	2
8 OZ.	ROQUEFORT CHEESE	250 G
8 OZ.	CREAM CHEESE	250 G
1 TBSP.	MAYONNAISE	15 ML
1	EGG	1
36	FRESH ASPARAGUS SPEARS, SNAP OFF ENDS	36
1/2 CUP	BUTTER, MELTED	125 ML

CUT CRUSTS OFF BREAD AND ROLL EACH SLICE FLAT WITH A ROLLING PIN. COMBINE CHEESES, MAYONNAISE AND EGG IN BLENDER AND SPREAD ON BREAD. TOP WITH 1 ASPARAGUS SPEAR AND ROLL UP. BRUSH WITH MELTED BUTTER, CUT INTO 3 PIECES AND PLACE ON UNGREASED COOKIE SHEET. (AT THIS POINT YOU MAY LAYER ROLLS BETWEEN WAXED PAPER AND PLACE IN AN AIRTIGHT CONTAINER AND FREEZE.) BAKE AT 350°F (180°C) FOR ABOUT 15 MINUTES, OR UNTIL LIGHTLY BROWNED. MAKES ABOUT 9 DOZEN.

HEAT MAKES OBJECTS EXPAND AND COLD MAKES THEM CONTRACT. THAT'S WHY THE DAYS ARE LONGER IN THE SUMMER AND SHORTER IN THE WINTER.

FRENCH BLANKETS

A QUESADILLA WITH A FRENCH TWIST . . . QUELLE SURPRISE!

	DIJON MUSTARD	
4	10" (25 CM) FLOUR TORTILLAS	4
6 OZ.	BRIE CHEESE, RIND REMOVED, ROOM TEMPERATURE	170 G
1	BUNCH FRESH SPINACH LEAVES, STEMS REMOVED	1
	OLIVE OIL	

AIOLI*

1/2 CUP	MAYONNAISE	125 ML
1	GARLIC CLOVE, MINCED	1
1 TSP.	LEMON JUICE	5 ML

SPREAD A THIN LAYER OF DIJON ON 1 TORTILLA. SPREAD BRIE ON SECOND TORTILLA THEN TOP WITH FRESH SPINACH LEAVES. PUT THE 2 TORTILLAS TOGETHER LIKE A SANDWICH. HEAT OLIVE OIL ON MEDIUM-LOW IN LARGE FRYING PAN AND BROWN TORTILLAS LIGHTLY ON BOTH SIDES UNTIL CHEESE MELTS.

TO MAKE AIOLI: BLEND INGREDIENTS TOGETHER..

TO SERVE, CUT TORTILLAS INTO WEDGES AND SERVE WARM WITH AIOLI DIP.

* AIOLI IS THE SALSA OF SOUTHERN FRANCE. IN PROVENCE IT'S USED AS A SAUCE FOR VEGETABLES, MEAT AND FISH.

PASADENA PINWHEELS

FAST 'N' EASY!

8 OZ.	CREAM CHEESE	250 G
2 TBSP.	MAYONNAISE	30 ML
4 OZ.	CAN DICED GREEN CHILIES, DRAINED	114 ML
1	LARGE TOMATO, SEEDED & CHOPPED	1
1/4 CUP	FINELY CHOPPED ONION	60 ML
1	LARGE GARLIC CLOVE, MINCED	1
1 TSP.	CHILI POWDER	5 ML
1/2 TSP.	SALT	2 ML
	FLOUR TORTILLAS	

BLEND CREAM CHEESE AND MAYONNAISE. STIR IN REMAINING INGREDIENTS. COVER AND REFRIGERATE FOR 2 HOURS. SPREAD CHEESE MIXTURE OVER EACH TORTILLA AND ROLL UP TIGHTLY. TRIM ENDS. REFRIGERATE UNTIL FIRM. SLICE AND PLACE PINWHEELS FLAT ON COOKIE SHEET. BROIL UNTIL LIGHTLY GOLDEN.

THE CREAM CHEESE MIXTURE IS ALSO A TASTY DIP TO SERVE WITH TACO OR CORN CHIPS.

I GOLF IN THE LOW 80'S. IF IT'S ANY HOTTER THAN THAT, I WON'T PLAY.

SMOKED SALMON QUESADILLAS

I	ANAHEIM PEPPER, CHARRED, PEELED & CUT INTO STRIPS	I
I	RED BELL PEPPER, CHARRED, PEELED & CUT INTO STRIPS	I
1/4 CUP	CHÈVRE (GOAT CHEESE)	60 ML
1/4 CUP	CREAM CHEESE, ROOM TEMPERATURE	60 ML
3	8" (20 CM) FLOUR TORTILLAS	3
I	AVOCADO, PEELED, PITTED & CUT INTO THIN SLICES	I
1/4 CUP	MINCED SHALLOTS	60 ML
2 OZ.	SMOKED SALMON, CUT INTO STRIPS	60 G

TO CHAR PEPPERS: PLEASE REFER TO "CHARRED PEPPER AND FETA DIP" ON PAGE 51.

IN A SMALL BOWL, MIX TOGETHER THE CHÈVRE AND CREAM CHEESE UNTIL SMOOTH AND CREAMY. SPREAD ONE-THIRD OF THE MIXTURE OVER HALF OF EACH TORTILLA. DIVIDE THE PEPPER STRIPS EVENLY OVER THE 3 HALVES OF THE TORTILLAS. LAYER THE AVOCADO SLICES OVER THE PEPPER STRIPS AND TOP WITH THE CHOPPED SHALLOTS. DIVIDE THE SALMON EVENLY ON THE TORTILLA HALVES. FOLD THE TORTILLAS OVER, PRESSING TO SEAL. HEAT A NONSTICK PAN OVER MEDIUM HEAT AND BROWN THE FOLDED TORTILLAS UNTIL THE CHEESE MELTS. TURN OVER AND BROWN ON THE OTHER SIDE. CUT EACH QUESADILLA INTO 4 WEDGES AND SERVE IMMEDIATELY.

STACKED PIZZA

FOR ADULTS ONLY.

7	SHEETS PHYLLO PASTRY	7
1/2 CUP	BUTTER, MELTED	125 ML
1/2 CUP	FRESHLY GRATED PARMESAN CHEESE	125 ML
1 1/2 CUPS	GRATED MOZZARELLA CHEESE	375 ML
1	ONION, THINLY SLICED	1
5-6	ROMA TOMATOES, THINLY SLICED	5-6
1 TSP.	OREGANO	5 ML
	SALT & PEPPER TO TASTE	
	FRESH HERB SPRIGS: THYME, OREGANO, ROSEMARY	

PREHEAT OVEN TO 375°F (190°C). THAW AND PREPARE PHYLLO FOLLOWING PACKAGE INSTRUCTIONS. BE SURE TO COVER EXTRA PHYLLO WITH A DAMP TOWEL WHILE BUILDING PIZZA. PLACE FIRST SHEET OF PHYLLO ON BAKING SHEET, BRUSH WITH BUTTER AND SPRINKLE WITH 1 TBSP. (15 ML) PARMESAN CHEESE. REPEAT UNTIL ALL SHEETS ARE USED. PRESS FIRMLY SO LAYERS WILL STICK TOGETHER. SPRINKLE TOP SHEET WITH MOZZARELLA AND ONIONS. ARRANGE TOMATO SLICES ON TOP. SEASON WITH OREGANO, SALT AND PEPPER. BAKE FOR 20-25 MINUTES, UNTIL EDGES ARE GOLDEN. DECORATE WITH HERBS AND CUT INTO SQUARES.

NOTE: OLIVES, ANCHOVIES, PEPPERS CAN ALSO BE USED - BUT DON'T OVERLOAD AS THIS IS A DELICATE CRUST!

CURRIED CHICKEN TRIANGLES

2 TSP.	BUTTER OR MARGARINE	10 ML
1/2	MEDIUM ONION, FINELY CHOPPED	1/2
1/2 CUP	FINELY CHOPPED CELERY	125 ML
1 TBSP.	FLOUR	15 ML
1 1/2 TSP.	CURRY POWDER	7 ML
1/4 TSP.	SALT	1 ML
1/2 CUP	CHICKEN BROTH	125 ML
1 1/2 CUPS	DICED COOKED CHICKEN	375 ML
1/4 CUP	FAT-FREE SOUR CREAM	60 ML
1/4 CUP	SKIM-MILK PLAIN YOGURT	60 ML
	PHYLLO PASTRY, THAWED	
	(ABOUT 1/3 OF PKG.)	
1/4 CUP	MELTED BUTTER	60 ML

MELT BUTTER IN SAUCEPAN. ADD ONION AND CELERY; COOK UNTIL SOFT. ADD FLOUR, CURRY POWDER AND SALT. STIR FOR 1 MINUTE. ADD CHICKEN BROTH; SIMMER FOR 2 MINUTES. REMOVE FROM HEAT; ADD CHICKEN, SOUR CREAM AND YOGURT. TO MAKE TRIANGLES, UNROLL PHYLLO AND LAY FLAT. CUT A 2" (5 CM) WIDE STRIP. COVER REMAINING PHYLLO WITH A DAMP CLOTH. BRUSH THE STRIP WITH BUTTER. PLACE 1 TSP. (5 ML) OF FILLING IN BOTTOM CORNER OF STRIP AND FOLD CORNER TO CORNER (FLAG FASHION) USING ENTIRE STRIP. FILLING SHOULD BE SEALED IN. CONTINUE UNTIL ALL FILLING IS USED. BRUSH TRIANGLES WITH BUTTER; BAKE AT 350°F (180°C) FOR 20-25 MINUTES. MAKES ABOUT 50.

TO FREEZE: BEFORE BAKING, FREEZE ON BAKING SHEET THEN PLACE FROZEN TRIANGLES IN PLASTIC BAGS. NO NEED TO THAW BEFORE COOKING.

SAMOSAS IN PHYLLO

THESE LOW-FAT APPETIZERS FREEZE WELL. NOW YOU'RE READY FOR LAST-MINUTE GUESTS!

FILLING:

I CUP	PEELED & FINELY CHOPPED POTATOES	250 ML
I TSP.	VEGETABLE OIL	5 ML
I	ONION, FINELY CHOPPED	I
2 TSP.	CURRY POWDER	10 ML
2 TSP.	CUMIN	10 ML
I TSP.	TURMERIC	5 ML
1/4 TSP.	SALT	I ML
	PINCH CAYENNE PEPPER	
1/2 LB.	LEAN GROUND BEEF	250 G
1/2 CUP	SMALL FROZEN PEAS	125 ML
3 TBSP.	BEEF BROTH	45 ML
I TBSP.	CURRANTS	15 ML
I TBSP.	LEMON JUICE	15 ML
2 TSP.	LIQUID HONEY	10 ML
9	SHEETS PHYLLO PASTRY	9
1/4 CUP	BUTTER, MELTED	60 ML

TO MAKE FILLING: COOK POTATOES IN BOILING WATER UNTIL TENDER BUT STILL FIRM; DRAIN AND SET ASIDE. IN NONSTICK PAN, HEAT OIL OVER MEDIUM HEAT AND COOK ONION, STIRRING, UNTIL SOFTENED. STIR IN CURRY POWDER, CUMIN, TURMERIC, SALT AND CAYENNE. STIR AND COOK FOR 2 MINUTES. ADD BEEF, BREAKING UP INTO SMALL PIECES; COOK UNTIL NO LONGER PINK. STIR IN POTATOES, PEAS, BEEF BROTH, CURRANTS, LEMON JUICE AND HONEY. COOK,

SAMOSAS IN PHYLLO

CONTINUED FROM PAGE 64.

GENTLY STIRRING, UNTIL PEAS ARE THAWED. COOL.
PLACE 1 SHEET OF PHYLLO ON WORK SURFACE (KEEP
A SLIGHTLY DAMP CLEAN CLOTH OVER THE OTHER
SHEETS SO THEY WILL NOT DRY OUT.) LIGHTLY BRUSH
PHYLLO WITH SOME OF THE BUTTER. USING A SHARP
KNIFE, CUT THE PHYLLO INTO 4, 3" (8 CM) WIDE
STRIPS. SPOON 1 TBSP. (15 ML) FILLING ONTO PHYLLO
ABOUT 1" (2.5 CM) FROM BOTTOM ON THE RIGHT
SIDE. FOLD THE LEFT SIDE OVER FILLING AND
CONTINUE FOLDING IN A TRIANGULAR SHAPE (FLAG-
FASHION) TO THE END OF THE STRIP. PRESS EDGES
TOGETHER AND PLACE ON BAKING SHEET. REPEAT
WITH REMAINING STRIPS. BRUSH TOPS LIGHTLY WITH
BUTTER. (THESE MAY BE FROZEN ON A COOKIE SHEET
AND STORED IN A FREEZER BAG.) DO NOT THAW. BAKE
AT 375°F (190°C) FOR 20 MINUTES, OR UNTIL
SAMOSAS ARE GOLDEN. MAKES 36 APPETIZERS.

SERVE WITH CORIANDER CHUTNEY OR A HOT MANGO
CHUTNEY OR GINGER PICKLE RELISH - ALL AVAILABLE
AT LARGE GROCERIES OR EASTERN SPECIALTY
STORES - EXPERIMENT! (PICTURED OPPOSITE PAGE 36.)

NEVER LEND YOUR CAR TO ANYONE TO WHOM YOU HAVE
GIVEN BIRTH - ERMA BOMBECK

CHICKEN SATAY WITH SPICY PEANUT DIPPING SAUCE

2	WHOLE BONELESS SKINLESS CHICKEN BREASTS	2
12	SMALL WOODEN SKEWERS, SOAKED IN WATER	12

GARLIC SOY MARINADE

2	GARLIC CLOVES, MINCED	2
¼ CUP	SOY SAUCE	60 ML
¼ CUP	LEMON JUICE	60 ML
2 TBSP.	OIL	30 ML

SPICY PEANUT DIPPING SAUCE

½ CUP	CHUNKY PEANUT BUTTER	125 ML
½ CUP	COCONUT MILK (LIGHT IS AVAILABLE)	125 ML
2 TBSP.	SWEET HOT CHILE SAUCE	30 ML
2 TBSP.	SOY SAUCE	30 ML
1	CLOVE GARLIC, MINCED	1
½ TSP.	CUMIN	2 ML

CUT CHICKEN IN ½" (1.3 CM) CUBES AND THREAD 4-5 PIECES ONTO EACH SKEWER. COMBINE MARINADE INGREDIENTS; POUR OVER SKEWERED CHICKEN AND MARINATE FOR 1 HOUR. TO SERVE, GRILL OR BROIL UNTIL BROWN, TURN AS NEEDED.

TO PREPARE SAUCE: COMBINE ALL INGREDIENTS IN A SMALL SAUCEPAN. BRING TO A BOIL; SIMMER 10 MINUTES, STIRRING FREQUENTLY. IF SAUCE BECOMES TOO THICK, ADD MORE COCONUT MILK.

TO SERVE, ARRANGE SKEWERED CHICKEN ON A PLATTER AROUND A BOWL OF PEANUT SAUCE FOR DIPPING. SERVES 4-6.

BUFFALO CHICKEN WINGS

HOT STUFF! PURISTS SAY YOU MUST SERVE WITH CELERY STICKS AND BLUE CHEESE DRESSING – SO DO IT!

CELERY STICKS, CUT IN STRIPS, STORE IN ICE WATER IN REFRIGERATOR

BLUE CHEESE DRESSING

1 OZ.	BLUE CHEESE, CRUMBLED	30 G
1/4 CUP	MAYONNAISE (NOT MIRACLE WHIP)	60 ML
1/4 CUP	SOUR CREAM OR YOGURT (FAT-FREE IS FINE)	60 ML

WINGS

1/4 CUP	BUTTER	60 ML
3-5 TBSP.	HOT RED PEPPER SAUCE	45-75 ML
1 1/2 TBSP.	RED WINE VINEGAR	22 ML
	OIL FOR DEEP-FRYING	
2 1/2 LBS.	CHICKEN WINGS, TIPS REMOVED, CUT IN 2	1.25 KG

PREPARE CELERY STICKS.

TO PREPARE DRESSING: MIX INGREDIENTS IN FOOD PROCESSOR AND CHILL UNTIL SERVING TIME.

TO PREPARE WINGS: MELT BUTTER IN LARGE SAUCEPAN. STIR IN HOT SAUCE, 3 TBSP. (45 ML) IS RELATIVELY MILD, AND VINEGAR. SET ASIDE. HEAT OIL IN A LARGE HEAVY FRYING PAN OR WOK (HEAT UNTIL A PIECE OF POTATO CRISPS QUICKLY). ADD WINGS A FEW AT A TIME, COOK ABOUT 10 MINUTES, OR UNTIL BROWN AND CRISP. REMOVE TO A PAPER TOWEL TO DRAIN. WHEN ALL WINGS ARE COOKED, REHEAT HOT SAUCE AND TOSS WITH WINGS TO COAT. SERVES 6-8.

GET OUT THE FINGER BOWLS FOR EVERYONE'S FAVORITE.

3 LBS.	CHICKEN WINGS, CUT IN 2, TIPS REMOVED	1.5 KG
½ CUP	KETCHUP (TRY "HOT" – IF YOU'RE NOT CHICKEN)	125 ML
¼ CUP	WATER	60 ML
¼ CUP	HONEY	60 ML
¼ CUP	RED WINE VINEGAR	60 ML
2 TBSP.	BROWN SUGAR	30 ML
I TBSP.	DIJON MUSTARD	15 ML
I TBSP.	WORCESTERSHIRE SAUCE	15 ML
I TBSP.	SOY SAUCE	15 ML
2 TBSP.	HOT PEPPER SAUCE	30 ML
2	GARLIC CLOVES, MINCED	2
2 TBSP.	DRIED MINCED ONIONS	30 ML

COVER A BROILER PAN WITH FOIL. POKE HOLES IN FOIL. ARRANGE WINGS IN SINGLE LAYER. PLACE UNDER BROILER UNTIL LIGHTLY BROWNED. IN A SAUCEPAN, COMBINE ALL REMAINING INGREDIENTS AND BRING TO A BOIL; REDUCE HEAT AND SIMMER FOR 5-10 MINUTES. USING TONGS, DIP EACH WING IN HOT SAUCE AND PLACE ON BAKING SHEET; BAKE AT 375°F (190°C) FOR 35-40 MINUTES. BASTE WITH REMAINING SAUCE DURING BAKING. DURING THE LAST FEW MINUTES, TURN ON BROILER AND CRISP WINGS. SERVES 6-8.

WHY IS THERE AN EXPIRATION DATE ON SOUR CREAM?

JELLY BALLS

RALLY 'ROUND THE CHAFING DISH!

I LB.	LEAN GROUND BEEF	500 G
I	EGG, BEATEN	I
1/2 CUP	FINE BREAD CRUMBS	125 ML
3 TBSP.	CHOPPED PARSLEY	45 ML
1/2 CUP	CHOPPED ONION	125 ML
I TSP.	WORCESTERSHIRE SAUCE	5 ML
	SALT & PEPPER TO TASTE	

CHILI GRAPE SAUCE:*

12 OZ.	BOTTLE CHILI SAUCE	341 ML
10 OZ.	JAR GRAPE JELLY	284 ML
I TSP.	LEMON JUICE	5 ML
2 TBSP.	BROWN SUGAR	30 ML
I TBSP.	SOY SAUCE	15 ML

MIX GROUND BEEF WITH EGG, BREAD CRUMBS, PARSLEY, ONION, WORCESTERSHIRE SAUCE, SALT AND PEPPER. ROLL INTO BALLS I" (2.5 CM) IN DIAMETER. HEAT CHILI SAUCE, JELLY, LEMON JUICE, BROWN SUGAR, AND SOY SAUCE IN A LARGE POT. BRING TO A BOIL AND ADD UNCOOKED MEATBALLS. SIMMER MEATBALLS IN SAUCE FOR 30 MINUTES. SERVE IN A CHAFING DISH. (AVEC TOOTHPICKS!) MAKES ABOUT 50 BALLS. FREEZES WELL.

* BELIEVE IT OR NOT - THIS SAUCE IS FANTASTIC. THE FLAVOR COMBINATION IS GREAT!

SHRIMP

3 LBS.	SHRIMP IN THE SHELL	1.5 KG
4	GARLIC CLOVES, PEELED	4
6	ALLSPICE BERRIES	6
1 TBSP.	RED PEPPER FLAKES	15 ML
1	BAY LEAF	1
6	SPRIGS FRESH PARSLEY	6
2	SPRIGS FRESH DILL	2
12 OZ.	BEER	341 ML
	SALT & PEPPER TO TASTE	

LEMON BUTTER DIPPING SAUCE

1/2 CUP	BUTTER	250 ML
	JUICE OF 1/2 LEMON	
1 TSP.	WORCESTERSHIRE SAUCE	5 ML
	SALT & PEPPER TO TASTE	

TO COOK SHRIMP: COMBINE ALL INGREDIENTS IN LARGE POT AND COVER. BRING TO A BOIL. TURN DOWN HEAT AND LET THE SHRIMP SIMMER 2 MINUTES. (DON'T OVERCOOK!) THEN REMOVE FROM HEAT AND DRAIN.

TO PREPARE SAUCE: HEAT BUTTER IN A SAUCEPAN UNTIL ALMOST BUBBLING. STIR IN LEMON JUICE AND WORCESTERSHIRE, SALT AND PEPPER TO TASTE.

SERVE SHRIMP HOT, IN THE SHELL. SPREAD OUT THE NEWSPAPER ON YOUR PATIO TABLE AND LET YOUR GUESTS "PEEL 'N' EAT". SERVE SAUCE INDIVIDUALLY TO 8 HAPPY GUESTS. (PICTURED OPPOSITE PAGE 37.)

SALADS

Arizona Fruit Salad
Romaine with Oranges and Pecans
Papaya Avocado Salad
Committee Salad
Marinated Artichoke and Mushroom Salad
Caesar Salad
Strawberry and Chèvre Salad
Spinach and Strawberry Salad
Fresh Spinach Salad
Christmas Salad
Layered Southwest Salad
Santa Fe Salad
Beet, Red Onion & Orange Salad
Broccoli Mandarin Salad
Greek Salad
Regina Beach Coleslaw
Killer Coleslaw
Spicy Noodle Salad
Orzo with Veggies
Fresh Orange Pasta Salad
Fiesta Chicken Tortilla Salad
Korean Chicken Salad
Layered Chicken Salad

DRESSINGS

Balsamic Vinaigrette
Roasted Garlic Caesar Dressing
Tarragon Mustard Dressing
Italian Dressing

ARIZONA FRUIT SALAD

GREAT WITH MEXICAN FARE.

SALAD

1	AVOCADO	1
2 TBSP.	LIME JUICE	30 ML
1	PAPAYA	1
2	ORANGES	2
1	GRAPEFRUIT	1
1	SMALL RED ONION	1
1/2	POMEGRANATE (OPTIONAL)	1/2

DRESSING

2 TBSP.	ORANGE JUICE	30 ML
2 TBSP.	LIME JUICE	30 ML
2 TSP.	LIQUID HONEY	10 ML
1/4 TSP.	HOT PEPPER FLAKES	1 ML
1/2 CUP	VEGETABLE OIL	125 ML

1	HEAD ROMAINE LETTUCE	1

TO MAKE SALAD: PEEL AND SLICE AVOCADO. SPRINKLE WITH 1 TBSP. (15 ML) LIME JUICE. PEEL, SEED AND SLICE PAPAYA THINLY. SPRINKLE WITH REMAINING LIME JUICE. PEEL ORANGES AND GRAPEFRUIT. CUT FRUIT INTO SEGMENTS. SLICE RED ONION. IN A LARGE BOWL, COMBINE AVOCADO, PAPAYA, ORANGE AND GRAPEFRUIT SEGMENTS AND ONION. SET ASIDE. IF USING POMEGRANATE, SCOOP OUT SEEDS AND SET ASIDE.

TO MAKE DRESSING: WHISK TOGETHER ORANGE JUICE, LIME JUICE, HONEY, PEPPER FLAKES AND OIL.

ARIZONA FRUIT SALAD

CONTINUED FROM PAGE 72.

BEFORE SERVING, POUR DRESSING OVER FRUIT AND
TOSS WELL. SPOON ONTO LETTUCE-LINED PLATTER.
SPRINKLE POMEGRANATE SEEDS OVER ALL. DELICIOUS
WITH OUR CHICKEN ENCHILADA CASSEROLE (PAGE 195).

ROMAINE WITH ORANGES AND PECANS

A REAL FAVORITE!

2	HEADS ROMAINE LETTUCE (WASH AND TEAR INTO BITE-SIZED PIECES)	2
1 CUP	PECANS HALVES, TOASTED	250 ML
2	ORANGES, PEELED & SLICED	2

DRESSING

1/4 CUP	VINEGAR	60 ML
1/2 CUP	VEGETABLE OIL	125 ML
1/4 CUP	SUGAR	60 ML
1 TSP.	SALT	5 ML
1/2	SMALL RED ONION, CHOPPED	1/2
1 TSP.	DRY MUSTARD	5 ML
2 TBSP.	WATER	30 ML

PLACE LETTUCE, PECANS AND ORANGES IN SALAD BOWL.
COMBINE DRESSING INGREDIENTS IN BLENDER. BLEND
UNTIL WELL MIXED. MAKE AHEAD AND REFRIGERATE
UNTIL READY TO TOSS SALAD. USE EXTRA DRESSING
AS A DIP FOR FRESH FRUIT! SERVES 6-8.

PAPAYA AVOCADO SALAD

I	HEAD OF ROMAINE LETTUCE	I
I	RIPE PAPAYA (PAPAYAS ARE RIPE WHEN THEY HAVE TURNED YELLOW)	I
I	LARGE AVOCADO, PEELED & SLICED	I
	RED ONION SLICES	

PAPAYA SEED DRESSING

1/4-1/2 CUP	SUGAR	60-125 ML
1/2 TSP.	DRY MUSTARD	2 ML
2 TSP.	SALT	10 ML
2 TBSP.	PAPAYA SEEDS	30 ML
1/2 CUP	WHITE WINE VINEGAR OR TARRAGON VINEGAR	125 ML
1/2 CUP	SALAD OIL	125 ML
2	GREEN ONIONS, FINELY CHOPPED	2

WASH AND DRY LETTUCE. TEAR INTO BITE-SIZED PIECES AND PLACE IN SALAD BOWL. HALVE AND PEEL PAPAYA. SCOOP OUT SEEDS AND SAVE 2 TBSP. (30 ML). SLICE PAPAYA. COMBINE DRESSING INGREDIENTS IN A BLENDER UNTIL PAPAYA SEEDS HAVE THE APPEARANCE OF GROUND PEPPER. STORE DRESSING IN REFRIGERATOR. JUST BEFORE SERVING, ADD PAPAYA, AVOCADO AND RED ONION SLICES TO LETTUCE. POUR DRESSING OVER SALAD AND TOSS. (YOU MIGHT HAVE SOME DRESSING LEFT OVER, BUT YOU'RE GOING TO WANT TO MAKE THIS SALAD AGAIN - SOON!) SERVES 6-8. (PICTURED OPPOSITE PAGE 55.)

COMMITTEE SALAD

WE ALL WORKED ON IT AND WE ALL LOVE IT.

DRESSING

1/2 CUP	OIL	125 ML
3 TBSP.	RED WINE VINEGAR	45 ML
1 TBSP.	LEMON JUICE	15 ML
2 TSP.	SUGAR	10 ML
1/2 TSP.	SALT	2 ML
1/2 TSP.	DRY MUSTARD	2 ML
1	GARLIC CLOVE, CRUSHED	1

SALAD

2 TBSP.	BUTTER	30 ML
1/2 CUP	SUNFLOWER SEEDS, SHELLED	125 ML
1/2 CUP	SLIVERED ALMONDS	125 ML
1	HEAD LEAF LETTUCE	1
2	GREEN ONIONS, FINELY CHOPPED	2
10 OZ.	CAN MANDARIN ORANGES, DRAINED	284 ML
1	RIPE AVOCADO, PEELED & SLICED	1

COMBINE ALL DRESSING INGREDIENTS IN A JAR; SHAKE TO BLEND. HEAT BUTTER IN FRYING PAN AND SAUTÉ SUNFLOWER SEEDS AND ALMONDS UNTIL GOLDEN BROWN. PREPARE REMAINING INGREDIENTS. ADD COOLED SEEDS AND ALMONDS. TOSS WITH DRESSING JUST BEFORE SERVING. SERVES 6.

THE TROUBLE WITH OPERA IS THERE'S TOO MUCH SINGING.

MARINATED ARTICHOKE AND MUSHROOM SALAD

MARINADE

½ CUP	TARRAGON VINEGAR	12 ML
2 TBSP.	WATER	30 ML
1 TBSP.	SUGAR	15 ML
1½ TSP.	SALT	7 ML
	DASH OF PEPPER	
1	GARLIC CLOVE, MINCED	1
½ CUP	SALAD OIL	125 ML

SALAD

14 OZ.	CAN ARTICHOKE HEARTS, DRAINED	398 ML
1 CUP	SLICED FRESH MUSHROOMS	250 ML
1	MEDIUM RED ONION, SLICED IN RINGS	1
1	HEAD ROMAINE LETTUCE, TORN INTO BITE-SIZED PIECES	1
½ CUP	CHOPPED FRESH PARSLEY	125 ML
	PAPRIKA	

COMBINE MARINADE INGREDIENTS AND MIX THOROUGHLY. TOSS ARTICHOKES, MUSHROOMS AND ONIONS WITH MARINADE. COVER AND REFRIGERATE AT LEAST 2 HOURS, STIRRING OCCASIONALLY. SERVE ON LETTUCE, USING MARINADE AS THE DRESSING. SPRINKLE WITH PARSLEY AND PAPRIKA. SERVES 6.

BEFORE THEY INVENTED DRAWING BOARDS, WHAT DID THEY GO BACK TO?

CAESAR SALAD

YOU'LL DESERVE THE "HAILS" WHEN YOU SERVE THIS CLASSIC.

1	LARGE HEAD ROMAINE LETTUCE	1
1	GARLIC CLOVE, MINCED	1
1/3 CUP	OIL	75 ML
	SALT & FRESH GROUND BLACK PEPPER TO TASTE	
1/4 TSP.	DRY MUSTARD	1 ML
1 1/2 TSP.	WORCESTERSHIRE SAUCE	7 ML
3 (OR MORE)	ANCHOVY FILETS, DRAINED	3 (OR MORE)
1	EGG	1
1-2 TBSP.	FRESH LEMON JUICE	15-30 ML
2 TBSP.	FRESHLY GRATED PARMESAN CHEESE	30 ML
	CROÛTONS	

WASH AND TEAR ROMAINE INTO BITE-SIZED PIECES. BLENDERIZE REMAINING INGREDIENTS, EXCEPT PARMESAN AND CROÛTONS. TOSS LETTUCE AND DRESSING. SPRINKLE ON PARMESAN AND CROÛTONS. TOSS AGAIN.

WHERE DO THEY GET THE SEEDS TO GROW SEEDLESS ORANGES?

STRAWBERRY AND CHÈVRE SALAD

WHEN NANNY (OR THE REST OF THE HERD) IS COMING FOR LUNCH. SERVE WITH BAGUETTE OR CROISSANTS AND A GLASS OF BUBBLY.

BALSAMIC RASPBERRY VINAIGRETTE

1	GARLIC CLOVE, MINCED	1
1/2 TSP.	HONEY DIJON MUSTARD	2 ML
2 TBSP.	RASPBERRY VINEGAR	30 ML
1 TBSP.	BALSAMIC VINEGAR	15 ML
1 TBSP.	BROWN SUGAR	15 ML
1/4 CUP	VEGETABLE OIL	60 ML

SALAD

6 CUPS	MIXED GREENS	1.5 L
1/2 CUP	CRUMBLED CHÈVRE (GOAT CHEESE) – BRIE IS GOOD TOO	125 ML
1/4 CUP	SLIVERED ALMONDS, TOASTED	60 ML
2 CUPS	HALVED STRAWBERRIES	500 ML
	SALT AND FRESHLY GROUND PEPPER TO TASTE	

TO PREPARE VINAIGRETTE: IN A SMALL BOWL, COMBINE GARLIC, MUSTARD, VINEGARS AND BROWN SUGAR. WHISK IN OIL.

TO PREPARE SALAD: IN A LARGE BOWL, TOSS GREENS WITH VINAIGRETTE. PLACE AN EQUAL PORTION ON 4 SALAD PLATES. TOP WITH CHEESE, NUTS AND STRAWBERRIES. SPRINKLE WITH SALT AND PEPPER.

EVER STOP TO THINK AND FORGET TO START AGAIN?

SPINACH AND STRAWBERRY SALAD

SPINACH - ENOUGH FOR YOUR CREW
STRAWBERRIES - SAME AS ABOVE!

POPPYSEED WORCESTERSHIRE DRESSING

1/3 CUP	WHITE SUGAR	75 ML
1/2 CUP	OIL	125 ML
1/4 CUP	WHITE VINEGAR	60 ML
2 TBSP.	SESAME SEEDS	30 ML
2 TBSP.	POPPY SEEDS	30 ML
1/4 TSP.	PAPRIKA	1 ML
1/2 TSP.	WORCESTERSHIRE SAUCE	2 ML
1 1/2 TSP.	MINCED ONION	7 ML

TEAR SPINACH INTO BITE-SIZED PIECES. CUT
STRAWBERRIES IN HALF. COMBINE DRESSING
INGREDIENTS AND MIX WELL. TOSS WITH SPINACH
AND STRAWBERRIES.

CHILD'S OBSERVATIONS ON LOVE:

"NO ONE IS SURE WHY IT HAPPENS, BUT I HEARD IT HAS
SOMETHING TO DO WITH HOW YOU SMELL . . . THAT'S WHY
PERFUME AND DEODORANT ARE SO POPULAR."

"I'M NOT RUSHING INTO BEING IN LOVE. I'M FINDING
FOURTH GRADE HARD ENOUGH."

FRESH SPINACH SALAD

DRESSING

I	GARLIC CLOVE, MINCED	I
2 TBSP.	CIDER OR RED WINE VINEGAR	30 ML
I TSP.	SUGAR	5 ML
1/2 TSP.	SALT	2 ML
I TSP.	DRY MUSTARD	5 ML
1/2 TSP.	FRESHLY GROUND PEPPER	2 ML
1/4 CUP	SALAD OIL	60 ML

SALAD

8 CUPS	CRISP YOUNG SPINACH, STEMS REMOVED	2 L
3	HARD-COOKED EGGS, GRATED	3
8	SLICES BACON, COOKED & CRUMBLED	8
4	GREEN ONIONS, FINELY CHOPPED	4
	FRESH MUSHROOMS, SLICED	
	FRESH CAULIFLOWER, SLICED	

TO MAKE DRESSING: BEAT ALL INGREDIENTS TOGETHER AND REFRIGERATE.

TO MAKE SALAD: PREPARE SALAD INGREDIENTS, TOSS WITH DRESSING JUST BEFORE SERVING. SERVES 4-6.

CHILD'S SUGGESTION FOR LOVE BALLAD:
"I'M IN LOVE WITH YOU MOST OF THE TIME, BUT DON'T BOTHER ME WHEN I'M WITH MY FRIENDS."

CHRISTMAS SALAD

... OR THE FIRST DAY OF SPRING, OR GROUND HOG DAY, OR SECRETARIES' DAY OR ....

SALAD

8 CUPS	SPINACH LEAVES	2 L
1	AVOCADO, THINLY SLICED	1
1/2 CUP	THINLY SLICED RED ONION	125 ML
1/2 CUP	DRIED CRANBERRIES OR 1 CUP (250 ML) POMEGRANATE SEEDS	125 ML

DRESSING

1/4 CUP	CRANBERRY JUICE CONCENTRATE	60 ML
1/4 CUP	WHITE WINE VINEGAR	60 ML
1 1/2 TSP.	DIJON MUSTARD	7 ML
1/4 TSP.	FRESHLY GROUND PEPPER	1 ML
1/2 CUP	VEGETABLE OIL	125 ML

TO MAKE SALAD: STEM SPINACH, TEAR INTO BITE-SIZED PIECES AND PLACE IN A LARGE SALAD BOWL. PLACE AVOCADO AND ONION OVER SPINACH.

TO MAKE DRESSING: COMBINE CRANBERRY JUICE CONCENTRATE, VINEGAR, MUSTARD, PEPPER AND OIL IN A JAR WITH A TIGHT-FITTING LID. SHAKE UNTIL WELL BLENDED. DRIZZLE OVER SALAD. SPRINKLE DRIED CRANBERRIES OR POMEGRANATE SEEDS OVER SALAD, TOSS GENTLY AND SERVE 6 GUESTS.

FAVORITE OXYMORONS: ACT NATURALLY, AIRLINE FOOD, GOOD GRIEF.

LAYERED SOUTHWEST SALAD

CREAMY RANCH DRESSING

1 CUP	COTTAGE CHEESE	250 ML
1 CUP	BUTTERMILK	250 ML
2 TBSP.	WHITE WINE VINEGAR	30 ML
1	LARGE GARLIC CLOVE, MINCED	1
1/2 TSP.	SALT	2 ML
1/2 TSP.	FRESHLY GROUND BLACK PEPPER	2 ML
1/2 TSP.	CUMIN	2 ML
1 TSP.	DRIED OREGANO LEAVES	5 ML

SALAD

1	JICAMA, 3/4 LB. (365 G) PEELED	1
14 OZ.	CAN BLACK BEANS, DRAINED & RINSED	398 ML
1 CUP	MILD SALSA	250 ML
1/2 CUP	DICED RED ONION	125 ML
10 OZ.	FRESH SPINACH, WASHED, STEMMED & CUT INTO PIECES	300 G
2 CUPS	FROZEN WHOLE KERNEL CORN, COOKED, DRAINED & COOLED	500 ML
2 CUPS	SHREDDED CHEDDAR CHEESE	500 ML

DRESSING: BLEND ALL INGREDIENTS IN BLENDER UNTIL SMOOTH. COVER AND REFRIGERATE 1 HOUR.

SALAD: CUT JICAMA INTO 6 WEDGES. SLICE CROSSWISE INTO 1/8" (3 MM) THICK SLICES. COMBINE BEANS, SALSA AND ONION IN MEDIUM BOWL. LAYER 1/2 OF SPINACH, JICAMA, BEAN MIXTURE, CORN AND 1 CUP (250 ML) OF DRESSING IN LARGE BOWL. REPEAT LAYERS. SPRINKLE WITH CHEESE; DRIZZLE WITH REMAINING DRESSING. COVER AND REFRIGERATE 1-2 HOURS. SERVE WITH JALAPEÑO CORN MUFFINS (PAGE 8). SERVES 6-8.

SANTA FE SALAD

CILANTRO LIME DRESSING

1/4 CUP	OLIVE OIL	60 ML
	JUICE OF 2 LIMES	
1/4 CUP	CHOPPED CILANTRO	60 ML
1 TSP.	CUMIN	5 ML
	SALT & FRESHLY GROUND PEPPER	
	TO TASTE	

SALAD

19 OZ.	CAN BLACK BEANS (TURTLE BEANS), RINSED & DRAINED	540 ML
1	RED BELL PEPPER, DICED	1
12 OZ.	CAN KERNEL CORN, DRAINED	341 ML
1/3 CUP	CHOPPED RED ONION	75 ML
1	JALAPEÑO PEPPER, SEEDED & MINCED	1

IN MEDIUM BOWL, WHISK TOGETHER OIL AND LIME JUICE. ADD CILANTRO, CUMIN, SALT AND PEPPER AND MIX WELL. STIR IN SALAD INGREDIENTS AND CORRECT SEASONING. SERVE AT ROOM TEMPERATURE. SERVES 6.

A MAN CELEBRATING HIS 50TH WEDDING ANNIVERSARY SAID TO HIS YOUNGER FRIEND: "I'M TAKING MY WIFE TO ASIA."

"THAT'S INTERESTING." SAID THE YOUNGER MAN, "IT'S OUR 25TH AND I'M TAKING MY WIFE THERE TOO!"

"THAT'S A PRETTY BIG PRESENT - WHAT WILL YOU DO FOR YOUR 50TH?"

"GO AND GET HER."

BEET, RED ONION AND ORANGE SALAD

SALAD

1½ LBS.	FRESH BEETS	750 G
½	RED ONION, THINLY SLICED	½
2	LARGE NAVAL ORANGES, PEELED & SECTIONED.	2

VINAIGRETTE

¼ CUP	RED WINE VINEGAR	60 ML
¼ CUP	FRESH ORANGE JUICE	60 ML
2 TSP.	DIJON MUSTARD	10 ML
2 TSP.	ORANGE ZEST	10 ML
½ CUP	OLIVE OIL	125 ML
	SALT & PEPPER TO TASTE	

TO MAKE SALAD: COOK BEETS IN BOILING SALTED WATER 30-40 MINUTES, OR UNTIL TENDER. DRAIN, REMOVE SKINS AND COOL. CUT INTO ¼" (1 CM) SLICES. PLACE BEETS, ONIONS AND ORANGE SLICES IN A SALAD BOWL.

TO MAKE VINAIGRETTE: WHISK VINAIGRETTE INGREDIENTS TOGETHER IN BOWL. POUR OVER SALAD. COVER AND REFRIGERATE FOR SEVERAL HOURS. SERVES 8.

STUDENT: "IS IT TRUE THAT HISTORY REPEATS ITSELF?"
HISTORY PROFESSOR: "YES, PARTICULARLY IF YOU FLUNK IT."

BROCCOLI MANDARIN SALAD

GREAT FOR BUFFETS OR PICNICS. EVERYONE WANTS THIS RECIPE.

DRESSING

2	EGGS	2
1/2 CUP	SUGAR	125 ML
1 TSP.	CORNSTARCH	5 ML
1 TSP.	DRY MUSTARD	5 ML
1/4 CUP	WHITE WINE VINEGAR	60 ML
1/4 CUP	WATER	60 ML
1/2 CUP	MAYONNAISE	125 ML

SALAD

4 CUPS	FRESH BROCCOLI FLORETS	1 L
1/2 CUP	RAISINS	125 ML
8	SLICES BACON, COOKED & CHOPPED	8
2 CUPS	SLICED FRESH MUSHROOMS	500 ML
1/2 CUP	SLIVERED TOASTED ALMONDS	125 ML
10 OZ.	CAN MANDARIN ORANGES, DRAINED	284 ML
1/2	RED ONION, SLICED	1/2

TO MAKE DRESSING: IN A SAUCEPAN, WHISK TOGETHER EGGS, SUGAR, CORNSTARCH AND DRY MUSTARD. ADD VINEGAR AND WATER AND COOK SLOWLY UNTIL THICKENED. REMOVE FROM HEAT AND STIR IN MAYONNAISE. COOL.

TO MAKE SALAD: MARINATE BROCCOLI IN DRESSING FOR SEVERAL HOURS. ADD REMAINING INGREDIENTS AND TOSS WELL. SERVES 6.

CLONES ARE PEOPLE TWO.

GREEK SALAD

ANY GREEK WHO BRINGS THIS IS BEARING A GIFT!

SALAD

1	HEAD ROMAINE LETTUCE, TORN	1
1	LARGE TOMATO, CUT IN WEDGES	1
1	GREEN PEPPER, CUT INTO STRIPS	1
1	SMALL RED ONION, SLICED & SEPARATED INTO RINGS	1
1	MEDIUM CUCUMBER, SEEDED & CHOPPED	1
1/4 CUP	GREEK OLIVES (KALAMATA)	60 ML
1/2 CUP	CRUMBLED FETA CHEESE	125 ML

DRESSING

6 TBSP.	OLIVE OIL	90 ML
2 TBSP.	FRESH LEMON JUICE	30 ML
1 TSP.	OREGANO	5 ML
	SALT & COARSELY GROUND PEPPER TO TASTE	

COMBINE ALL SALAD INGREDIENTS, EXCEPT FETA CHEESE, IN A LARGE SALAD BOWL. BEAT DRESSING INGREDIENTS UNTIL WELL BLENDED. POUR OVER SALAD, TOSS WELL AND SPRINKLE ON FETA CHEESE.

AS A VARIATION, SERVE IN A PITA POCKET!

MY HUSBAND THINKS THAT HEALTH FOOD IS ANYTHING HE EATS BEFORE THE EXPIRATION DATE.

REGINA BEACH COLESLAW

A MUST WITH OUR BEST HOMEMADE FISH 'N' CHIPS (PAGE 179).

SLAW

3 LBS.	CABBAGE SHREDDED	1.5 KG
2	LARGE CARROTS, COARSELY GRATED	2
1	WHITE ONION, CHOPPED	1
1½ CUPS	SUGAR	375 ML

DRESSING

1 CUP	SALAD OIL	250 ML
1 CUP	VINEGAR	250 ML
½ CUP	SUGAR	125 ML
2 TBSP.	SALT	30 ML
1 TBSP.	CELERY SEED	15 ML

PUT VEGETABLES IN A LARGE BOWL, SPRINKLE SUGAR OVER TOP. IN A SAUCEPAN, BOIL DRESSING INGREDIENTS UNTIL THE SUGAR HAS DISSOLVED. POUR OVER VEGETABLES AND MIX WELL. PACK INTO STERILIZED JARS. THIS SALAD WILL KEEP UP TO 2 WEEKS IN THE REFRIGERATOR. GREAT FOR A CROWD. MAKES 3 QUARTS (3 L). DRAIN BEFORE SERVING.

THESE DAYS, IF A LITTLE OLD LADY IS SITTING AT A SPINNING WHEEL CHANCES ARE SHE'S IN LAS VEGAS.

KILLER COLESLAW

ANOTHER FOREVER FAVORITE!

SALAD INGREDIENTS

1/2	CABBAGE, CHOPPED	1/2
5	GREEN ONIONS, CHOPPED	5
1/4 CUP	SLIVERED ALMONDS, TOASTED	60 ML
1/4 CUP	SUNFLOWER SEEDS, TOASTED (OR SESAME SEEDS)	60 ML
3 OZ.	PKG. JAPANESE NOODLE SOUP MIX, (SAVE SEASONING PACKAGE FOR DRESSING)	85 G

DRESSING

1/4 CUP	RICE (OR WHITE) VINEGAR	60 ML
1/4 CUP	SALAD OIL	60 ML
	SEASONING PACKAGE FROM NOODLES	

COMBINE ALL SALAD INGREDIENTS EXCEPT NOODLES.
BEFORE SERVING, CRUSH NOODLES, COMBINE WITH
SALAD INGREDIENTS AND TOSS WITH DRESSING.
SERVES 6. IF THERE'S ANY LEFT OVER - SAVE IT!
KIDS LOVE IT THE NEXT DAY!

OUTSIDE OF A DOG, A MAN'S BEST FRIEND IS A BOOK; INSIDE
OF A DOG, IT IS VERY DARK.

SPICY NOODLE SALAD

THIS DRESSING CAN BE PREPARED UP TO 1 WEEK IN ADVANCE - IN FACT, THE FLAVOR IMPROVES.

DRESSING

1/3 CUP	SOY SAUCE	75 ML
1/4 CUP	WHITE WINE VINEGAR	60 ML
2 TBSP.	CHILI SAUCE	30 ML
2 TBSP.	SUGAR	30 ML
2 TBSP.	SESAME OIL	30 ML
1"	CHUNK FRESH GINGER, PEELED & FINELY CHOPPED	2.5 CM
4	GARLIC CLOVES, MINCED	4
2 TSP.	CHILI FLAKES	10 ML
	FRESHLY GROUND BLACK PEPPER	
1/4 CUP	VEGETABLE OIL	60 ML

SPAGHETTINI OR VERMICELLI
GRATED CARROTS
GREEN ONION, THINLY SLICED

IN A MEDIUM BOWL, WHISK SOY SAUCE WITH VINEGAR, CHILI SAUCE, SUGAR, SESAME OIL, GINGER, GARLIC, CHILI FLAKES AND PEPPER. GRADUALLY WHISK IN VEGETABLE OIL IN A THIN STREAM. REFRIGERATE UNTIL READY TO USE. WHISK AGAIN JUST BEFORE USING. MAKES ABOUT 1 1/2 CUPS (375 ML).

TOSS WITH COOKED PASTA, CARROTS AND GREEN ONIONS.

I INTEND TO LIVE FOREVER - SO FAR, SO GOOD!

A GREAT COMPLEMENT TO GRILLED MEATS.

SALAD

6 OZ.	SNOW PEAS, TRIMMED	170 G
2 CUPS	ORZO	500 ML
1½ CUPS	CHERRY TOMATOES, CUT IN QUARTERS & SEEDED	375 ML
1 CUP	SEEDED, CHOPPED CUCUMBER	250 ML
½ CUP	CHOPPED GREEN ONIONS	125 ML
½ CUP	CHOPPED FRESH PARSLEY	125 ML
2 TSP.	GRATED LEMON RIND	10 ML
	SALT & PEPPER TO TASTE	

LEMON GARLIC DRESSING

¼ CUP	FRESH LEMON JUICE	60 ML
2 TBSP.	WHITE WINE VINEGAR	30 ML
2 TSP.	GRATED LEMON RIND	10 ML
1 TSP.	MINCED GARLIC	5 ML
½ CUP	OIL	125 ML
	SALT & PEPPER	
	LETTUCE	

TO MAKE SALAD: BRING A LARGE POT OF SALTED WATER TO A BOIL. ADD SNOW PEAS AND COOK FOR 1 MINUTE. USING A SLOTTED SPOON, REMOVE PEAS TO A STRAINER; RINSE UNDER COLD WATER AND DRAIN ON PAPER TOWEL. ADD ORZO TO SAME POT AND BOIL UNTIL TENDER BUT STILL FIRM TO BITE, ABOUT 10 MINUTES. DRAIN; COOL AND PLACE IN A LARGE BOWL. ADD SNOW PEAS,

ORZO WITH VEGGIES

CONTINUED FROM PAGE 90.

TOMATOES, CUCUMBER, ONIONS, PARSLEY AND LEMON RIND. SEASON WITH SALT AND PEPPER.

TO MAKE DRESSING: COMBINE LEMON JUICE, VINEGAR, LEMON RIND AND GARLIC IN MEDIUM BOWL. GRADUALLY BLEND IN OIL. SEASON TO TASTE WITH SALT AND PEPPER.

POUR HALF OF THE DRESSING OVER SALAD AND TOSS TO COAT. COVER SALAD AND REMAINING DRESSING AND CHILL. LET SIT AT LEAST 6 HOURS. BRING TO ROOM TEMPERATURE BEFORE SERVING. TO SERVE, TOSS SALAD WITH REMAINING DRESSING TO COAT GENEROUSLY. LINE SHALLOW SERVING BOWL WITH LETTUCE AND MOUND SALAD IN BOWL. SERVES 6-8. (PICTURED OPPOSITE PAGE 54.)

IT'S BETTER TO BE NOUVEAU RICHE THAN NEVER TO HAVE BEEN RICHE AT ALL.

FRESH ORANGE PASTA SALAD

ATTRACTIVE, LIGHT AND ZESTY

<u>ORANGE DILL DRESSING</u>

	GRATED PEEL OF ½ ORANGE	
	JUICE OF 1 ORANGE	
3 TBSP.	VEGETABLE OIL	45 ML
½ TSP.	SEASONING SALT	2 ML
½ TSP.	DRIED DILLWEED	2 ML
2 CUPS	SPIRAL PASTA	500 ML
2	ORANGES - PEELED AND CUT INTO	2
	SEMICIRCULAR SLICES	
2 CUPS	BROCCOLI FLORETS, COOKED	500 ML
	TENDER-CRISP	
½ CUP	SLICED CELERY	125 ML
½ CUP	SLICED GREEN ONIONS	125 ML
	PEPPER & SALT TO TASTE	

IN A LARGE BOWL, COMBINE ORANGE PEEL, ORANGE
JUICE, OIL, SEASONING SALT, AND DILL-WEED. COOK
PASTA ACCORDING TO PACKAGE DIRECTIONS. DRAIN.
TO DRESSING, ADD PASTA, ORANGE SLICES, BROCCOLI,
CELERY, ONIONS, SALT AND PEPPER. GENTLY TOSS.
COVER AND CHILL. SERVE WITH CHEESE BUNS.
SERVES 6-8.

IF THE WORLD IS GETTING SMALLER, WHY DO THE
POSTAL RATES KEEP GOING UP?

FIESTA CHICKEN TORTILLA SALAD

A DELICIOUS DINNER SALAD FOR 2 - MUY SABROSO!
- DON'T BE SHY, USE YOUR FINGERS FOR THE
TORTILLA STRIPS.

I	WHOLE BONELESS, SKINLESS CHICKEN BREAST	I
I TBSP.	TABASCO	15 ML
	VEGETABLE OIL FOR FRYING	
3	SOFT CORN TORTILLAS, IN 1/4" (1 CM) STRIPS	3
	SALT TO SPRINKLE	
4 CUPS	ROMAINE LETTUCE, SLICED IN STRIPS	I L
1/2	RED PEPPER, CUT IN STRIPS	1/2

DRESSING

4 TBSP.	TOASTED SESAME SEEDS	60 ML
2 TBSP.	WHITE WINE VINEGAR	30 ML
I TBSP.	DIJON MUSTARD	15 ML
1/2 CUP	VEGETABLE OIL	125 ML
	SALT & PEPPER TO TASTE	

TO PREPARE CHICKEN: CUT CHICKEN BREAST INTO 1/4"
(1 CM) STRIPS AND TOSS WITH THE TABASCO. HEAT
OIL, 1/4" (1 CM) DEEP, UNTIL HOT IN HEAVY FRYING
PAN. FRY TORTILLA STRIPS QUICKLY UNTIL GOLDEN.
SET ON PAPER TOWEL TO DRAIN. SEASON WITH SALT.
POUR OFF ALL BUT A LITTLE OIL AND SAUTÉ
CHICKEN FOR 2-3 MINUTES. SET ASIDE.

TO PREPARE DRESSING: COMBINE ALL INGREDIENTS IN
BLENDER AND BLEND UNTIL SMOOTH.

TO PREPARE SALAD: PLACE LETTUCE, PEPPERS AND
CHICKEN IN A BOWL AND TOSS WITH DRESSING.
SERVE ON INDIVIDUAL PLATES AND ARRANGE TORTILLA
STRIPS ON TOP.

KOREAN CHICKEN SALAD

A PERFECT SUMMER MEAL. THE ONLY THING THAT'S DIFFICULT IS FINDING THE KOREAN CHICKENS!

3 LBS.	BONELESS SKINLESS CHICKEN BREASTS	1.5 KG

MARINADE

¼ CUP	SOY SAUCE	60 ML
2 TBSP.	OIL	30 ML
2 TBSP.	SHERRY OR WHITE WINE	30 ML
½ TSP.	GROUND GINGER	2 ML
½ TSP.	CINNAMON	2 ML
2	GARLIC CLOVES, FINELY CHOPPED	2

SALAD VEGGIES

2 CUPS	SHREDDED ICEBERG LETTUCE	500 ML
1 CUP	THINLY SLICED CUCUMBER	250 ML
1 CUP	THINLY SLICED CARROTS	250 ML
⅔ CUP	CHOPPED GREEN ONION	150 ML
1 CUP	BEAN SPROUTS	250 ML
¾ CUP	SLIVERED ALMONDS, TOASTED & SALTED	175 ML
2 TBSP.	SESAME SEEDS, TOASTED	30 ML

DRESSING

½ TSP.	DRY MUSTARD	2 ML
½ TSP.	SALT	2 ML
½ TSP.	TABASCO SAUCE	2 ML
1 TBSP.	SOY SAUCE	15 ML
¼ CUP	CORN OIL	60 ML
¼ CUP	SESAME OIL	60 ML
4 TSP.	LEMON JUICE	20 ML

KOREAN CHICKEN SALAD

CONTINUED FROM PAGE 94.

CUT CHICKEN BREASTS IN HALF. COMBINE MARINADE INGREDIENTS. THOROUGHLY COAT CHICKEN IN MARINADE. PLACE IN SHALLOW ROASTING PAN. POUR REMAINDER OF MARINADE OVER TOP AND COOK, UNCOVERED, AT 400°F (200°C) FOR 40 MINUTES, TURNING AT HALF TIME. (IF YOUR TEAM IS LOSING — HAVE ANOTHER BEER!) COOL COOKED CHICKEN AND CUT IN THIN STRIPS. PREPARE SALAD VEGGIES AND PLACE IN LARGE BOWL. WHISK TOGETHER ALL DRESSING INGREDIENTS. JUST BEFORE SERVING, TOSS THE CHICKEN AND VEGGIES WITH DRESSING, ALMONDS AND SESAME SEEDS. ENJOY! SERVES 6.

WHY DOES IT TAKE SO LITTLE TIME FOR A CHILD WHO IS AFRAID OF THE DARK TO BECOME A TEENAGER WHO WANTS TO STAY OUT ALL NIGHT?

LAYERED CHICKEN SALAD

A REAL WINNER! PREPARE THIS SALAD THE NIGHT BEFORE AND SERVE FOR LUNCH TO 8-10 DELIGHTED GUESTS.

SALAD

4-5 CUPS	SHREDDED ICEBERG LETTUCE	1-1.25 L
1/4 LB.	BEAN SPROUTS	125 G
8 OZ.	CAN WATER CHESTNUTS, SLICED	227 G
1	MEDIUM-SIZED CUCUMBER, THINLY SLICED	1
1/2 CUP	THINLY SLICED GREEN ONIONS	125 ML
2 CUPS	SNOW PEAS (OR FROZEN IS FINE)	250 ML
4 CUPS	COOKED CHICKEN, CUT INTO STRIPS	1 L

DRESSING

2 CUPS	MAYONNAISE	500 ML
2 TSP.	CURRY POWDER	10 ML
1/2 TSP.	GROUND GINGER	2 ML
1 TBSP.	SUGAR	15 ML
12	CHERRY TOMATOES, HALVED	12

SPREAD LETTUCE EVENLY IN A 4-QUART (4 L) GLASS BOWL. TOP WITH 1 LAYER EACH OF SPROUTS, WATER CHESTNUTS, CUCUMBER, ONIONS, PEAS AND CHICKEN. (MAKE SURE PEAS ARE DRY). STIR TOGETHER MAYONNAISE, CURRY, GINGER AND SUGAR. SPREAD EVENLY OVER THE SALAD. DECORATE WITH HALVED CHERRY TOMATOES. COVER AND REFRIGERATE UNTIL READY TO SERVE. (YOU MAY WANT TO MAKE EXTRA MAYONNAISE MIXTURE TO SERVE ON THE SIDE.)

BALSAMIC VINAIGRETTE

DRIZZLE OVER A VARIETY OF GREENS: BIBB, LEAF, ENDIVE, RADICCHIO, ARUGULA (YOU CAN BUY THIS COMBO PACKAGED AT MOST STORES.)

1/3 CUP	BALSAMIC VINEGAR	75 ML
1/4 CUP	OLIVE OIL	60 ML
1/4 CUP	DRY WHITE WINE	60 ML
	JUICE OF 1 LIME	
	SALT & FRESHLY GROUND PEPPER	
	TO TASTE	

POUR VINEGAR INTO A SMALL BOWL AND GRADUALLY WHISK IN OIL. WHISK IN WINE AND LIME JUICE, SEASON AND STORE IN REFRIGERATOR. JUST BEFORE SERVING, SHAKE WELL AND DRIZZLE OVER GREENS.

ROASTED GARLIC CAESAR DRESSING

1	GARLIC BULB, ROASTED	1
1-2	ANCHOVIES	1-2
1 TSP.	DIJON MUSTARD	5 ML
1 TSP.	WORCESTERSHIRE SAUCE	5 ML
2 TBSP.	BALSAMIC VINEGAR	30 ML
2 TBSP.	OLIVE OIL	30 ML
1/4 CUP	GRATED PARMESAN CHEESE	60 ML
1/2 CUP	YOGURT	125 ML
	SALT AND PEPPER TO TASTE	

TO ROAST GARLIC: REMOVE LOOSE SKINS, RUB BULB WITH OIL AND WRAP IN FOIL. BAKE IN A 350°F (180°C) OVEN FOR ABOUT 1 HOUR.

TO MAKE DRESSING: CUT TOP OFF ROASTED GARLIC AND SQUEEZE INTO FOOD PROCESSOR. ADD REMAINING INGREDIENTS; BLEND UNTIL SMOOTH.

TARRAGON MUSTARD DRESSING

MAHVALOUS!! ON SALMON OR SEAFOOD.

1	LARGE EGG	1
1 TBSP.	DIJON MUSTARD	15 ML
2 TBSP.	TARRAGON WINE VINEGAR	30 ML
1-2 TSP.	TARRAGON	5-10 ML
	SALT & PEPPER TO TASTE	
1¼ CUPS	VEGETABLE OIL	300 ML

USING A FOOD PROCESSOR, BLEND TOGETHER EGG, MUSTARD, VINEGAR AND SEASONINGS. WITH MACHINE RUNNING, DRIZZLE IN OIL. MIXTURE WILL BE THICK AND SHINY.

I'M NOT GOING TO VACUUM UNTIL THEY MAKE A MODEL YOU CAN RIDE ON!

ITALIAN DRESSING

1 CUP	OLIVE OIL	250 ML
¼ CUP	WHITE WINE VINEGAR	60 ML
1 TBSP.	FRESH LEMON JUICE	15 ML
¾ TSP.	OREGANO	4 ML
½ TSP.	DRY MUSTARD	2 ML
¼ TSP.	THYME	1 ML
1	GARLIC CLOVE, MINCED	1
1 TSP.	MINCED ONION	5 ML
1 TSP.	HONEY	5 ML
	SALT & PEPPER TO TASTE	

COMBINE ALL INGREDIENTS. BLENDERIZE AND STORE IN REFRIGERATOR. MAKES ABOUT 1½ CUPS (375 ML).

SOUPS

Cold Cucumber Soup
Gazpacho
Fresh Tomato Bisque
Red Pepper Soup
Champagne Squash Soup
Carrot Soup
Corn Chowder
French Onion Soup Au Gratin
Tortilla Soup
Moroccan Chicken-Vegetable Soup
Shooter's Soup
War Wonton Soup
Hamburger Soup
Best of Bridge Bean Soup

COLD CUCUMBER SOUP

A DELICIOUS COLD SOUP. MAKE THE DAY BEFORE.
(YOU'LL NEED A BLENDER.)

2-8"	ENGLISH CUCUMBERS	2-20 CM
2 TBSP.	BUTTER	30 ML
1/4 CUP	CHOPPED GREEN ONIONS	60 ML
4 CUPS	CHICKEN BROTH	1 L
1 TBSP.	WHITE WINE VINEGAR	15 ML
1/2 TSP.	DRIED TARRAGON (OR MORE)	2 ML
3 TBSP.	CREAM OF WHEAT (QUICK COOKING)	45 ML
	SALT & WHITE PEPPER	
1 CUP	FAT-FREE SOUR CREAM	250 ML

CUT 12 PAPER-THIN SLICES OF CUCUMBER (SKIN ON)
TO BE USED FOR GARNISH AND RESERVE. PEEL
REMAINING CUCUMBERS AND CHOP INTO CHUNKS. IN
A LARGE POT, MELT BUTTER; STIR IN ONIONS AND
COOK 1 MINUTE OVER MODERATE HEAT. ADD CUCUMBER
CHUNKS, CHICKEN BROTH, VINEGAR AND TARRAGON.
BRING TO A BOIL. STIR IN CREAM OF WHEAT.
SIMMER, UNCOVERED, FOR 20 MINUTES. BLENDERIZE
(IF TOO THICK, ADD SMALL AMOUNT OF CHICKEN
BROTH OR MILK). SEASON TO TASTE WITH SALT AND
WHITE PEPPER. LET COOL AND ADD SOUR CREAM TO
SOUP IN BLENDER. CHILL UNTIL READY TO SERVE.
SERVE WITH 2 THIN SLICES OF RESERVED CUCUMBER
ON TOP. SERVES 6.

ISN'T IT INCREDIBLE THAT THE NEWS FROM ALL OVER
THE WORLD ALWAYS FITS EXACTLY INTO THE NEWSPAPER.

GAZPACHO

A CHILLED TOMATO SOUP - PERFECT ON A HOT DAY!

3 LBS.	FRESH TOMATOES, PEELED & CUT UP (6 CUPS/1.5 L)	1.5 KG
1	ONION, CUT IN CHUNKS	1
½ CUP	GREEN PEPPER CHUNKS	125 ML
½ CUP	CUCUMBER CHUNKS	125 ML
2 CUPS	TOMATO JUICE	500 ML
1	GARLIC CLOVE, MINCED	1
½ TSP.	CUMIN	2 ML
1 TSP.	SALT	5 ML
1 TSP.	PEPPER	5 ML
¼ CUP	OLIVE OIL	60 ML
¼ CUP	WHITE WINE VINEGAR	60 ML

GARNISH:

½ CUP	FINELY CHOPPED GREEN ONION	125 ML
½ CUP	FINELY CHOPPED GREEN PEPPER	125 ML
½ CUP	CROÛTONS	125 ML

IMMERSE TOMATOES IN BOILING WATER FOR
2 MINUTES. DRAIN AND SKIN. IN BLENDER OR FOOD
PROCESSOR COMBINE TOMATOES, ONION, GREEN
PEPPER AND CUCUMBER. WHIRL BUT LEAVE A LITTLE
BIT CHUNKY. TRANSFER TO LARGE TUREEN. ADD JUICE,
GARLIC, CUMIN, SALT AND PEPPER. COVER AND CHILL
WELL. BEFORE SERVING, STIR IN OIL AND VINEGAR.
GARNISH AND SERVE COLD.

FRESH TOMATO BISQUE

3 LBS.	FRESH RIPE TOMATOES	1.5 KG
	(6 CUPS/1.5 L)	
1/3 CUP	BUTTER	75 ML
2 CUPS	DRY BREAD CRUMBS	500 ML
1 1/2 TSP.	SALT	7 ML
	GROUND PEPPER	
3	GARLIC CLOVES, MINCED	3
6 CUPS	WATER	1.5 L
1 1/2 CUPS	CREAM	375 ML
2 EGG	YOLKS, BEATEN	

PURÉE TOMATOES (SEEDS AND SKINS INCLUDED).
STRAIN THROUGH SIEVE. HEAT BUTTER; ADD
TOMATOES AND SIMMER FOR 5 MINUTES. ADD CRUMBS,
SALT, PEPPER, GARLIC AND WATER; BRING TO A BOIL.
BEAT CREAM INTO EGG YOLKS. ADD TO TOMATO
PURÉE, STIRRING CONSTANTLY. HEAT TO SERVING
TEMPERATURE. DO NOT BOIL. SERVES 8.

WHY IS A PACKAGE SENT BY LAND CARRIER CALLED A
SHIPMENT, WHILE A PACKAGE SENT BY SHIP IS CALLED
CARGO?

WELL WORTH THE EFFORT! THE PERFECT LIGHT LUNCHEON STARTER SERVED HOT OR COLD. MAY BE PREPARED THE DAY BEFORE.

4	LARGE RED PEPPERS	4
2 TBSP.	BUTTER OR MARGARINE	30 ML
1	LARGE RED ONION, CHOPPED	1
2	GARLIC CLOVES, MINCED	2
4 CUPS	CHICKEN BROTH	1 L
1 TBSP.	LEMON JUICE OR GIN	15 ML
	SALT TO TASTE	
1/2 TSP.	GROUND PEPPER	2 ML
	FRESH BASIL FOR GARNISH	

CUT PEPPERS IN THIRDS; REMOVE SEEDS AND PLACE CUT SIDE DOWN ON A COOKIE SHEET. BROIL UNTIL SKINS ARE BLACKENED AND PUFFED. REMOVE FROM SHEET AND PLACE IN A PAPER BAG TO STEAM. MELT BUTTER AND SAUTÉ ONIONS AND GARLIC UNTIL SOFT. REMOVE COOLED PEPPERS FROM BAG AND PEEL OFF SKINS. CUT INTO CHUNKS AND ADD TO ONIONS AND GARLIC. COOK FOR 2-3 MINUTES. ADD BROTH, COVER AND SIMMER 20 MINUTES. ADD LEMON JUICE OR GIN. IN A BLENDER OR FOOD PROCESSOR, WHIRL 1/3 OF THE MIXTURE AT A TIME UNTIL SMOOTH. (STRAIN IF YOU WISH.) SEASON WITH SALT AND PEPPER. GARNISH WITH BASIL. SERVES 4-6.

WHAT'S ANOTHER WORD FOR SYNONYM?

CHAMPAGNE SQUASH SOUP

WHEN YOU WANT TO FUSS . . .

4 LBS.	SQUASH, ACORN OR BUTTERNUT	2 KG
2	MEDIUM ONIONS, HALVED & THINLY SLICED	2
2 TBSP.	BUTTER	30 ML
1/4 CUP	CHAMPAGNE (YOU'LL FIND SOME WAY TO USE THE REMAINDER OF THE BOTTLE)	60 ML
4-5 CUPS	CHICKEN BROTH	1-1.25 L
2 TBSP.	BUTTER	30 ML
1/2 TSP.	NUTMEG	2 ML
	SALT & PEPPER TO TASTE	
1/4 CUP	SOUR CREAM	60 ML

PREHEAT OVEN TO 350°F (180°C). LINE A COOKIE SHEET WITH FOIL. QUARTER SQUASH. SCOOP OUT SEEDS. PLACE SKIN-SIDE UP ON COOKIE SHEET AND BAKE 1-1 1/2 HOURS, UNTIL SQUASH IS TENDER. (YOU MAY MICROWAVE, USING THE SAME METHOD, COVERED WITH PLASTIC WRAP, ON HIGH UNTIL A SKEWER CAN PENETRATE THE SKIN, ABOUT 10 MINUTES.) COOL. SCOOP OUT PULP AND PURÉE IN BATCHES IN FOOD PROCESSOR. SAUTÉ ONIONS IN 2 TBSP. (30 ML) BUTTER. ADD CHAMPAGNE. COOK UNTIL LIQUID IS ABSORBED AND ONIONS ARE GOLDEN BROWN, STIRRING OFTEN. PURÉE ONIONS IN FOOD PROCESSOR WITH A LITTLE OF THE SQUASH PURÉE. IN LARGE SAUCEPAN, COMBINE ONION AND SQUASH PURÉES. WHISK IN BROTH TO DESIRED CONSISTENCY. COVER AND HEAT THROUGH OVER MEDIUM HEAT, STIRRING OCCASIONALLY. WHISK IN 2 TBSP. (30 ML) BUTTER.

CHAMPAGNE SQUASH SOUP

CONTINUED FROM PAGE 104.

SEASON WITH NUTMEG, SALT AND PEPPER. TO DECORATE, DROP A SMALL SPOONFUL OF SOUR CREAM IN EACH BOWL OF SOUP AND SWIRL WITH A KNIFE. SERVES 6-8. (PICTURED OPPOSITE PAGE 108.)

CARROT SOUP

SOMETHING ELSE TO DO WITH YOUR CARROTS!

1/4 CUP	BUTTER	60 ML
2 CUPS	FINELY CHOPPED ONION	500 ML
12	LARGE CARROTS, PEELED & SLICED	12
4 CUPS	CHICKEN BROTH	1 L
1 CUP	FRESH ORANGE JUICE	250 ML
	SALT & PEPPER TO TASTE	
	GRATED ORANGE ZEST	

MELT BUTTER IN POT AND ADD ONIONS, COOKING OVER LOW HEAT UNTIL LIGHTLY BROWNED. ADD CARROTS AND BROTH AND BRING TO A BOIL. REDUCE HEAT. COVER AND COOK UNTIL CARROTS ARE VERY TENDER, ABOUT 30 MINUTES. POUR THROUGH A STRAINER, RESERVING BROTH. ADD STRAINED VEGETABLES IN BATCHES TO FOOD PROCESSOR OR BLENDER AND PURÉE UNTIL SMOOTH. RETURN PURÉE TO POT, ADD ORANGE JUICE AND RESERVED BROTH. SEASON TO TASTE. ADD ORANGE ZEST. SIMMER UNTIL HEATED THROUGH. SERVES 6-8.

CORN CHOWDER

RICH AND CREAMY – AND HEALTHY TOO!

10 OZ.	PKG. FROZEN KERNEL CORN	300 G
1	LARGE PEELED POTATO, CHOPPED	1
1	MEDIUM ONION, CHOPPED	1
1	SMALL RED OR ORANGE PEPPER, CHOPPED	1
10 OZ.	CAN CHICKEN BROTH	284 ML
6 OZ.	CAN EVAPORATED SKIM MILK	160 ML
1/4 CUP	APPLE JUICE	60 ML
1/2 TSP.	CUMIN	2 ML
	SALT & FRESHLY GROUND PEPPER TO TASTE	
	FRESH CILANTRO LEAVES (OPTIONAL)	

COMBINE ALL INGREDIENTS IN A LARGE SAUCEPAN. BRING TO A BOIL; REDUCE HEAT AND SIMMER, COVERED, FOR 10 MINUTES, UNTIL POTATO IS TENDER. PUT 2 CUPS (500 ML) OF THE CHOWDER INTO A BLENDER AND PURÉE UNTIL SMOOTH. RETURN TO SAUCEPAN, COOK AND STIR UNTIL HEATED THROUGH. SERVES 4.

I USED TO WISH MY COMPUTER WERE AS EASY TO USE AS MY TELEPHONE. THAT WISH HAS COME TRUE SINCE I NO LONGER KNOW HOW TO USE MY TELEPHONE.

FRENCH ONION SOUP AU GRATIN

THIS IS THE BEST!

4	LARGE ONIONS, THINLY SLICED	4
1/4 CUP	BUTTER	60 ML
4	10 OZ. (284 ML) CANS BEEF BROTH	4
1/2 CUP	DRY SHERRY	125 ML
2 TSP.	WORCESTERSHIRE SAUCE	10 ML
	DASH OF PEPPER	
6	SLICES FRENCH BREAD, 1/2" (1.3 CM) THICK, TOASTED	6
3/4 CUP	GRATED PARMESAN CHEESE	175 ML
1-2 CUPS	GRATED MOZZARELLA CHEESE	250-500 ML

IN A LARGE SAUCEPAN, COOK ONIONS IN BUTTER UNTIL TENDER BUT NOT BROWN. ADD BEEF BROTH, SHERRY, WORCESTERSHIRE SAUCE AND PEPPER AND BRING TO A BOIL. POUR INTO INDIVIDUAL OVENPROOF BOWLS. FLOAT A SLICE OF TOASTED FRENCH BREAD IN EACH. SPRINKLE WITH PARMESAN AND TOP WITH MOZZARELLA. PLACE UNDER BROILER AND HEAT UNTIL CHEESE BUBBLES. SERVE WITH A SALAD AND GARLIC BREAD. SCRUMPTIOUS! SERVES 6.

ISN'T IT A BIT UNNERVING THAT DOCTORS CALL WHAT THEY DO "PRACTICE"?

TORTILLA SOUP

SOUP

2 TBSP.	OIL	30 ML
3	CORN TORTILLAS, CUT INTO 1" (2.5 CM) PIECES	3
½ CUP	FINELY CHOPPED ONION	125 ML
3	GARLIC CLOVES, MINCED	3
1	JALAPEÑO PEPPER, SEEDED & MINCED	1
2	ANAHEIM CHILIES, ROASTED, PEELED, SEEDED & FINELY CHOPPED	2
8	ROMA TOMATOES, SEEDED & DICED	8
2 TBSP.	TOMATO PASTE	30 ML
2 TSP.	CUMIN	10 ML
¼ TSP.	CAYENNE PEPPER	1 ML
5 CUPS	CHICKEN BROTH	1.2 L
1 CUP	PICANTE SAUCE (MEDIUM)	250 ML
2	WHOLE COOKED CHICKEN BREASTS, SHREDDED	2
1	RIPE AVOCADO, PITTED, PEELED & DICED	1

GARNISH

½ CUP	GRATED MONTEREY JACK CHEESE	125 ML
⅓ CUP	CHOPPED FRESH CILANTRO (OPTIONAL)	75 ML
2	CORN TORTILLAS	2

TO MAKE SOUP: HEAT THE OIL IN A LARGE POT. ADD THE TORTILLAS, REDUCE HEAT AND COOK UNTIL THEY ARE GOLDEN BROWN AND SLIGHTLY CRISP. ADD THE ONION AND COOK 3 MINUTES LONGER; ADD GARLIC AND JALAPEÑO CHILI AND COOK ANOTHER 2 MINUTES.

CONTINUED ON PAGE 109.

Champagne Squash Soup, page 104

Tortilla Soup, page 108

CONTINUED FROM PAGE 108.

ADD THE ANAHEIM CHILIES, TOMATOES AND TOMATO PASTE;COOK FOR 10 MINUTES. STIR IN THE CUMIN AND CAYENNE. SLOWLY WHISK IN THE CHICKEN BROTH AND PICANTE SAUCE. SIMMER THE SOUP FOR ABOUT 20 MINUTES, OR UNTIL SLIGHTLY REDUCED. ADD THE SHREDDED CHICKEN AND AVOCADO AND HEAT UNTIL WARMED THROUGH.

TO MAKE GARNISH: PREHEAT OVEN TO 350°F (180°C). CUT TORTILLAS INTO STRIPS. PLACE THE STRIPS ON A BAKING SHEET AND BAKE FOR 10-15 MINUTES, OR UNTIL CRISP.

TO SERVE, LADLE SOUP INTO 6 BOWLS AND GARNISH WITH THE GRATED CHEESE, CILANTRO AND BAKED TORTILLA STRIPS. SERVES 6. (PICTURED ON OPPOSITE PAGE.)

THE DIFFERENCE BETWEEN A PESSIMIST AND AN OPTIMIST: THE PESSIMIST SAYS, "THINGS ARE SO BAD, THEY CAN'T GET ANY WORSE." AND THE OPTIMIST SAYS, "OH YES THEY CAN!"

MOROCCAN CHICKEN-
VEGETABLE SOUP

SEEMS LIKE A LONG WAY TO GO FOR A GOOD BOWL
OF SOUP.

3 LBS.	CUT-UP CHICKEN, SKIN & FAT REMOVED	1.5 KG
2	LARGE RED ONIONS, CHOPPED	2
6	CARROTS, PEELED & SLICED	6
6	GARLIC CLOVES, MINCED (YES – ALL OF IT!)	6
2	BAY LEAVES	2
1/2 TSP.	SALT	2 ML
1/2 TSP.	TURMERIC	2 ML
1/2 TSP.	CINNAMON	2 ML
1 TSP.	CUMIN	5 ML
8 CUPS	CHICKEN BROTH	2 L
1/3 CUP	COUSCOUS	75 ML
1/2 CUP	SLICED GREEN ONIONS	125 ML

PLACE CHICKEN PIECES IN DUTCH OVEN WITH ONIONS,
CARROTS, GARLIC, BAY LEAVES, SEASONINGS AND CHICKEN
BROTH. BRING TO A BOIL AND REDUCE HEAT TO LOW.
SIMMER FOR 1 HOUR, STIRRING OCCASIONALLY. REMOVE
CHICKEN PIECES FROM SOUP AND REMOVE BONES. CUT
CHICKEN INTO BITE-SIZED PIECES AND RETURN TO POT.
ADD COUSCOUS AND GREEN ONIONS. SIMMER UNTIL
HEATED THROUGH. SERVES 6.

FAVORITE OXYMORONS: NEW CLASSIC, CHILDPROOF, TAPED
LIVE, PLASTIC GLASSES.

SHOOTER'S SOUP

LISA, OUR PHOTOGRAPHER, CREATED THIS TERRIFIC THAI RECIPE. A GREAT LUNCH FOR THE LADIES.

2	SKINLESS, BONELESS CHICKEN BREASTS	2
1 TSP.	GRATED GINGER ROOT	5 ML
2	GARLIC CLOVES, MINCED	2
1/4 CUP	FRESH LIME JUICE	60 ML
2	10 OZ. (284 ML) CANS CHICKEN BROTH	2
1 1/2	CANS WATER	425 ML
1	RIPE PAPAYA, PEELED & CUBED	1
4	GREEN ONIONS, SLICED	4
2 TBSP.	CHOPPED CILANTRO	30 ML
1-2 TBSP.	FRESH LIME JUICE	15-30 ML
1 TSP.	CHILI OIL OR CAYENNE, TO TASTE	5 ML

CUT CHICKEN IN BITE-SIZED PIECES. MARINATE IN GINGER, GARLIC AND LIME JUICE FOR 1/2 HOUR. ADD CHICKEN AND MARINADE TO BROTH AND WATER. BRING TO BOIL; REDUCE TO SIMMER FOR ABOUT 5 MINUTES. ADD PAPAYA. SIMMER 3 MINUTES. ADD GREEN ONIONS, CILANTRO, LIME JUICE AND CHILI OIL. SERVE WITH BREAD STICKS. SERVES 4.

BOY'S COMMENT TO HIS MOM - "DADDY TOOK ME TO THE ZOO AND ONE OF THE ANIMALS PAID $46.20 ACROSS THE BOARD."

WAR WONTON SOUP

CELEBRATE CHINESE NEW YEAR WITH THIS SAVORY SOUP.

3	10 OZ. (284 ML) CANS CHICKEN BROTH	3
3 CUPS	WATER	750 ML
1 TSP.	SESAME OIL	5 ML
3	THIN SLICES FRESH GINGER	3
1 CUP	LEFTOVER RARE ROAST BEEF (OR COOKED SLICED CHICKEN), CUT IN STRIPS	250 ML
1/2 LB.	RAW SHRIMP, PEELED & DEVEINED	250 G
1-2 CUPS	FRESH PEAPODS	250-500 ML
1 CUP	THINLY CHOPPED CARROTS	250 ML
8 OZ.	CAN SLICED WATER CHESTNUTS, DRAINED	236 ML
14 OZ.	CAN BABY CORN COBS, DRAINED	398 ML
3	STALKS BOK CHOY, CHOPPED	3
4 OZ.	PKG. FROZEN WONTONS	115 G
1 CUP	THINLY SLICED GREEN ONIONS	250 ML

IN LARGE POT COMBINE BROTH, WATER, OIL AND GINGER. BRING TO BOIL. ADD REMAINING INGREDIENTS, EXCEPT WONTONS & GREEN ONIONS. REDUCE HEAT AND SIMMER 12 MINUTES. MEANWHILE, COOK WONTONS ACCORDING TO PACKAGE DIRECTIONS. DRAIN, ADD WONTONS TO BROTH MIXTURE AND SPRINKLE WITH GREEN ONIONS. MAKES ENOUGH FOR 8 LARGE SERVINGS.

IF A PARSLEY FARMER IS SUED, CAN THEY GARNISH HIS WAGES?

HAMBURGER SOUP

DON'T BE DECEIVED BY THE NAME, THIS IS A FAMILY FAVORITE. FREEZES VERY WELL.

1½ LBS.	LEAN GROUND BEEF	750 G
1	MEDIUM ONION, FINELY CHOPPED	1
28 OZ.	CAN TOMATOES	796 ML
2 CUPS	WATER	500 ML
3	10 OZ. (284 ML) CANS CONSOMMÉ	3
10 OZ.	CAN TOMATO SOUP	284 ML
4	CARROTS, FINELY CHOPPED	4
1	BAY LEAF	1
3	CELERY STALKS, FINELY CHOPPED	3
	PARSLEY	
½ TSP.	THYME	2 ML
	PEPPER TO TASTE	
½ CUP	BARLEY	125 ML

BROWN MEAT AND ONIONS. DRAIN WELL. COMBINE ALL INGREDIENTS IN LARGE POT. SIMMER, COVERED, A MINIMUM OF 2 HOURS. SERVES 10.

THEY SAY THAT A DOG IS A MAN'S BEST FRIEND. I DON'T THINK SO. HOW MANY FRIENDS HAVE YOU HAD NEUTERED?

BEST OF BRIDGE BEAN SOUP

YOUR NEXT FAMILY FAVORITE! THE VERY THING FOR A COLD WINTER'S NIGHT.

I LB.	HOT ITALIAN SAUSAGE	500 G
2	SMOKED PORK HOCKS OR 2-3 CUPS (500-750 ML) CUBED HAM	2
3	MEDIUM POTATOES, PEELED & CUBED	3
2	MEDIUM ONIONS, DICED	2
3	CELERY STALKS WITH LEAVES, CHOPPED	3
5	CARROTS, PEELED & DICED	5
I	GREEN PEPPER, SEEDED & CHOPPED	I
I CUP	CHOPPED FRESH PARSLEY OR 2 TBSP. (30 ML) DRIED	250 ML
3	14 OZ. (398 ML) CANS KIDNEY BEANS	3
14 OZ.	CAN TOMATO SAUCE	398 ML
28 OZ.	CAN TOMATOES, CHOPPED	796 ML
I-2 TSP.	SALT	5-10 ML
I TSP.	PEPPER	5 ML
I TSP.	HOT PEPPER SAUCE	5 ML
2	BAY LEAVES	2
I TSP.	WORCESTERSHIRE SAUCE	5 ML
2	GARLIC CLOVES, CRUSHED	2

BOIL SAUSAGE TO REMOVE EXCESS FAT; CUT INTO BITE-SIZED PIECES. SKIN PORK HOCKS AND REMOVE EXCESS FAT. BROWN SAUSAGE AND PORK HOCKS IN A LARGE, HEAVY POT. DRAIN. ADD ALL OTHER INGREDIENTS AND ADD JUST ENOUGH WATER TO COVER. BRING TO A BOIL THEN REDUCE TO SIMMER. COVER AND COOK FOR 2-3 HOURS. REMOVE PORK HOCKS AND CUT MEAT INTO BITE-SIZED PIECES. RETURN MEAT TO POT. SERVE WITH CRUSTY BREAD. SERVES 8-10.

HINDSIGHT: SITTING ON YOUR GLASSES!

PIZZA

Fast and Easy Pizza Crust
Pear and Cambozola Pizza
Mexican Pizza
Pizza Primavera

POCKETS & WRAPS

Tuna Terrific
Turkey, Apple and Spinach Pockets
Turkey, Blue Cheese 'N' Pear Wrap
Zucchini, Peppers & Feta Cheese Wrap
Teriyaki Ginger Steak Wrap
Tex-Mex Fajitas

FAST AND EASY PIZZA CRUST

PUT THIS TOGETHER WHEN YOU COME HOME FROM WORK - TAKES ABOUT 20 MINUTES.

³/₄ CUP	WARM WATER	175 ML
1 TBSP.	ACTIVE DRY YEAST (1 PKG.)	15 ML
1 TSP.	SUGAR	5 ML
1¹/₂ CUPS	FLOUR	375 ML
¹/₄ TSP.	SALT	1 ML
1 TBSP.	YELLOW CORNMEAL	15 ML
1 TBSP.	OLIVE OIL	15 ML
	CORNMEAL TO SPRINKLE	

PREHEAT OVEN TO 450°F (230°C). LIGHTLY OIL A 12" (30 CM) PIZZA PAN. IN A SMALL BOWL, MIX WARM WATER, YEAST AND SUGAR TOGETHER. LET SIT UNTIL YEAST ACTIVATES, ABOUT 5 MINUTES. IN A LARGE BOWL, STIR TOGETHER FLOUR, SALT AND CORNMEAL. ADD YEAST MIXTURE AND OLIVE OIL AND KNEAD TO A SMOOTH DOUGH, ABOUT 10 MINUTES. SPRINKLE A WORK SURFACE WITH CORNMEAL AND ROLL DOUGH INTO A 13" (33 CM) CIRCLE AND PLACE ON PIZZA PAN. CRIMP EDGES AND ADD YOUR FAVORITE TOPPINGS. BAKE FOR 10-15 MINUTES. MAKES 1, 12" (30 CM) PIZZA.

IF YOU CAN'T SWIM, IS IT REALLY NECESSARY TO WAIT A HALF AN HOUR AFTER EATING BEFORE YOU GO IN THE WATER?

PEAR AND CAMBOZOLA PIZZA

THIS IS SOOO GOOD!

12"	PIZZA CRUST (PAGE 116) OR PURCHASED PIZZA CRUST	30 CM
	OLIVE OIL TO BRUSH ON CRUST	
14 OZ.	CAN PEARS, DRAINED AND SLICED IN THIN STRIPS	398 ML
2 TBSP.	TOASTED PINE NUTS	30 ML
3 OZ.	CAMBOZOLA CHEESE, SLICED OR CRUMBLED	85 G
	FRESHLY GROUND PEPPER	

PREHEAT OVEN TO 450°F (230°C). BRUSH CRUST WITH OLIVE OIL, ARRANGE PEARS ON CRUST IN PINWHEEL PATTERN, SPRINKLE WITH PINE NUTS, TOP WITH CHEESE AND A SPRINKLE OF PEPPER. BAKE 10-15 MINUTES, UNTIL CRUST IS GOLDEN.

ANOTHER GOOD IDEA: FOR APPLE AND BRIE PIZZA, SAUTÉ SLICED APPLES IN BUTTER AND BROWN SUGAR. SPRINKLE WITH CINNAMON. DOT PIZZA CRUST WITH BROKEN PIECES OF BRIE CHEESE, ARRANGE APPLES ON TOP AND SPRINKLE WITH CHOPPED WALNUTS AND FRESH ROSEMARY. BAKE AS ABOVE.

FAVORITE OXYMORONS: TEMPORARY TAX INCREASE, TIGHT SLACKS, TWELVE-OUNCE POUND CAKE, EXACT ESTIMATE.

RANCHERO SAUCE

2 TBSP.	VEGETABLE OIL	30 ML
I CUP	FINELY CHOPPED ONION	250 ML
I	GARLIC CLOVE, MINCED	I
4 CUPS	FINELY CHOPPED FRESH OR CANNED TOMATOES	I L
2	ANAHEIM OR OTHER MILD CHILIES, CORED, SEEDED & CHOPPED	2
I TSP.	SUGAR	5 ML
	SALT & FRESHLY GROUND PEPPER TO TASTE	
2 TBSP.	MINCED CILANTRO	30 ML
12"	PIZZA CRUST (PAGE 116) OR PURCHASED PIZZA CRUST	30 CM

TOPPING

I CUP	RANCHERO SAUCE	250 ML
½ LB.	HOT SAUSAGE, COOKED, CRUMBLED & DRAINED	250 G
I½ CUPS	GRATED MONTEREY JACK CHEESE	375 ML
½ CUP	THINLY SLICED RED ONION	125 ML
I	RED, YELLOW OR GREEN BELL PEPPER, SLICED IN STRIPS	I
I	PICKLED JALAPEÑO PEPPER, SEEDED & DICED	I

TO PREPARE SAUCE: IN LARGE SKILLET, HEAT OIL OVER MEDIUM HEAT AND ADD ONION. COOK 2 MINUTES, STIRRING CONSTANTLY. ADD GARLIC AND COOK 2 MINUTES MORE, OR UNTIL ONION IS TRANSLUCENT. ADD TOMATOES, CHILIES, SUGAR, SALT AND PEPPER. SIMMER UNTIL SLIGHTLY THICKENED, ABOUT 15 MINUTES, STIRRING

MEXICAN PIZZA

CONTINUED FROM PAGE 118.

OCCASIONALLY. STIR IN CILANTRO. THIS RECIPE MAKES 4 CUPS (1 L) AND WILL KEEP REFRIGERATED FOR UP TO 1 WEEK. ALSO DELICIOUS USED AS A PASTA SAUCE.

TO PREPARE PIZZA: PREHEAT OVEN TO 500°F (260°C). SPREAD RANCHERO SAUCE EVENLY OVER ROLLED PIZZA DOUGH. COVER WITH COOKED SAUSAGE AND SPRINKLE CHEESE OVER ALL. EVENLY DISTRIBUTE ONION, PEPPER AND PICKLED JALAPEÑO OVER CHEESE. BAKE PIZZA IN THE LOWER THIRD OF OVEN UNTIL CRUST IS BROWNED AND CHEESE IS MELTED, ABOUT 15-20 MINUTES.

IF MEN CAN RUN THE WORLD, WHY CAN'T THEY STOP WEARING NECKTIES? HOW INTELLIGENT IS IT TO START THE DAY BY TYING A LITTLE NOOSE AROUND YOUR NECK?

PIZZA PRIMAVERA

12"   PIZZA CRUST (PAGE 116) OR   30 CM
               PURCHASED PIZZA CRUST

VEGETABLE TOPPINGS

MARINATED ARTICHOKE HEARTS,
RESERVE MARINADE
ASPARAGUS TIPS OR BROCCOLI FLORETS
RED PEPPER CUT IN THIN STRIPS
MARINATED SUN-DRIED TOMATOES,
CUT IN THIN SLIVERS
ROMA TOMATOES, THINLY SLICED
FETA CHEESE, CRUMBLED
BASIL, DRIED OR FRESH
PITTED OLIVES, SLICED
GRATED MOZZARELLA CHEESE
TO SPRINKLE

PREHEAT OVEN TO 450°F (230°C). BRUSH CRUST WITH
SOME OF RESERVED ARTICHOKE MARINADE. SPRINKLE
WITH ANY OR ALL OF THE TOPPINGS LISTED. TOP
WITH MOZZARELLA CHEESE AND BAKE 10-15 MINUTES,
OR UNTIL CRUST IS GOLDEN.

I CAN REMEMBER WHEN YOU USED TO KISS YOUR MONEY
GOOD-BYE. NOW YOU DON'T EVEN GET A CHANCE TO BLOW
IN ITS EAR.

TUNA TERRIFIC

A PERFECTLY POPULAR PITA POCKET.

<u>CURRY TUNA FILLING</u>

7 OZ.	CAN TUNA	170 G
1	CELERY STALK, FINELY CHOPPED	1
2	GREEN ONIONS, FINELY CHOPPED	2
1	GRANNY SMITH APPLE, CORED & CHOPPED	1
2 TSP.	FRESH LEMON JUICE	10 ML
1 TSP.	CURRY POWDER	5 ML
3 TBSP.	MAYONNAISE (FAT-FREE – ALL THE BETTER FOR YOU!)	45 ML
2	PITA ROUNDS, CUT IN HALF LETTUCE	2

DRAIN TUNA AND PUT IN BOWL. ADD REMAINING FILLING INGREDIENTS, MIX WELL. CHILL TO LET FLAVORS GET TO KNOW EACH OTHER. TO SERVE, PLACE ONE HALF OF A PITA INTO THE OTHER HALF. THIS MAKES A STURDIER POCKET. LINE EACH POCKET WITH LETTUCE AND SPOON HALF THE TUNA MIXTURE INTO EACH POCKET. SERVES 2.

IF A MAN IS STANDING IN THE MIDDLE OF THE FOREST SPEAKING AND THERE IS NO WOMAN AROUND TO HEAR HIM – IS HE STILL WRONG?

TURKEY, APPLE AND SPINACH POCKETS

FAST 'N' HEALTHY.

DIJON HONEY DRESSING

1/3 CUP	FAT-FREE SOUR CREAM	75 ML
1 TBSP.	HONEY	15 ML
1 TSP.	DIJON MUSTARD	5 ML
2	LARGE PITA BREAD ROUNDS	2
1 CUP	TORN FRESH SPINACH OR ROMAINE LEAVES	250 ML
	THINLY SLICED RED ONION, TO TASTE	
6 OZ.	THINLY SLICED, COOKED TURKEY OR CHICKEN BREAST	170 G
1	SMALL APPLE, CORED & THINLY SLICED	1

TO MAKE DRESSING: IN A SMALL BOWL, STIR TOGETHER SOUR CREAM, HONEY AND MUSTARD. SET ASIDE.

CUT EACH PITA BREAD ROUND IN HALF CROSSWISE. OPEN EACH PITA HALF TO FORM A POCKET. LAYER SPINACH, ONION, TURKEY AND APPLE. DRIZZLE WITH MUSTARD DRESSING. SERVES 4.

HELP STAMP OUT AND ERADICATE SUPERFLUOUS REDUNDANCY.

TURKEY, BLUE CHEESE 'N' PEAR WRAP

SANDWICH BORED? TRY THIS!

1 TBSP.	OLIVE OIL	15 ML
1/2 CUP	COARSELY CHOPPED PECANS	125 ML
1/4 TSP.	SALT	1 ML
1/2 LB.	SLICED, SMOKED OR COOKED TURKEY, CUT IN THIN STRIPS	250 G
1	LARGE PEAR, CORED & DICED	1
3 CUPS	ROMAINE LETTUCE CUT IN STRIPS	750 ML
1/3 CUP	RAISINS	75 ML
1/4-1/3 CUP	CRUMBLED BLUE CHEESE	60-75 ML
1 TBSP.	FRESH LEMON JUICE	15 ML
4	10" (25 CM) FLOUR TORTILLAS	4

HEAT OIL IN FRYING PAN. ADD NUTS AND SALT. SAUTÉ ABOUT 2 MINUTES. IN LARGE BOWL, ADD NUTS TO TURKEY, PEAR, LETTUCE, RAISINS, BLUE CHEESE, AND LEMON JUICE. TOSS TO COAT WELL.

WRAP & ROLL: PLACE EACH FLOUR TORTILLA ON A PIECE OF WAXED PAPER. PILE 1/4 OF THE FILLING IN A STRIP ABOUT 1/3 OF THE WAY FROM THE BOTTOM OF TORTILLA. FOLD BOTTOM OVER FILLING AND ROLL ONCE. THEN FOLD 1 SIDE OVER AND CONTINUE TO ROLL TORTILLA, LEAVING THE SIDE OPEN. BE CAREFUL NOT TO ROLL IN THE WAXED PAPER. WHEN FINISHED, ROLL FILLED TORTILLAS IN THEIR WAXED PAPER WITH THE TOP OPEN SO PAPER CAN BE PEELED DOWN AS THEY ARE EATEN. (PICTURED OPPOSITE PAGE 126.)

ZUCCHINI, PEPPERS AND FETA CHEESE WRAP

BALSAMIC VINAIGRETTE

2 TBSP.	BALSAMIC VINEGAR	30 ML
1/4 CUP	OLIVE OIL	60 ML
	SALT & FRESHLY GROUND PEPPER	
	TO TASTE	
1	SMALL RED ONION, SLICED	1
1 TBSP.	OIL	15 ML
1	MEDIUM ZUCCHINI, HALVED &	1
	SLICED IN STRIPS	
1	SMALL GREEN PEPPER, SLICED	1
	IN STRIPS	
1	SMALL RED PEPPER, SLICED	1
	IN STRIPS	
1/2 CUP	BEAN SPROUTS	125 ML
1/2 CUP	COOKED COUSCOUS (OPTIONAL)	125 ML
2-3	FLOUR TORTILLAS	2-3
2 OZ.	FETA CHEESE (GOAT CHEESE IS	60 G
	GOOD TOO!)	

COMBINE ALL VINAIGRETTE INGREDIENTS. IN A
FRYING PAN, SAUTÉ ONION IN OIL. ADD ZUCCHINI AND
PEPPERS AND STIR BRIEFLY. ADD BEAN SPROUTS; STIR,
THEN ADD COUSCOUS AND MIX WELL. COOK FOR
30 SECONDS; ADD VINAIGRETTE AND MIX WELL. TO
SERVE, DISTRIBUTE MIXTURE EVENLY ON TORTILLAS,
CRUMBLE CHEESE OVER VEGETABLE MIXTURE AND ROLL
UP. MMMMMM! MMMMMMM! SERVES 2-3. (PICTURED
OPPOSITE PAGE 126.)

— TERIYAKI GINGER STEAK WRAP —

1/2 LB.	SIRLOIN STEAK, THINLY SLICED	250 G
4 TSP.	MINCED FRESH GINGER	20 ML
2 TBSP.	OIL	30 ML
1	MEDIUM RED ONION, THINLY SLICED	1
2 CUPS	SLICED FRESH MUSHROOMS	500 ML
1/2	RED PEPPER, SLICED	1/2
1/2	GREEN PEPPER, SLICED	1/2
1 1/2 CUPS	COOKED BASMATI RICE	375 ML
1/4 CUP	TERIYAKI SAUCE	60 ML
1 TBSP.	HOT & SPICY SZECHUAN SAUCE	15 ML
1 TSP.	SESAME OIL	5 ML
1 CUP	BEAN SPROUTS	250 ML
4	10" (25 CM) FLOUR TORTILLAS	4

TOSS STEAK SLICES WITH GINGER AND LET STAND FOR AT LEAST 1/2 HOUR. HEAT OIL IN LARGE FRYING PAN AND SAUTÉ ONION, STEAK AND GINGER UNTIL STEAK IS BROWN. ADD MUSHROOMS AND STIR-FRY. ADD PEPPERS AND RICE. STIR IN SAUCES AND SESAME OIL. ADD BEAN SPROUTS JUST BEFORE YOU'RE READY TO WRAP AND ROLL, DIVIDE MIXTURE EVENLY BETWEEN TORTILLAS. ROLL 1 END OVER FILLING, THEN BOTH SIDES OVER. ROLL AGAIN UNTIL YOU HAVE A CLOSED PACKAGE. CUT WRAP IN HALF DIAGONALLY. ADJUST YOUR OBI! (PICTURED OPPOSITE PAGE 126.)

THE REPAIRMAN WILL NEVER HAVE SEEN A MODEL LIKE YOURS.

TEX-MEX FAJITAS

OLÉ YOUSE GRINGOS!!

2 LBS.	FLANK STEAK (1 LB. SERVES 3 PEOPLE) OR 3 CHICKEN BREASTS, SKINNED, BONED & HALVED	1 KG

FAJITA MARINADE

1/2 CUP	VEGETABLE OIL	125 ML
1/3 CUP	FRESH LIME JUICE	75 ML
1/3 CUP	RED WINE VINEGAR (ELIMINATE FOR CHICKEN)	75 ML
1/3 CUP	CHOPPED ONION	75 ML
1 TSP.	SUGAR	5 ML
1 TSP.	OREGANO	5 ML
	SALT & PEPPER TO TASTE	
1/4 TSP.	CUMIN	1 ML
2	GARLIC CLOVES, MINCED	2
6	LARGE FLOUR TORTILLAS	6

TOPPINGS

ONION SLICES, SAUTÉED
GREEN & RED PEPPER STRIPS, SAUTÉED
SHREDDED LETTUCE
GUACAMOLE, SOUR CREAM & SALSA

COMBINE MARINADE INGREDIENTS IN SHALLOW CASSEROLE. SCORE BOTH SIDES OF STEAK. ADD MEAT. COVER AND REFRIGERATE SEVERAL HOURS. REMOVE FROM MARINADE AND BAR-B-QUE. SLICE IN THIN STRIPS ACROSS THE GRAIN. WRAP IN WARM TORTILLAS WITH ONIONS AND PEPPERS AND ANY OR ALL OF THE OTHER TOPPINGS. SERVES 6 GRINGOS.

Wraps — Turkey / Teriyaki Steak / Zucchini, pages 123–125

Vegetable Frittata, page 34

PASTA

Fettuccine with Sambuca and Cranberries
Fresh Pear and Curry Pasta
Spicy Penne
Pasta with Peppers
Pasta Fasta
Gnocchi with Red Pepper Sauce
Red and White Tortellini
Alfredo Sauce
Gourmet Macaroni and Cheese
Bow Ties with Lemon Chicken
Lemon Fettuccine with Chicken
Chicken with Spaghettini
Traditional Lasagne
"Death to Dieters" Chicken Lasagna
Broccoli Lasagne Au Gratin
Pesto Lasagne
Linguine with Red Clam Sauce
Linguine with White Clam Sauce
Fettuccine with Asparagus and Shrimp

FETTUCCINE WITH SAMBUCA AND CRANBERRIES

PASTA FOR COMPANY - ESTUPENDO!

1/4 CUP	BUTTER	60 ML
2	WHOLE BONELESS, SKINLESS CHICKEN BREASTS, CUBED	2
2	GARLIC CLOVES, MINCED	2
3 CUPS	WHIPPING CREAM	750 ML
1/4 CUP	SAMBUCA LIQUEUR	60 ML
1/4 CUP	ORANGE JUICE CONCENTRATE	60 ML
1/2 CUP	FRESHLY GRATED PARMESAN CHEESE	125 ML
1/4 TSP.	NUTMEG	1 ML
	SALT & PEPPER TO TASTE	
14 OZ.	CAN ARTICHOKES (10-12 COUNT), DRAINED & CHOPPED	398 ML
3 OZ.	PKG. DRIED CRANBERRIES	85 G
1 LB.	FETTUCCINE	500 G
	CHOPPED FRESH PARSLEY & ORANGE ZEST FOR GARNISH	

IN A LARGE FRYING PAN, HEAT BUTTER AND SAUTÉ CUBED CHICKEN AND GARLIC UNTIL BARELY COOKED (DO NOT OVER COOK!). REMOVE CHICKEN FROM PAN AND SET ASIDE. ADD WHIPPING CREAM, SAMBUCA AND ORANGE JUICE TO PAN AND STIR WELL. ADD PARMESAN, NUTMEG, SALT AND PEPPER, STIRRING UNTIL SMOOTH. SIMMER FOR 5 MINUTES. ADD CHOPPED ARTICHOKES, CRANBERRIES AND CHICKEN; SIMMER AND STIR FOR 10 MINUTES. THAT'S IT FOR THE SAUCE! NOW, COOK THE FETTUCCINE ACCORDING TO PACKAGE DIRECTIONS. CAREFULLY FOLD SAUCE INTO PASTA AND GARNISH WITH PARSLEY AND ORANGE ZEST. SERVE WITH GARLIC TOAST. SERVES 6-8.

FRESH PEAR AND CURRY PASTA

VEGETARIAN DINNER FOR 2.

1/2	SMALL ONION, CHOPPED	1/2
2 TBSP.	OIL	30 ML
2	GARLIC CLOVES, MINCED	2
1 TBSP.	MEDIUM CURRY PASTE	15 ML
1 TSP.	TOMATO PASTE	5 ML
2 TBSP.	HONEY	30 ML
2 CUPS	VEGETABLE OR CHICKEN BROTH	500 ML
1	UNPEELED RIPE PEAR, SLICED IN THIN WEDGES	1
2	ROMA TOMATOES, CHOPPED	2
2 TBSP.	CREAM OR MILK	30 ML
3 TBSP.	CHOPPED CILANTRO	45 ML
	PASTA FOR 2: ROTINI, BOW TIES OR SHELLS	

IN A FRYING PAN OVER MEDIUM HEAT, SAUTÉ ONION IN OIL UNTIL SOFT. ADD GARLIC AND CURRY PASTE AND STIR 2-3 MINUTES. ADD TOMATO PASTE AND HONEY AND STIR ANOTHER 2 MINUTES. ADD BROTH, INCREASE HEAT TO MEDIUM HIGH AND BOIL GENTLY, REDUCING LIQUID TO LESS THAN 1 CUP (250 ML). (THIS TAKES ABOUT 15 MINUTES; NOW IS A GOOD TIME TO START COOKING THE PASTA.) ADD PEAR SLICES AND COOK FOR 1 MINUTE. ADD TOMATOES AND CREAM AND STIR ANOTHER 2 MINUTES. STIR IN CHOPPED CILANTRO. POUR OVER PASTA AND TOSS GENTLY. IF YOUR DINNER COMPANION INSISTS ON MEAT, SERVE WITH GRILLED CHICKEN BREAST OR PORK TENDERLOIN. MIXED GREENS AND BALSAMIC VINAIGRETTE (PAGE 97) IS A PERFECT COMPLEMENT.

SPICY PENNE

EASY AND GOOD!

2 TBSP.	OLIVE OIL	30 ML
4	GARLIC CLOVES, MINCED	4
1/2 TSP.	HOT RED PEPPER FLAKES	2 ML
28 OZ.	CAN CRUSHED ITALIAN TOMATOES	796 ML
1 TSP.	SALT	5 ML
1/2 TSP.	FRESHLY GROUND PEPPER	2 ML
1/4 CUP	CHOPPED FRESH PARSLEY	60 ML
1 LB.	PENNE NOODLES	500 G
1/2 CUP	FRESHLY GRATED PARMESAN CHEESE	125 ML

IN A LARGE HEAVY FRYING PAN, HEAT OIL, ADD
GARLIC AND PEPPER FLAKES. DO NOT BROWN. STIR IN
TOMATOES, SALT AND PEPPER. COOK FOR 10-15 MINUTES,
OR UNTIL THICKENED. STIR IN HALF OF THE PARSLEY.
SET ASIDE. IN A LARGE POT OF BOILING, SALTED
WATER, COOK PENNE FOR 10-15 MINUTES. DRAIN WELL.
REHEAT SAUCE AND POUR OVER PENNE. SPRINKLE WITH
PARMESAN AND REMAINING PARSLEY. TOSS WELL. SERVE
IN INDIVIDUAL PASTA BOWLS. SERVES 6.

CANDY IS DANDY BUT ASPARTAME IS PHENYLKETONURIC.

PASTA WITH PEPPERS

AFTER FIVE AND STILL ALIVE!

4	PEPPERS, USE MIXTURE OF RED, GREEN & YELLOW	4
1/3 CUP	OLIVE OIL	75 ML
3	GARLIC CLOVES, MINCED	3
1/2 LB.	SPAGHETTINI	250 G
2 CUPS	GRATED ASIAGO OR FRESHLY GRATED PARMESAN CHEESE	500 ML

CUT PEPPERS INTO STRIPS. SAUTÉ IN OIL WITH GARLIC. COOK PASTA ACCORDING TO PACKAGE DIRECTIONS. DRAIN. POUR PEPPER-OIL MIXTURE OVER HOT PASTA AND TOSS WITH GRATED CHEESE. SERVES 4 AS A SIDE DISH.

IF THE DOCTOR TELLS YOU TO TAKE AN ASPIRIN A DAY FOR YOUR HEART, HOW DO YOU KNOW WHEN YOU'VE GOT A HEADACHE?

PASTA FASTA

AFTER A BUSY DAY - YOU'VE GOT IT MADE!

2 CUPS	HALVED CHERRY TOMATOES	500 ML
1/2 CUP	CHOPPED FRESH BASIL	125 ML
2	GARLIC CLOVES, MINCED	2
3 TBSP.	OLIVE OIL	45 ML
	SALT & PEPPER TO TASTE	
	ENOUGH ROTINI OR PENNE FOR 2	
1 CUP	GRATED MOZZARELLA CHEESE	250 ML

IN THE MORNING: COMBINE TOMATOES, BASIL, GARLIC, OLIVE OIL, SALT AND PEPPER. COVER AND REFRIGERATE.

DINNERTIME: COOK THE PASTA ACCORDING TO PACKAGE DIRECTIONS. DRAIN AND RETURN TO POT. ADD MARINATED VEGGIES (DON'T DRAIN) AND CHEESE. TOSS, COVER. SET ASIDE FOR 5 MINUTES, UNTIL CHEESES MELT. PLACE IN YOUR FAVORITE PASTA BOWL AND SERVE IMMEDIATELY. GOOD WITH BAGUETTE STICKS (PAGE 20). (PICTURED OPPOSITE PAGE 144.) SERVES 2.

I COULDN'T REPAIR YOUR BRAKES, SO I MADE YOUR HORN LOUDER.

GNOCCHI WITH RED PEPPER SAUCE

3 TBSP.	OLIVE OIL	45 ML
3	RED PEPPERS, CUT INTO ¼" (1 CM) PIECES	3
1	LARGE ONION, FINELY CHOPPED	1
4	GARLIC CLOVES, MINCED	4
1½ TSP.	DRIED BASIL	7 ML
½ TSP.	PEPPER	2 ML
¼ TSP.	SALT	1 ML
28 OZ.	CAN PLUM TOMATOES, DRAINED & CHOPPED	796 ML
1 CUP	CHICKEN BROTH	250 ML
1 TBSP.	BALSAMIC VINEGAR	15 ML
½ TSP.	SUGAR	2 ML
1½ LBS.	FRESH OR FROZEN GNOCCHI	750 G
	FRESHLY GRATED PARMESAN CHEESE	

IN A LARGE FRYING PAN, HEAT OIL OVER MEDIUM-HIGH HEAT. COOK RED PEPPERS, ONION, GARLIC, BASIL, PEPPER AND SALT, STIRRING OFTEN, FOR ABOUT 10 MINUTES, OR UNTIL ONIONS ARE SOFTENED. ADD TOMATOES, BROTH, VINEGAR AND SUGAR; BRING TO BOIL. REDUCE HEAT AND SIMMER FOR 10 MINUTES.

IN LARGE POT OF BOILING SALTED WATER, COOK GNOCCHI ACCORDING TO PACKAGE DIRECTIONS OR UNTIL THEY FLOAT TO SURFACE. DRAIN; RETURN TO POT AND TOSS GENTLY WITH THE SAUCE. SERVES 4.

DON'T FORGET TO PASS THE PARMESAN!

RED AND WHITE TORTELLINI

TORTELLINI IN TWO SAUCES.

TOMATO SAUCE

1 TBSP.	BUTTER	15 ML
2	GARLIC CLOVES, MINCED	2
1/4 CUP	CHOPPED ONION	60 ML
14 OZ.	CAN TOMATO SAUCE	398 ML
12 OZ.	TORTELLINI, FRESH OR FROZEN	340 G

MUSHROOM PARMESAN SAUCE

2 TBSP.	BUTTER	30 ML
2 CUPS	SLICED FRESH MUSHROOMS	500 ML
1/4 CUP	CHOPPED GREEN ONION	60 ML
2 TBSP.	FLOUR	30 ML
2 CUPS	MILK	500 ML
2/3 CUP	GRATED PARMESAN CHEESE	150 ML
	SALT & PEPPER	
1 1/2 CUPS	GRATED MOZZARELLA CHEESE	375 ML
	GRATED PARMESAN CHEESE	

TO MAKE TOMATO SAUCE: MELT BUTTER AND SAUTÉ GARLIC AND ONION UNTIL TENDER. ADD TOMATO SAUCE AND BRING TO BOIL. REDUCE HEAT, COVER AND SIMMER 10 MINUTES.

COOK TORTELLINI ACCORDING TO PACKAGE DIRECTIONS.

TO MAKE MUSHROOM SAUCE: MELT BUTTER AND SAUTÉ MUSHROOMS AND GREEN ONION UNTIL TENDER. SPRINKLE WITH FLOUR AND GRADUALLY

CONTINUED FROM PAGE 134.

STIR IN MILK. COOK AND STIR OVER MEDIUM HEAT UNTIL MIXTURE THICKENS TO CONSISTENCY OF MUSHROOM SOUP. REMOVE FROM HEAT. STIR IN PARMESAN CHEESE, SALT AND PEPPER TO TASTE. ADD MUSHROOM PARMESAN SAUCE TO COOKED, DRAINED TORTELLINI.

TO SERVE: SPREAD TOMATO SAUCE OVER BOTTOM OF A LARGE SHALLOW CASSEROLE. SPOON TORTELLINI MUSHROOM MIXTURE ON TOP LEAVING A RED BORDER OF TOMATO SAUCE. SPRINKLE WITH MOZZARELLA CHEESE AND ADDITIONAL PARMESAN CHEESE. PLACE UNDER BROILER UNTIL CHEESE IS MELTED AND GOLDEN. SERVE IMMEDIATELY. SERVES 4-6.

POSTED NEXT TO A TRAY OF PENNIES AT CASHIER'S COUNTER: "NEED A PENNY, TAKE A PENNY: NEED TWO PENNIES, GET A JOB!"

ALFREDO SAUCE

BASIC AND A BREEZE TO MAKE. SERVE WITH ANY PASTA. OUR FAVORITE IS FETTUCCINE OR TORTELLINI.

1/3 CUP	BUTTER	75 ML
1 1/2 CUPS	WHIPPING CREAM	375 ML
3-4 CUPS	COOKED PASTA	750 ML-1 L
1 CUP	FRESHLY GRATED PARMESAN	250 ML
1/4 CUP	MILK	60 ML
1 TSP.	SALT	5 ML
1/2 TSP.	PEPPER	2 ML
DASH OF	NUTMEG	

IN A LARGE FRYING PAN, MELT BUTTER OVER HIGH HEAT UNTIL IT TURNS LIGHT BROWN. ADD 1/2 CUP (125 ML) OF CREAM AND BOIL, STIRRING CONSTANTLY, UNTIL MIXTURE BECOMES SHINY AND LARGE BUBBLES FORM. SET ASIDE IF MAKING AHEAD.

COOK PASTA ACCORDING TO PACKAGE DIRECTIONS. OVER MEDIUM HEAT ADD PASTA TO SAUCE, MIXING WITH 2 FORKS TO COAT WELL. ADD PARMESAN CHEESE, REMAINING CREAM AND MILK, A LITTLE OF EACH AT A TIME UNTIL ALL ARE COMBINED. SEASON WITH SALT, PEPPER AND NUTMEG, ADDING MORE OF EACH IF DESIRED. SERVES 4-6.

BAROQUE: WHEN YOU ARE OUT OF MONET.

GOURMET MACARONI AND CHEESE

COMFORT FOOD.

2½ CUPS	MACARONI	625 ML
¼ CUP	BUTTER	60 ML
¼ CUP	FLOUR	60 ML
2 CUPS	MILK	500 ML
1 TSP.	SALT	5 ML
1 TSP.	SUGAR	5 ML
½ LB.	PROCESSED CHEESE, CUBED (VELVEETA)	250 G
⅔ CUP	SOUR CREAM (FAT-FREE IS FINE)	150 ML
1⅓ CUPS	COTTAGE CHEESE	325 ML
2 CUPS	GRATED OLD CHEDDAR CHEESE	500 ML
1½ CUPS	SOFT BREADCRUMBS	375 ML
2 TBSP.	BUTTER	30 ML
	PAPRIKA	

COOK AND DRAIN MACARONI AND PLACE IN A
2½-QUART (2.5 L). GREASED CASSEROLE. MELT BUTTER
OVER MEDIUM HEAT; STIR IN FLOUR; MIX WELL. ADD
MILK AND COOK OVER MEDIUM HEAT, STIRRING
CONSTANTLY UNTIL SAUCE THICKENS. ADD SALT, SUGAR
AND CHEESE. MIX WELL. MIX SOUR CREAM AND
COTTAGE CHEESE INTO SAUCE. POUR OVER MACARONI.
MIX WELL. SPRINKLE CHEDDAR CHEESE AND CRUMBS
OVER TOP. DOT WITH BUTTER AND SPRINKLE WITH
PAPRIKA. MAY BE FROZEN AT THIS POINT. BAKE AT
350°F (180°C) FOR 45-50 MINUTES. SERVES 6.

THE FACE OF A CHILD CAN SAY IT ALL - ESPECIALLY
THE MOUTH PART OF THE FACE.

BOW TIES WITH LEMON CHICKEN

2	BONELESS, SKINLESS CHICKEN BREAST HALVES	2
3/4 LB.	BOW-TIE PASTA	365 G
10 OZ.	BAG PREWASHED SPINACH, TRIMMED, TORN INTO BITE-SIZED PIECES	300 G
1	MEDIUM ONION, HALVED LENGTHWISE & THINLY SLICED CROSSWISE	1
1 1/2 CUPS	CHICKEN BROTH	375 ML
1/4 CUP	WHITE WINE	60 ML
1 TSP.	GRATED LEMON ZEST	5 ML
3 TBSP.	FRESH LEMON JUICE	45 ML
2 TSP.	MINCED GARLIC	10 ML
	SALT & PEPPER TO TASTE	
1/4 CUP	CHICKEN BROTH	60 ML
1 TBSP.	FLOUR	15 ML
2 TSP.	CHOPPED FRESH THYME	10 ML
2 TSP.	BUTTER	10 ML

POACH CHICKEN IN WATER TO COVER FOR
5 MINUTES, OR UNTIL NO LONGER PINK IN
THE MIDDLE. CUT INTO BITE-SIZED PIECES. IN
LARGE POT, COOK PASTA ACCORDING TO PACKAGE
DIRECTIONS. WHEN COOKED, ADD SPINACH
TO PASTA AND BOIL UNTIL WILTED, ABOUT
10-20 SECONDS. DRAIN AND RETURN TO POT. COAT
FRYING PAN WITH COOKING SPRAY. SAUTÉ ONION
OVER MEDIUM-LOW HEAT, STIRRING OCCASIONALLY,
UNTIL WELL BROWNED AND CARAMELIZED, ABOUT
7 MINUTES. STIR IN BROTH, WHITE WINE,

BOW TIES WITH LEMON CHICKEN

CONTINUED FROM PAGE 138.

LEMON ZEST, JUICE, GARLIC, SALT AND PEPPER. SIMMER 2 MINUTES. WHISK TOGETHER BROTH AND FLOUR. STIR INTO MIXTURE. SIMMER AND STIR, UNTIL SLIGHTLY THICKENED. ADD THYME AND BUTTER AND STIR IN CHICKEN. REMOVE FROM HEAT AND POUR OVER PASTA AND SPINACH IN POT. TOSS TO MIX. SERVES 4.

LEMON FETTUCCINE WITH CHICKEN

DEE-LICIOUS AND INCREDIBLY EASY.

3/4 LB.	FETTUCCINE	365 G
1/4 CUP	MELTED BUTTER	60 ML
1 CUP	HALF & HALF CREAM	250 ML
1	LEMON, JUICE & GRATED RIND	1
1	SKINLESS, BONELESS CHICKEN BREAST, COOKED & CUBED	1
1/2 CUP	PINE NUTS	125 ML

COOK PASTA ACCORDING TO PACKAGE DIRECTIONS. COMBINE BUTTER, CREAM, LEMON JUICE AND GRATED RIND. TOSS WITH PASTA, CHICKEN AND PINE NUTS.

CHICKEN WITH SPAGHETTINI

A NIFTY NOODLE DISH WITH A WONDERFUL
TARRAGON FLAVOR.

2	CHICKEN BREASTS, SKINNED & BONED	2
1/4 CUP	BUTTER OR MARGARINE	60 ML
3	GARLIC CLOVES, MINCED	3
1	ONION, FINELY CHOPPED	1
3	MEDIUM TOMATOES, CHOPPED	3
1 TBSP.	DRIED TARRAGON OR BASIL	15 ML
3/4 LB.	SPAGHETTINI OR LINGUINE	365 G
3 TBSP.	DRY WHITE WINE OR VERMOUTH	45 ML
1/4 CUP	CHICKEN BROTH	60 ML
1 CUP	MILK	250 ML
1/4 TSP.	EACH SALT & PEPPER	1 ML
1/2 CUP	CHOPPED FRESH PARSLEY	125 ML
	FRESHLY GRATED PARMESAN CHEESE	

CUT CHICKEN INTO CUBES AND SAUTÉ IN BUTTER,
STIRRING UNTIL OPAQUE. TRANSFER TO A PLATE. ADD
GARLIC AND ONION TO FRYING PAN. SAUTÉ UNTIL
SOFTENED. ADD TOMATOES AND TARRAGON AND COOK
3 MINUTES. COOK SPAGHETTINI ACCORDING TO
PACKAGE DIRECTIONS. DRAIN. MEANWHILE, POUR
WINE AND BROTH INTO FRYING PAN AND COOK UNTIL
REDUCED BY TWO-THIRDS. STIR IN MILK, SALT AND
PEPPER AND COOK UNTIL SLIGHTLY THICKENED. ADD
COOKED CHICKEN AND ACCUMULATED JUICES; SIMMER
UNTIL HEATED THROUGH. STIR IN 1/3 CUP (75 ML)
PARSLEY AND TOSS WITH HOT PASTA IN LARGE
SERVING BOWL. TOP WITH REMAINING PARSLEY. PASS
THE PARMESAN. SERVES 4.

TRADITIONAL LASAGNE

MEAT SAUCE

1½ LBS.	LEAN GROUND BEEF	750 G
I CUP	DICED ONIONS	250 ML
I	GARLIC CLOVE, MINCED	I
19 OZ.	CAN ITALIAN TOMATOES	540 ML
14 OZ.	CAN TOMATO SAUCE	398 ML
5½ OZ.	CAN TOMATO PASTE	156 ML
½ CUP	RED WINE	125 ML
2 TBSP.	WORCESTERSHIRE SAUCE	30 ML
I TSP.	SUGAR	5 ML
	SALT & PEPPER TO TASTE	
I TSP.	BASIL	5 ML
I TSP.	OREGANO	5 ML
8	LASAGNE NOODLES, COOKED ACCORDING TO PACKAGE DIRECTIONS	8
2 CUPS	RICOTTA OR COTTAGE CHEESE	500 ML
I LB.	SLICED MOZZARELLA CHEESE	500 G
½ CUP	GRATED PARMESAN CHEESE	125 ML

BROWN BEEF, ONIONS AND GARLIC. DRAIN OFF FAT.
ADD TOMATOES, TOMATO SAUCE, PASTE, WINE,
WORCESTERSHIRE SAUCE, SUGAR AND SEASONINGS.
COVER AND SIMMER FOR I HOUR. IN A 9 X 13" (23 X
33 CM) PAN, LAYER ½ OF THE MEAT SAUCE, ½ OF
THE NOODLES, ½ OF THE RICOTTA CHEESE AND ½
OF THE MOZZARELLA CHEESE. REPEAT LAYERS. SPRINKLE
WITH PARMESAN AND BAKE AT 350°F (180°C) FOR
40 MINUTES. LET SIT FOR 10 MINUTES BEFORE
SERVING. SERVE WITH CAESAR SALAD (PAGE 77). THE
MEAT SAUCE MAY BE SERVED OVER ANY COOKED PASTA.

"DEATH TO DIETERS" CHICKEN LASAGNE

3 CUPS	FRESH MUSHROOMS, SLICED	750 ML
2 CUPS	CHOPPED ONION	500 ML
2 PKGS.	KNORRS HOLLANDAISE SAUCE, (PREPARED ACCORDING TO PACKAGE DIRECTIONS) YIELD 3 CUPS (750 ML)	750 ML
8	LASAGNE NOODLES, COOKED	8
2 LBS.	CHICKEN OR TURKEY BREAST, COOKED & THINLY SLICED SALT & PEPPER TO TASTE	1 KG
1 TSP.	DRIED BASIL	5 ML
1 TSP.	DRIED OREGANO	5 ML
3 CUPS	SHREDDED MOZZARELLA CHEESE	750 ML
1 CUP	GRATED PARMESAN CHEESE	250 ML
1 LB.	FRESH ASPARAGUS, COOKED TENDER-CRISP	500 KG

SPRAY A NON-STICK FRYING PAN WITH COOKING SPRAY. SAUTÉ MUSHROOMS AND ONIONS UNTIL SOFT. SPREAD A SMALL AMOUNT OF HOLLANDAISE ON THE BOTTOM OF A 9 X 13" (23 X 33 CM) PAN. PLACE A LAYER OF NOODLES ON TOP, THEN COVER WITH HALF OF THE CHICKEN AND SPRINKLE WITH SALT AND PEPPER TO TASTE. TOP WITH HALF OF THE MUSHROOM AND ONION MIXTURE, THEN HALF OF THE REMAINING HOLLANDAISE AND SPRINKLE WITH HALF OF THE BASIL AND OREGANO. TOP THIS WITH HALF OF THE MOZZARELLA AND PARMESAN CHEESES. PLACE ALL OF THE ASPARAGUS NEATLY IN A LAYER OVER CHEESE. REPEAT THE

"DEATH TO DIETERS" CHICKEN LASAGNE

CONTINUED FROM PAGE 142.

LAYERS, ENDING WITH THE CHEESES. COOK, UNCOVERED, AT 350°F (180°C) OVEN FOR 35 MINUTES, OR UNTIL HOT AND BUBBLY. LET STAND FOR 10 MINUTES BEFORE CUTTING. SERVE A SALAD WITH A TART DRESSING TO OFFSET THE RICHNESS. SERVES 10-12.

BROCCOLI LASAGNE AU GRATIN

5 CUPS	FRESH BROCCOLI FLORETS	1.25 L
24 OZ.	JAR SPICY SPAGHETTI SAUCE	750 ML
8	LASAGNE NOODLES, COOKED	8
2 CUPS	RICOTTA CHEESE	500 ML
2	EGGS, SLIGHTLY BEATEN	2
2 CUPS	SHREDDED MOZZARELLA CHEESE	500 ML
1/2 CUP	GRATED PARMESAN CHEESE	125 ML

PARBOIL BROCCOLI FOR 1 MINUTE. SPREAD A THIN LAYER OF SPAGHETTI SAUCE IN A 9 X 13" (23 X 33 CM). COVER WITH 4 LASAGNE NOODLES. MIX TOGETHER BROCCOLI, RICOTTA CHEESE AND EGGS. SPREAD 1/2 OF MIXTURE OVER NOODLES. TOP WITH 1/2 OF REMAINING SPAGHETTI SAUCE, 1/2 MOZZARELLA AND 1/2 PARMESAN. REPEAT LAYERS. BAKE AT 350°F (180°C) FOR 30-35 MINUTES. SERVES 8-10. (PICTURED OPPOSITE PAGE 145.)

PESTO LASAGNE

GOOD AS A SIDE DISH WITH BAR-B-QUED CHICKEN OR STEAK.

TOMATO SAUCE

4	GARLIC CLOVES, MINCED	4
2	ONIONS, CHOPPED	2
1/3 CUP	OLIVE OIL	75 ML
28 OZ.	CAN CRUSHED TOMATOES	796 ML
	SALT TO TASTE	

PESTO

1 CUP	FRESH BASIL	250 ML
1/2 CUP	PINE NUTS	125 ML
1/3 CUP	GRATED PARMESAN	75 ML
1/3 CUP	OLIVE OIL	75 ML

BÉCHAMEL SAUCE

3 TBSP.	BUTTER	45 ML
1/4 CUP	FLOUR	60 ML
1/4 TSP.	NUTMEG	1 ML
	SALT & PEPPER TO TASTE	
2 CUPS	MILK	500 ML
8-10	LASAGNA NOODLES	8-10
1 LB.	BOCCONCINI OR MOZZARELLA CHEESE, SLICED	500 G
1/2 CUP	GRATED PARMESAN CHEESE	125 ML

TO MAKE TOMATO SAUCE: SAUTÉ GARLIC AND ONION IN OIL UNTIL SOFTENED. ADD TOMATOES AND SALT. COOK UNTIL THICKENED. SET ASIDE.

CONTINUED ON PAGE 145.

Broccoli Lasagne, page 143

CONTINUED FROM PAGE 144.

TO MAKE THE PESTO: PURÉE ALL INGREDIENTS IN FOOD PROCESSOR. SET ASIDE.

TO MAKE THE BÉCHAMEL SAUCE: MELT BUTTER, ADD FLOUR AND SEASONINGS AND STIR FOR A FEW MINUTES. ADD MILK, STIRRING CONSTANTLY. COOK SLOWLY UNTIL THICKENED.

TO MAKE LASAGNE: COOK PASTA ACCORDING TO PACKAGE DIRECTIONS. DRAIN, PLUNGE INTO COLD WATER AND SET ASIDE. LADLE $1/3$ OF BÉCHAMEL SAUCE INTO BOTTOM OF 9 X 13" (23 X 33 CM) PAN. THEN LAYER PASTA, TOMATO SAUCE, CHEESE AND PESTO. REPEAT LAYERS AND FINISH WITH GRATED PARMESAN. BAKE AT 350°F (180°C) OR 40 MINUTES. SERVES 12.

HEAVY MEDDLE: WHAT YOU GET WHEN YOUR MOTHER-IN-LAW SHOWS UP TO HELP WITH THE BABY.

LINGUINE WITH RED CLAM SAUCE

1	MEDIUM ONION, CHOPPED	1
3-4	GARLIC CLOVES, MINCED	3-4
3	CELERY STALKS, SLICED	3
3 TBSP.	OLIVE OIL	45 ML
28 OZ.	CAN ITALIAN TOMATOES	796 ML
1 TSP.	SALT	5 ML
2	7 OZ. (189 ML) CANS BABY CLAMS, WITH LIQUID	2
1	BAY LEAF	1
1 TSP.	DRIED OREGANO	5 ML
8	SLICES BACON, COOKED & CRUMBLED	8
	COARSELY GROUND BLACK PEPPER TO TASTE	
	LINGUINE FOR 4 PEOPLE	

IN MEDIUM FRYING PAN SAUTÉ ONION, GARLIC AND CELERY IN OIL UNTIL LIGHTLY GOLDEN. ADD NEXT 7 INGREDIENTS AND SIMMER, COVERED, FOR 1 HOUR OR MORE. JUST BEFORE SERVING, COOK LINGUINE. DRAIN WELL. MIX WITH HALF THE CLAM SAUCE AND TOSS. SERVE IN BOWLS AND PASS THE REMAINING SAUCE.

IF LOVE IS BLIND, WHY IS LINGERIE SO POPULAR?

LINGUINE WITH WHITE CLAM SAUCE

THIS IS A SMOOTH WHITE CLAM SAUCE – THE ULTIMATE!

1	GARLIC CLOVE, MASHED	1
1	MEDIUM ONION, FINELY CHOPPED	1
2 TSP.	OLIVE OIL	10 ML
½ CUP	DRY WHITE WINE	125 ML
2 CUPS	CHICKEN BROTH	500 ML
2	5 OZ. (142 G) CANS BABY CLAMS, RESERVE LIQUID	2
4 OZ.	CAN SHRIMP, DRAINED (OPTIONAL)	113 G
4 OZ.	CAN CRABMEAT, DRAINED (OPTIONAL)	113 G
	DASH OF FRESH GROUND PEPPER	
3	DASHES TABASCO	3
1 TSP.	OREGANO	5 ML
8 OZ.	LIGHT CREAM CHEESE (CUT INTO SMALL PIECES)	250 G
1 LB.	LINGUINE NOODLES	500 G
	GRATED PARMESAN CHEESE	
	CHOPPED FRESH PARSLEY	

IN A 4-QUART (1 L) SAUCEPAN, SAUTÉ GARLIC AND ONION IN OIL UNTIL SOFT. DO NOT BROWN. ADD WINE, CHICKEN BROTH AND CLAM LIQUID. ADD PEPPER, TABASCO AND OREGANO. SIMMER FOR 15 MINUTES. ADD CREAM CHEESE; STIR INTO SAUCE UNTIL WELL BLENDED. ADD CLAMS AND, IF DESIRED, OTHER SEAFOOD. COOK LINGUINE ACCORDING TO PACKAGE DIRECTIONS. DRAIN WELL AND ADD TO SAUCE. LET PASTA REST IN SAUCE FOR 5 MINUTES TO ABSORB FLAVORS. SERVE IN A PASTA BOWL AND SPRINKLE WITH PARMESAN AND PARSLEY. SERVE IMMEDIATELY TO 6 LINGUINE LOVERS!

FETTUCCINE WITH ASPARAGUS AND SHRIMP

1 LB.	LARGE SHRIMP, SHELLED & DEVEINED	500 G
1	LEMON, JUICE & GRATED RIND	1
1/4-1/2 TSP.	HOT RED PEPPER FLAKES	1-2 ML
1/2 TSP.	SALT	2 ML
16 OZ.	PKG. FETTUCCINE OR LINGUINE	500 G
1 TBSP.	VEGETABLE OIL	15 ML
1	MEDIUM ONION, DICED	1
2	RED PEPPERS, SLICED IN STRIPS	2
1/2 TSP.	SALT	2 ML
1 TBSP.	VEGETABLE OIL	15 ML
1 LB.	FRESH ASPARAGUS, CUT IN 3" (8 CM) PIECES	500 G
1/2 CUP	WATER	125 ML
1 TBSP.	SOY SAUCE	15 ML

IN A BOWL, MIX SHRIMP WITH LEMON JUICE, PEPPER FLAKES AND SALT. COOK FETTUCCINE ACCORDING TO PACKAGE DIRECTIONS. KEEP WARM IN POT. HEAT OIL AND STIR-FRY ONION, PEPPER STRIPS AND SALT UNTIL PEPPERS ARE TENDER-CRISP; REMOVE TO BOWL. IN SAME PAN HEAT OIL AND ADD ASPARAGUS AND SHRIMP MIXTURE. STIR-FRY UNTIL ASPARAGUS ARE TENDER-CRISP AND SHRIMP TURN OPAQUE, ABOUT 3 MINUTES. STIR IN PEPPER MIXTURE AND WATER; HEAT THROUGH. TO SERVE, TOSS FETTUCCINE WITH SHRIMP MIXTURE AND SOY SAUCE. SPRINKLE WITH GRATED LEMON RIND. SERVES 4.

VEGGIES

Grilled Veggies with Oil and Balsamic Vinegar
Asparagus Vinaigrette
Tolerable Brussels Sprouts
Tomatoes Florentine
Sesame Broccoli
Green Beans Guido
Teriyaki Portobello Mushrooms
Parmesan Portobellos
Spaghetti Squash Primavera
Nifty Carrots
Gingered Carrot Purée
Holiday Parsnips
Turnip Puff
Sweet Potato Supreme
Roasted New Potatoes with Rosemary
Elsie's Potatoes
Gruyère Scalloped Potatoes
Butter-Baked Taters
Schwarties Hash Browns
Wild Rice Broccoli Casserole
Wild Rice and Artichoke Hearts
Wild Rice, Orzo and Mushroom Casserole
Orzo with Parmesan & Basil
Risotto
Curried Apple and Sweet Potato Pilaf
Barber's Best Chili
Calico Bean Pot
Vegetable Couscous

GRILLED VEGGIES WITH
OIL AND BALSAMIC VINEGAR

A LICENSE TO GRILL! TRY SERVING AS A SANDWICH ON TOASTED FOCACCIA.

1	SMALL EGGPLANT	1
1	SMALL ZUCCHINI	1
1	RED PEPPER	1
1	YELLOW PEPPER	1
1	RED ONION	1
3 TBSP.	OLIVE OIL	45 ML
3 TBSP.	BALSAMIC VINEGAR	45 ML
	FRESHLY GROUND PEPPER	

FIRE UP THE GRILL! CUT EGGPLANT AND ZUCCHINI INTO THICK DIAGONAL SLICES (LEAVE THE SKINS ON). QUARTER AND SEED PEPPERS. CUT ONION INTO 4 THICK SLICES (A WOODEN TOOTHPICK INSERTED INTO EACH SLICE WILL KEEP IT TOGETHER ON THE GRILL). IN A SMALL BOWL, COMBINE OLIVE OIL AND BALSAMIC VINEGAR; BRUSH ON ALL SIDES OF VEGGIES. SPRINKLE WITH FRESHLY GROUND PEPPER. SPRAY GRILL WITH COOKING SPRAY AND GRILL VEGGIES UNTIL TENDER, TURNING ONCE. SERVES 4.

WHERE ARE WE GOING? AND WHAT'S WITH THIS HANDBASKET?

ASPARAGUS VINAIGRETTE

AN ELEGANT SPRING VEGETABLE.

1 LB.	FRESH ASPARAGUS	500 G

DRESSING

1 TBSP.	DIJON MUSTARD	15 ML
2 TBSP.	WHITE WINE VINEGAR	30 ML
3 TBSP.	FRESH LEMON JUICE	45 ML
1 TSP.	SUGAR	5 ML
	SALT & PEPPER TO TASTE	
1/3 CUP	VEGETABLE OIL	75 ML
	LEMON ZEST	

TO PREPARE ASPARAGUS: PLACE ASPARAGUS IN SMALL AMOUNT OF BOILING WATER AND COOK FOR 2 MINUTES. (ASPARAGUS WILL TURN BRIGHT GREEN AND SHOULD STILL BE CRUNCHY.) REMOVE ASPARAGUS AND PLUNGE INTO ICE WATER. WHEN COOL, DRY AND PLACE ON SERVING PLATTER.

TO PREPARE DRESSING: PLACE ALL INGREDIENTS IN A BOWL AND WHISK TOGETHER. POUR OVER ASPARAGUS AND GARNISH WITH LEMON ZEST. SERVE WITH SWISS APPLE QUICHE (PAGE 22) OR POTLATCH SALMON (PAGE 176). SERVES 4-6. (PICTURED ON FRONT COVER AND OPPOSITE PAGE 163.)

BEFORE CREDIT CARDS, WE ALWAYS KNEW EXACTLY HOW MUCH WE WERE BROKE.

TOLERABLE BRUSSELS SPROUTS

IF YOU HAVE TO HAVE THEM - TRY THESE - THEY'RE DELICIOUS!

4 CUPS	(2 LBS./1 KG) FRESH BRUSSELS SPROUTS	1 L
1/2 CUP	CHOPPED ONION	125 ML
2 TBSP.	BUTTER	30 ML
1 TBSP.	FLOUR	15 ML
1 TBSP.	PACKED BROWN SUGAR	15 ML
1/2 TSP.	SALT	2 ML
1/2 TSP.	DRY MUSTARD	2 ML
1/2 CUP	MILK	125 ML
1 CUP	FAT-FREE SOUR CREAM	250 ML
1 TBSP.	PARSLEY	15 ML

WASH AND TRIM SPROUTS; COOK UNTIL TENDER. SAUTÉ ONION IN BUTTER UNTIL TRANSLUCENT. STIR IN FLOUR, SUGAR, SALT AND MUSTARD. ADD MILK AND COOK SLOWLY UNTIL THICKENED. BLEND IN SOUR CREAM. ADD SPROUTS AND HEAT THROUGH. SPRINKLE WITH PARSLEY BEFORE SERVING. SERVES 6.

WHY IS THE ALPHABET IN THAT ORDER? IS IT BECAUSE OF THAT SONG?

TOMATOES FLORENTINE

6	FAIRLY FIRM TOMATOES	6
	(NOT A CHORUS LINE!)	
10 OZ.	PKG. FROZEN, CHOPPED SPINACH	283 G
1 TBSP.	INSTANT MINCED ONION	15 ML
1	GARLIC CLOVE, MINCED	
1 TSP.	OREGANO	5 ML
	DASH OF NUTMEG	
1 CUP	GRATED CHEDDAR CHEESE	250 ML
	FRESHLY GRATED PARMESAN CHEESE	

SLICE OFF TOP OF TOMATOES AND SCOOP OUT PULP.
CHOP AND DRAIN THE PULP. THAW SPINACH AND DRAIN
WELL. COMBINE SPINACH, PULP, ONION, SPICES AND
GRATED CHEESE. FILL TOMATOES AND TOP WITH
PARMESAN. BAKE AT 350°F (180°C). FOR 20-30 MINUTES.
SERVES 6. WONDERFUL WITH BEEF EXTRAORDINAIRE.
(PAGE 212).

SESAME BROCCOLI

2 LBS.	FRESH BROCCOLI	1 KG
2 TBSP.	SALAD OIL	30 ML
2 TBSP.	VINEGAR	30 ML
2 TBSP.	SOY SAUCE	30 ML
4 TBSP.	SUGAR	60 ML
2 TBSP.	TOASTED SESAME SEEDS	30 ML

POUR BOILING WATER OVER BROCCOLI AND LET STAND
5 MINUTES. DRAIN. HEAT REMAINING INGREDIENTS
AND POUR OVER BROCCOLI IN A CASSEROLE. HEAT IN
OVEN BEFORE SERVING. SERVES 8.

GREEN BEANS GUIDO

2 TBSP.	VEGETABLE OIL	30 ML
4 CUPS	SLICED FRESH MUSHROOMS	1 L
2 TBSP.	CHOPPED ONION	30 ML
1	GARLIC CLOVE, MINCED	1
1	RED PEPPER, CUT IN STRIPS	1
10 OZ.	PKG. FROZEN WHOLE GREEN BEANS	285 G
1 TBSP.	CHOPPED FRESH BASIL OR	15 ML
	1½ TSP. (7 ML) DRIED BASIL	
½ CUP	GRATED PARMESAN CHEESE	125 ML

HEAT OIL IN LARGE SKILLET OVER MEDIUM HEAT. ADD MUSHROOMS, ONION, GARLIC AND RED PEPPER. COOK UNTIL ONION IS SOFT, ABOUT 5 MINUTES. ADD BEANS AND BASIL. CONTINUE TO COOK, STIRRING FREQUENTLY, UNTIL BEANS ARE TENDER-CRISP, ABOUT 10 MINUTES. ADD SEVERAL SPOONFULS OF CHEESE AND MIX WELL. PLACE IN SHALLOW CASSEROLE AND SPRINKLE REMAINING CHEESE ON TOP. SERVES 4.

WHY DOES AN INSPIRING SIGHT LIKE A SUNRISE ALWAYS HAVE TO TAKE PLACE AT SUCH AN INCONVENIENT TIME?

TERIYAKI PORTOBELLO MUSHROOMS

ONE BIG STEAK PLUS ONE BIG MUSHROOM EQUALS DINNER FOR TWO!

1 TBSP.	BUTTER	15 ML
2 TBSP.	OIL	30 ML
1	GARLIC CLOVE, MINCED	1
1	PORTOBELLO MUSHROOM, THICKLY SLICED	1
2 TBSP.	THICK TERIYAKI SAUCE	30 ML
1 TBSP.	LEMON JUICE	15 ML
1 TBSP.	WHITE WINE (VERMOUTH IS FINE)	15 ML
	SALT & PEPPER TO TASTE	

HEAT BUTTER AND OIL. SAUTÉ GARLIC AND MUSHROOM SLICES FOR 5 MINUTES. ADD TERIYAKI SAUCE, LEMON JUICE AND WINE. CONTINUE TO COOK, STIRRING UNTIL MUSHROOMS SOAK UP THE LIQUID. SPRINKLE WITH SALT AND PEPPER. SERVES 2.

PARMESAN PORTOBELLOS

2 TBSP.	SLICED SHALLOTS	30 ML
2	GARLIC CLOVES, CHOPPED	2
2 TBSP.	OLIVE OIL	30 ML
1/4 CUP	BUTTER	60 ML
1 LB.	SLICED PORTOBELLO MUSHROOMS	500 G
1/4 CUP	BALSAMIC VINEGAR	60 ML
1/3 CUP	GRATED PARMESAN CHEESE	75 ML
	PEPPER TO TASTE	

CLEAN TOPS OF MUSHROOMS WITH BRUSH OR MOIST PAPER TOWEL. DON'T PEEL THEM – YOU'LL LOSE THE FLAVOR! SAUTÉ SHALLOTS AND GARLIC IN OIL AND BUTTER FOR 2-3 MINUTES. ADD MUSHROOMS, STIRRING UNTIL GOLDEN. ADD VINEGAR AND STIR WELL TO DEGLAZE PAN. ADD THE CHEESE AND STIR UNTIL MELTED. SEASON WITH PEPPER AND SERVE IMMEDIATELY. SERVES 4.

SPAGHETTI SQUASH PRIMAVERA

A WONDERFUL VEGETARIAN DINNER - OR - IF YOU'RE
NOT INTO THAT, SERVE WITH BEEF, BOOZE AND A
GOOD STOGIE!

1	MEDIUM SPAGHETTI SQUASH	1
1/3 CUP	BUTTER	75 ML
2	MEDIUM ONIONS, DICED	2
1/2 LB.	MUSHROOMS, SLICED	250 G
1	GARLIC CLOVE, MINCED	1
1 1/2 CUPS	BROCCOLI FLORETS	375 ML
1 CUP	PEAS	250 ML
1	MEDIUM ZUCCHINI, SLICED	1
4	CARROTS, CUT DIAGONALLY	4
1 CUP	MILK OR HALF & HALF CREAM	250 ML
1/2 CUP	CHICKEN BROTH	125 ML
1/4 CUP	FRESH BASIL LEAVES OR	60 ML
	1 TBSP. (15 ML) DRIED BASIL	
1	RED BELL PEPPER, SLICED	1
6	GREEN ONIONS, CHOPPED	6
12	SMALL CHERRY TOMATOES	12
1 1/2 CUPS	GRATED PARMESAN CHEESE	375 ML

CUT SQUASH IN HALF LENGTHWISE AND REMOVE SEEDS.
PLACE CUT-SIDE DOWN IN A BAKING DISH, ADD 1"
(2.5 CM) OF WATER AND BAKE AT 375°F (190°C) FOR
1 HOUR. (OR MICROWAVE USING THE SAME METHOD,
COVERED, ON HIGH UNTIL A SKEWER CAN PENETRATE
THE SKIN, ABOUT 20 MINUTES.) MELT BUTTER IN A
LARGE FRYING PAN AND SAUTÉ ONIONS, MUSHROOMS
AND GARLIC UNTIL SOFT. ADD BROCCOLI, PEAS, ZUCCHINI
AND CARROTS. STIR. ADD MILK, CHICKEN BROTH AND
BASIL. BOIL BRISKLY TO REDUCE SAUCE A LITTLE,

SPAGHETTI SQUASH PRIMAVERA

CONTINUED FROM PAGE 156.

ABOUT 2 MINUTES. ADD RED PEPPER, GREEN ONIONS, CHERRY TOMATOES AND CHEESE. HEAT THOROUGHLY. USING A FORK, SCRAPE STRANDS OF SQUASH INTO A LARGE, HEATED, SHALLOW CASSEROLE. TOP IMMEDIATELY WITH HOT VEGETABLE MIXTURE. SERVE WITH EXTRA PARMESAN CHEESE. SERVES 8-10.

NIFTY CARROTS

EVEN GOOD FOR YOUR HEARING!

5-6	LARGE CARROTS PEELED, SLICED & COOKED UNTIL TENDER-CRISP (RESERVE COOKING WATER)	5-6
1/4 CUP	RESERVED CARROT WATER	60 ML
1/4 CUP	MAYONNAISE	60 ML
1/4 CUP	SOUR CREAM (FAT-FREE IS FINE)	60 ML
2 TBSP.	FINELY CHOPPED ONION	30 ML
1 TBSP.	HORSERADISH	15 ML
	SALT AND PEPPER TO TASTE	
1 TBSP.	BUTTER, MELTED	15 ML
1/2 CUP	BREAD CRUMBS	125 ML

PLACE COOKED CARROTS IN A SHALLOW CASSEROLE. COMBINE CARROT WATER, MAYONNAISE, SOUR CREAM, ONION, HORSERADISH, SALT AND PEPPER AND POUR OVER CARROTS. COMBINE BUTTER AND BREAD CRUMBS AND SPRINKLE OVER TOP. BAKE AT 375°F (190°C) FOR 30 MINUTES. SERVES 6.

GINGERED CARROT PURÉE

SPICY YET SWEET!

3 LBS.	CARROTS, CUT INTO 1" (2.5 CM) PIECES	1.5 KG
3 TBSP.	BUTTER	45 ML
1 TBSP.	GRATED FRESH GINGER OR	15 ML
	1/2 TSP. (2 ML) GROUND GINGER	
1/4 TSP.	SALT	1 ML
1/4 TSP.	PEPPER	1 ML
1/4 CUP	HALF & HALF CREAM	60 ML

BOIL CARROTS UNTIL VERY TENDER, 25-30 MINUTES. DRAIN AND TRANSFER TO A FOOD PROCESSOR. ADD REMAINING INGREDIENTS. WHIRL, SCRAPING SIDES OCCASIONALLY, UNTIL FAIRLY SMOOTH. PLACE "SIDE-BY-SIDE" IN SERVING DISH WITH HOLIDAY PARSNIPS.

HOLIDAY PARSNIPS

ENHANCED BY A LITTLE TASTE OF NUTMEG.

3 LBS.	PARSNIPS, PEELED & SLICED	1.5 KG
3 TBSP.	BUTTER	45 ML
1/4 TSP.	NUTMEG	1 ML
1/4 TSP.	SALT	1 ML
1/4 TSP.	WHITE PEPPER	1 ML
1/4 CUP	HALF & HALF CREAM	60 ML

BOIL PARSNIPS UNTIL VERY TENDER (15-20 MINUTES). DRAIN. IN A FOOD PROCESSOR, WHIRL UNTIL FAIRLY SMOOTH. ADD BUTTER, NUTMEG, SALT AND PEPPER. GIVE IT A WHIRL. ADD CREAM AND WHIRL AGAIN. THIS MAY BE MADE A DAY AHEAD. ARE YOU DIZZY YET? SERVE WITH GINGERED CARROT PURÉE.

TURNIP PUFF

IDEAL FOR THANKSGIVING AND CHRISTMAS DINNERS.

6 CUPS	CUBED TURNIPS	1.5 L
2 TBSP.	BUTTER	30 ML
2	EGGS, BEATEN	2
3 TBSP.	FLOUR	45 ML
1 TBSP.	BROWN SUGAR	15 ML
1 TSP.	BAKING POWDER	5 ML
	SALT & PEPPER TO TASTE	
	PINCH NUTMEG	
1/2 CUP	FINE BREAD CRUMBS	125 ML
2 TBSP.	BUTTER, MELTED	30 ML

COOK TURNIPS UNTIL TENDER. DRAIN AND MASH. ADD BUTTER AND EGGS. BEAT WELL. (THIS MUCH CAN BE DONE THE DAY AHEAD.) COMBINE FLOUR, SUGAR, BAKING POWDER, SALT, PEPPER AND NUTMEG. STIR INTO TURNIPS. BUTTER A CASSEROLE AND PUT IN TURNIP MIXTURE. COMBINE CRUMBS AND BUTTER. SPRINKLE ON TOP. BAKE AT 375°F (190°C) FOR 25 MINUTES, OR UNTIL LIGHT BROWN ON TOP. SERVES 6.

BRIDE TO NEW HUSBAND: "THERE YOU ARE DARLING - MY FIRST MEAL COOKED JUST THE WAY YOU BETTER LIKE IT!"

SWEET POTATO SUPREME

GREAT WITH HAM OR TURKEY.

4 CUPS	COOKED, MASHED SWEET POTATOES	1 L
2 TBSP.	CREAM OR MILK	30 ML
1 TSP.	SALT	5 ML
1/4 TSP.	PAPRIKA	1 ML
1/2 CUP	BROWN SUGAR, PACKED	125 ML
1/3 CUP	BUTTER	75 ML
1 CUP	PECAN HALVES, TO COVER CASSEROLE	250 ML

THOROUGHLY MIX POTATOES, CREAM, SALT AND PAPRIKA. SPREAD IN GREASED CASSEROLE. MAKE THE TOPPING BY HEATING BROWN SUGAR AND BUTTER OVER LOW HEAT, STIRRING CONSTANTLY, UNTIL BUTTER IS BARELY MELTED. (IT IS IMPORTANT NOT TO COOK AFTER BUTTER IS MELTED, OR THE TOPPING WILL HARDEN WHEN CASSEROLE IS HEATED.) SPREAD TOPPING OVER POTATOES AND COVER WITH PECAN HALVES. REFRIGERATE UNTIL READY TO HEAT. THIS CASSEROLE MAY BE WARMED IN AN OVEN OF ANY TEMPERATURE. SHOULD BE BUBBLING HOT BEFORE SERVING. SERVES 6-8.

CLASSICAL RADIO STATION MORNING PROGRAM: "BAROQUE AND EGGS".

ROASTED NEW POTATOES WITH ROSEMARY

8	MEDIUM NEW RED POTATOES	8
1/4 CUP	OLIVE OIL	60 ML
2-3	GARLIC CLOVES, MINCED	2-3
2 TBSP.	CHOPPED FRESH ROSEMARY	30 ML

WASH POTATOES AND CUT INTO QUARTERS. ARRANGE IN SHALLOW BAKING DISH AND TOSS WITH OIL, GARLIC AND ROSEMARY. BAKE AT 375°F (190°C). FOR I HOUR, TURNING OCCASIONALLY. SERVES 4-6. IF THE TINY RED POTATOES ARE AVAILABLE USE THEM. THEY'RE THE BEST.

ELSIE'S POTATOES

A MUST WITH TURKEY DINNER . . . CAN BE MADE AHEAD AND FROZEN.

5 LBS.	POTATOES OR 9 LARGE	2.5 KG
8 OZ.	LOW-FAT CREAM CHEESE	250 G
I CUP	FAT-FREE SOUR CREAM	250 ML
2 TSP.	ONION SALT	10 ML
I TSP.	SALT	5 ML
	PINCH OF PEPPER	
2 TBSP.	BUTTER	30 ML

COOK AND MASH POTATOES. ADD ALL INGREDIENTS, EXCEPT BUTTER, AND COMBINE. PUT INTO LARGE GREASED CASSEROLE. DOT WITH BUTTER. BAKE, COVERED, AT 350°F (180°C). FOR 30 MINUTES. IF MAKING AHEAD, COVER AND REFRIGERATE OR FREEZE. THAW BEFORE BAKING. SERVES 10-12.

GRUYÈRE SCALLOPED POTATOES

2	GARLIC CLOVES, MINCED	2
2½ CUPS	HALF & HALF CREAM	625 ML
6	BAKING POTATOES, PEELED	6
2 TBSP.	FLOUR	30 ML
3 CUPS	GRATED GRUYÈRE CHEESE	750 ML
	SALT AND PEPPER TO TASTE	

STIR GARLIC INTO CREAM AND SET ASIDE. SLICE
POTATOES INTO PAPER-THIN ROUNDS AND TOSS WITH
FLOUR. ARRANGE HALF THE POTATOES IN A 9 X 13"
(23 X 33 CM) GLASS BAKING DISH. SPRINKLE WITH
HALF OF THE CHEESE; POUR HALF OF THE CREAM
MIXTURE OVER TOP. SPRINKLE WITH SALT AND PEPPER.
REPEAT LAYERS. COVER AND BAKE AT 325°F (160°C)
FOR 1 HOUR. REMOVE COVER AND CONTINUE BAKING
FOR ½ HOUR, OR UNTIL POTATOES ARE TENDER.

SIGN ON DOOR: "DOORBELL BROKEN. PLEASE KNOCK LOUDLY
TO ACTIVATE DOG."

Curried Apple and Sweet Potato Pilaf, page 169

Asparagus Vinaigrette, page 151

BUTTER-BAKED TATERS

¼ CUP	BUTTER	60 ML
3 TBSP.	GREEN ONIONS, FINELY CHOPPED	45 ML
3	LARGE POTATOES, PEELED	3
	SALT AND PEPPER TO TASTE	
2 TBSP.	GRATED PARMESAN CHEESE	30 ML

PREHEAT OVEN TO 500°F (290°C). MELT BUTTER IN A FRYING PAN, ADD ONION AND SAUTÉ UNTIL TENDER. HALVE POTATOES LENGTHWISE, THEN SLICE CROSSWISE INTO ⅛" (3 MM) THICK SLICES. IMMEDIATELY LINE UP IN BUTTERED 9 X 13" (23 X 33 CM) BAKING PAN WITH SLICES OVERLAPPING. POUR BUTTER MIXTURE OVER POTATOES. SEASON WITH SALT AND PEPPER. BAKE 20 MINUTES. REMOVE FROM OVEN AND SPRINKLE WITH PARMESAN CHEESE. BAKE AN ADDITIONAL 5-7 MINUTES, OR UNTIL CHEESE IS SLIGHTLY BROWNED AND MELTED. SERVES 4.

VARIATIONS: SOME LIKE 'EM HOT!

I CUP	GRATED CHEDDAR CHEESE	250 ML
I CUP	CORNFLAKES, CRUSHED	250 ML
I TSP.	CAYENNE PEPPER	5 ML

COMBINE CHEESE, CORNFLAKES AND CAYENNE. SPRINKLE OVER BUTTERED POTATOES AND BAKE AT 400°F (200°C) FOR 30 MINUTES, OMITTING THE PARMESAN CHEESE.

COUNTING CALORIES HAS BEEN FOR MANY PEOPLE, A WEIGH OF LIFE.

SCHWARTIES HASH BROWNS

GREAT FOR BUFFETS! FREEZES WELL.

2 LBS.	FROZEN HASH BROWNS	1 KG
2 CUPS	FAT-FREE SOUR CREAM	500 ML
2	10 OZ. (284 ML) CANS MUSHROOM SOUP	2
1/4 CUP	MELTED BUTTER	60 ML
	GRATED ONION & SALT TO TASTE	
2 CUPS	GRATED LIGHT CHEDDAR CHEESE	500 ML
2 TBSP.	PARMESAN CHEESE	30 ML

THAW POTATOES SLIGHTLY. MIX FIRST 6 INGREDIENTS IN A 9 X 13" (23 X 33 CM) BAKING DISH. SPRINKLE PARMESAN ON TOP. BAKE AT 350°F (180°C) FOR 1 HOUR. SERVES 8-10.

WILD RICE BROCCOLI CASSEROLE

THIS COMPLEMENTS ANY MEAT OR FOWL.

6 OZ.	PKG. UNCLE BEN'S WILD RICE MIXTURE	170 G
2	HEADS BROCCOLI, CUT INTO FLORETS	2
2	10 OZ. (284 ML) CANS MUSHROOM SOUP	2
2 CUPS	GRATED CHEDDAR CHEESE	500 ML

COOK RICE MIXTURE AS DIRECTED. COOK BROCCOLI UNTIL CRUNCHY. MIX SOUP AND 1 1/2 CUPS (375 ML) CHEESE. BUTTER A CASSEROLE. ALTERNATE SOUP MIXTURE, BROCCOLI AND RICE IN LAYERS. SPRINKLE WITH REMAINING 1/2 CUP (125 ML) CHEESE. COOK AT 350°F (180°C). FOR 1 HOUR. SERVES 6.

WILD RICE AND ARTICHOKE HEARTS

1 CUP	UNCOOKED WILD RICE	250 ML
10 OZ.	CAN CONSOMMÉ	284 ML
1 3/4 CUPS	WATER	425 ML
1/2 TSP.	SALT	2 ML
3 TBSP.	BUTTER	45 ML
1/3 CUP	CHOPPED ONION	75 ML
2	GARLIC CLOVES, MINCED	2
2	6 OZ. (175 ML) JARS MARINATED ARTICHOKE HEARTS	2
1 TBSP.	FRESH, CHOPPED PARSLEY	15 ML
1/4 TSP.	OREGANO	1 ML

WASH AND DRAIN WILD RICE. PLACE RICE, CONSOMMÉ, WATER AND SALT IN SAUCEPAN. HEAT TO BOILING; REDUCE HEAT AND SIMMER, COVERED, UNTIL TENDER, ABOUT 45 MINUTES.

IN A LARGE FRYING PAN, MELT BUTTER AND SAUTÉ ONION AND GARLIC UNTIL SOFT. DRAIN AND CUT ARTICHOKES INTO QUARTERS. ADD TO FRYING PAN WITH COOKED RICE, PARSLEY AND OREGANO. STIR UNTIL HEATED THROUGH. SERVES 4-6.

MEN WAKE UP AS GOOD-LOOKING AS THEY WENT TO BED. WOMEN SOMEHOW DETERIORATE DURING THE NIGHT.

WILD RICE, ORZO AND MUSHROOM CASSEROLE

A GREAT MAKE-AHEAD.

1 CUP	ORZO	250 ML
1 CUP	WILD RICE	250 ML
2½ CUPS	BEEF BROTH	625 ML
8 CUPS	SLICED MUSHROOMS	2 L
1 TBSP.	OIL	15 ML
2 TBSP.	BUTTER	30 ML
¼ CUP	FRESH PARSLEY	60 ML

COOK ORZO ACCORDING TO PACKAGE DIRECTIONS.
COOK THE WILD RICE IN THE BROTH ACCORDING TO
PACKAGE DIRECTIONS. SAUTÉ MUSHROOMS IN OIL
AND BUTTER AND COOK UNTIL LIQUID HAS ALMOST
EVAPORATED. ADD MUSHROOMS AND PARSLEY TO RICE
AND ORZO. MIX WELL. THIS MAY BE PREPARED
AHEAD AND REFRIGERATED. BRING TO ROOM
TEMPERATURE AND BAKE AT 350°F (180°C) FOR
30 MINUTES, UNTIL HEATED THROUGH. SERVES 6-8.

THERE ARE TWO TIMES WHEN A MAN DOESN'T
UNDERSTAND A WOMAN - BEFORE MARRIAGE AND AFTER
MARRIAGE.

ORZO WITH PARMESAN AND BASIL

THE PASTA THAT LOOKS LIKE RICE - GREAT WITH CHICKEN OR FISH.

3 TBSP.	BUTTER	45 ML
1½ CUPS	ORZO	375 ML
3 CUPS	CHICKEN BROTH	750 ML
½ CUP	GRATED PARMESAN CHEESE	125 ML
6 TBSP.	CHOPPED FRESH BASIL OR	90 ML
	1½ TSP. (7 ML) DRIED BASIL	
	SALT & PEPPER TO TASTE	

MELT BUTTER IN SKILLET OVER MEDIUM-HIGH HEAT. ADD ORZO AND SAUTÉ 2 MINUTES, UNTIL SLIGHTLY BROWN. ADD BROTH AND BRING TO A BOIL. REDUCE HEAT, COVER AND SIMMER UNTIL ORZO IS TENDER AND LIQUID IS ABSORBED, ABOUT 20 MINUTES. MIX IN PARMESAN AND BASIL. SEASON WITH SALT AND PEPPER. TRANSFER TO SHALLOW BOWL. SERVES 6.

VARIATION: FOR A CREAMIER PASTA DISH, TRY STIRRING IN 2 TBSP. (30 ML) PLAIN YOGURT THINNED WITH A LITTLE MILK.

POLITICALLY CORRECT SEMANTICS: SNOW W.A.S.P. AND THE SEVEN VERTICALLY IMPAIRED MINERS.

THE CLASSIC COMPLEMENT TO OSSO BUCO (PAGE 210).

½ CUP	BUTTER OR MARGARINE	125 ML
½ CUP	FINELY CHOPPED ONION	125 ML
1½ CUPS	UNCOOKED RICE	375 ML
3½ CUPS	CHICKEN BROTH	875 ML
½ CUP	DRY WHITE WINE	125 ML
1 TSP.	CRUSHED SAFFRON	5 ML
2 TBSP.	CHICKEN BROTH	30 ML
2 TBSP.	FRESHLY GRATED PARMESAN CHEESE	30 ML

MELT ¼ CUP (60 ML) BUTTER IN MEDIUM SAUCEPAN AND SAUTÉ ONION UNTIL TRANSLUCENT. ADD THE RICE AND STIR TO MIX. ADD BROTH AND WINE AND BRING TO BOIL. COVER AND COOK OVER LOW HEAT FOR 25 MINUTES, STIRRING OCCASIONALLY. STIR IN ¼ CUP (60 ML) OF BUTTER. SOFTEN SAFFRON IN 2 TBSP. (30 ML) OF CHICKEN BROTH; ADD TO RICE AND COOK, UNCOVERED, OVER LOW HEAT FOR 4 MORE MINUTES. TO SERVE, SPRINKLE WITH PARMESAN CHEESE. SERVES 6-8.

THE EARLY BIRD GETS THE WORM, BUT THE SECOND MOUSE GETS THE CHEESE.

CURRIED APPLE AND SWEET POTATO PILAF

1 TBSP.	OLIVE OIL	15 ML
1/2 CUP	CHOPPED GREEN ONIONS	125 ML
2	GARLIC CLOVES, MINCED	2
1 CUP	UNCOOKED LONG-GRAIN RICE	250 ML
2 CUPS	WATER	500 ML
1 1/2 CUPS	PEELED & DICED SWEET POTATO	375 ML
2 CUPS	PEELED & CUBED GRANNY SMITH APPLES	500 ML
1/2 CUP	FROZEN GREEN PEAS	125 ML
1/4 CUP	CURRANTS	60 ML
1/2 TSP.	CURRY POWDER	2 ML
1/2 TSP.	CUMIN	2 ML
1/4 TSP.	SALT	1 ML
	PEPPER TO TASTE	

HEAT OIL IN A MEDIUM SAUCEPAN OVER MEDIUM-HIGH HEAT. ADD ONIONS AND GARLIC; SAUTÉ 1 MINUTE. STIR IN RICE AND SAUTÉ 1 MINUTE. ADD WATER AND SWEET POTATO; BRING TO A BOIL. COVER, REDUCE HEAT, AND SIMMER 15 MINUTES, OR UNTIL LIQUID IS ALMOST ABSORBED. STIR IN APPLE, PEAS, CURRANTS AND SEASONINGS. COVER AND SIMMER 3 MINUTES, OR UNTIL THOROUGHLY HEATED. A GREAT ACCOMPANIMENT FOR HAM. SERVES 4-6. (PICTURED OPPOSITE PAGE 162.)

HAPPINESS IS WHEN YOUR PLANE AND LUGGAGE ARRIVE AT THE SAME TIME.

BARBER'S BEST CHILI

A VEGETARIAN VERSION.

1½ CUPS	CHOPPED ONION	375 ML
2	GREEN PEPPERS, CHOPPED	2
3	CELERY STALKS, CHOPPED	3
4	GARLIC CLOVES, MINCED	4
2 TBSP.	OIL	30 ML
2	28 OZ. (796 ML) CANS TOMATOES	2
14 OZ.	CAN KIDNEY BEANS	398 ML
14 OZ.	CAN BROWN BEANS	398 ML
2 CUPS	SLICED FRESH MUSHROOMS	500 ML
1½ CUPS	WATER	375 ML
½ CUP	RAISINS	125 ML
¼ CUP	VINEGAR	60 ML
1	BAY LEAF	1
1 TBSP.	CHILI POWDER	15 ML
1 TBSP.	PARSLEY	15 ML
1½ TSP.	BASIL	7 ML
1½ TSP.	OREGANO	7 ML
½ TSP.	PEPPER	2 ML
¼ TSP.	TABASCO	1 ML
1 CUP	CASHEWS (OPTIONAL)	250 ML
	GRATED CHEDDAR CHEESE	
	SOUR CREAM	

SAUTÉ ONION, GREEN PEPPER, CELERY AND GARLIC IN OIL UNTIL TENDER. ADD TOMATOES AND BEANS WITH LIQUID, ALONG WITH REMAINING INGREDIENTS, EXCEPT CASHEWS, CHEESE AND SOUR CREAM. COVER AND SIMMER FOR 1 HOUR. UNCOVER AND SIMMER ANOTHER HOUR. REMOVE BAY LEAF (IF YOU CAN FIND IT). IF USING

BARBER'S BEST CHILI

CONTINUED FROM PAGE 170.

CASHEWS, ADD AT THE END. SERVE WITH GRATED CHEDDAR CHEESE AND A DOLLOP OF SOUR CREAM. SERVES 8-10 – DEPENDING ON WHAT SIZE YOUR BARBERS ARE!

CALICO BEAN POT

THE WORLD'S BEST BEAN CASSEROLE!

8	SLICES BACON	8
I CUP	CHOPPED ONION	250 ML
14 OZ.	CAN GREEN BEANS, DRAINED	398 ML
14 OZ.	CAN LIMA BEANS, DRAINED	398 ML
14 OZ.	CAN PORK & BEANS	398 ML
14 OZ.	CAN KIDNEY BEANS, DRAINED	398 ML
3/4 CUP	BROWN SUGAR, FIRMLY PACKED	175 ML
1/2 CUP	VINEGAR	125 ML
1/2 TSP.	GARLIC SALT	2 ML
1/2 TSP.	DRY MUSTARD	2 ML
	PEPPER TO TASTE	

CUT BACON INTO SMALL PIECES AND COOK UNTIL CRISP. COOK ONION UNTIL SOFT. ADD REMAINING INGREDIENTS IN A 2½-QUART (2.5 L) CASSEROLE. BAKE AT 350°F (180°C) FOR I HOUR, UNCOVERED. PERFECT WITH HAMBURGERS OR BAR-B-QUED BEEF. SERVES 12.

1	ONION, CHOPPED	1
1	RED PEPPER, CHOPPED	1
1	GREEN PEPPER, CHOPPED	1
2 TBSP.	OLIVE OIL	30 ML
1-2	GARLIC CLOVES, MINCED	1-2
1½ TSP.	PAPRIKA	7 ML
¼ TSP.	CAYENNE PEPPER	1 ML
2 CUPS	CHICKEN OR VEGETABLE BROTH	500 ML
3-4	ROMA TOMATOES, CHOPPED	3-4
1 CUP	FROZEN PEAS	250 ML
1 CUP	GARBANZO BEANS, DRAINED (CHICK-PEAS)	250 ML
2	CARROTS, PEELED & CHOPPED	2
1 CUP	COUSCOUS	250 ML
14 OZ.	CAN ARTICHOKE HEARTS, DRAINED & QUARTERED	398 ML
1	LEMON, CUT IN WEDGES	
	FRESH PARSLEY, CHOPPED	

SAUTÉ ONION AND PEPPERS IN OIL UNTIL THEY
BEGIN TO SOFTEN. STIR IN GARLIC, PAPRIKA AND
CAYENNE PEPPER. ADD BROTH, TOMATOES, PEAS,
GARBANZO BEANS AND CARROTS. COVER AND SIMMER
FOR 5 MINUTES. ADD COUSCOUS TO VEGETABLE
MIXTURE. COVER AND SIMMER 1 MINUTE MORE.
REMOVE FROM HEAT AND LET STAND 5 MINUTES.
WHEN SERVING, FLUFF COUSCOUS WITH FORK. GARNISH
WITH ARTICHOKE HEARTS, LEMON WEDGES AND
PARSLEY. SERVES 6-8. SERVE WITH CHICKEN IN
PHYLLO (PAGE 196) (PICTURED OPPOSITE PAGE 180.)

FISH

Poached Salmon with Piquant Sauce and Veggies
Potlatch Salmon
Grilled Halibut and Peppers Julienne
Red Snapper Parmesan
O-Sole-O-Mio
Fish 'N' Chips

SEAFOOD

Orange Stir-Fried Shrimp
Shrimp and Scallop Supreme

CHICKEN

Lime-Grilled Chicken
Orange-Rosemary Chicken
Honey-Mustard Chicken
Bare-Naked Chicken
Ginger Chicken Stir-Fry
Sweet and Spicy Cashew Chicken
Crunchy Garlic Chicken
Oven-Fried Chicken
Layered Chicken Tortilla
El Grando Chicken Quesadillas
Southwestern Chicken Chili
Chicken Enchilada Casserole
Chicken in Phyllo
Chicken Breasts Zelda
Chicken Breasts Stuffed with Asparagus
Chicken Pot Pie
Chicken in Wine
Classy Chicken
Japanese Chicken Wings

POACHED SALMON WITH PIQUANT SAUCE AND VEGGIES

A DELICIOUS DINNER FOR 4. SERVE WITH STEAMED RICE.

PIQUANT SAUCE

3 TBSP.	LOW-FAT MAYONNAISE	45 ML
1 TBSP.	CHOPPED FRESH DILL, OR 1 TSP. (5 ML) DRY DILL	15 ML
1 TBSP.	SKIM MILK	15 ML
1 TBSP.	CAPERS	15 ML
2 TSP.	JUICE FROM CAPERS	10 ML
1½ TSP.	DIJON MUSTARD	7 ML
¼ TSP.	GRATED LEMON RIND	1 ML

SALMON

1 LB.	SALMON FILLET	500 G
3 CUPS	WATER	750 ML
1	SMALL LEMON, THINLY SLICED	
2 TSP.	INSTANT CHICKEN BOUILLON POWDER	10 ML

VEGETABLES

1½ CUPS	WATER	375 ML
1 TSP.	INSTANT CHICKEN BOUILLON POWDER	5 ML
3	MEDIUM CARROTS, SLICED INTO MATCHSTICKS	3
1	MEDIUM ZUCCHINI (UNPEELED), SLICED INTO MATCHSTICKS	1
	CHOPPED FRESH DILL FOR GARNISH	

TO PREPARE PIQUANT SAUCE: COMBINE ALL INGREDIENTS IN SMALL BOWL AND SET ASIDE.

POACHED SALMON WITH PIQUANT SAUCE AND VEGGIES

CONTINUED FROM PAGE 174.

TO POACH SALMON: REMOVE ANY SMALL BONES WITH TWEEZERS AND CUT SALMON INTO 4 PIECES. IN LARGE FRYING PAN, BRING 3 CUPS (750 ML) WATER TO A BOIL. ADD LEMON SLICES AND CHICKEN BOUILLON POWDER. COVER AND SIMMER FOR 5 MINUTES. ADD SALMON AND HEAT TO BOILING. REDUCE HEAT TO LOW; COVER AND SIMMER 8-10 MINUTES, UNTIL FISH FLAKES EASILY WHEN TESTED WITH FORK.

TO PREPARE VEGGIES: WHILE FISH IS POACHING, HEAT WATER AND BOUILLON TO BOILING. ADD CARROTS; REDUCE HEAT TO LOW; COVER AND SIMMER 2 MINUTES. ADD ZUCCHINI; HEAT TO BOILING; COVER AND SIMMER 2 MINUTES LONGER, OR UNTIL VEGETABLES ARE TENDER-CRISP. DRAIN. ARRANGE SALMON, STEAMED RICE, AND VEGETABLES ON A WARM PLATTER. GARNISH WITH DILL.

REMEMBER WHEN A HARD DRIVE WAS A LONG TRIP AND NOT A COMPUTER PART?

POTLATCH SALMON

A WONDERFUL WAY TO BAR-B-QUE A WHOLE SALMON.

1	WHOLE SALMON, BUTTERFLIED	1
2 TBSP.	BUTTER, SOFTENED	30 ML
	JUICE OF 1 LEMON	
2 TSP.	DRY MUSTARD	10 ML
2/3-1 CUP	BROWN SUGAR	150-250 ML

TO BUTTERFLY SALMON: REMOVE HEAD, TAIL AND FINS. RUN SHARP KNIFE DOWN BACKBONE UNTIL SALMON OPENS FLAT. PLACE SKIN-SIDE DOWN ON A GREASED SHEET OF FOIL. SPREAD BUTTER OVER FISH. SPRINKLE LIBERALLY WITH LEMON JUICE AND MUSTARD. COVER WITH 1/4-1/2" (1-1.3 CM) BROWN SUGAR.

TO COOK: PLACE SALMON ON BAR-B-QUE, LOWER LID AND COOK OVER LOW HEAT FOR 20-30 MINUTES. SALMON IS COOKED WHEN FLESH FLAKES. DON'T OVERCOOK!NOW IS THE TIME TO REMOVE THE BONES. LIFT BACKBONE AT ONE END AND GENTLY REMOVE IN ONE PIECE. THE BOTTOM LINE: DEE-LISHUS!! SERVES 6-8.

START OFF EVERY DAY WITH A SMILE AND GET IT OVER WITH.

GRILLED HALIBUT AND PEPPERS JULIENNE

A POTPOURRI OF PEPPERS - THE PERFECT PARTNER FOR YOUR FAVORITE FISH. SERVE WITH ORZO WITH PARMESAN AND BASIL (PAGE 167).

1	RED PEPPER	1
1	GREEN PEPPER	1
1	YELLOW PEPPER	1
1	ONION	1
2	CELERY STALKS	2
1	TOMATO	1
2 TBSP.	BUTTER OR MARGARINE	30 ML
1 TSP.	CHOPPED FRESH PARSLEY	5 ML
	A GENEROUS SPRINKLE OF: PAPRIKA,	
	CURRY POWDER & CAYENNE	
	SALT & PEPPER TO TASTE	
2/3 CUP	WHITE WINE	150 ML
4	HALIBUT STEAKS	4
	SPRINKLING OF PAPRIKA & PEPPER	

CUT PEPPERS (REMOVE SEEDS), ONION AND CELERY INTO THIN STRIPS. COARSELY CHOP THE TOMATO. MELT BUTTER IN SKILLET. ADD PREPARED VEGGIES AND ALL REMAINING INGREDIENTS, EXCEPT THE FISH. SIMMER 5 MINUTES. WHILE VEGGIES ARE COOKING, PREPARE AND COOK FISH. BRUSH WITH OIL AND SPRINKLE WITH PAPRIKA AND PEPPER. GRILL UNTIL FISH IS OPAQUE AND FLAKES EASILY, ABOUT 4 MINUTES EACH SIDE. SPOON SIMMERED VEGGIES AND PAN JUICES OVER FISH. GOOD FOR YOUR BOD AND GREAT FOR YOUR CULINARY REPUTATION!! SERVES 4.

RED SNAPPER PARMESAN

¾ LB.	RED SNAPPER	365 G
1 TBSP.	LEMON JUICE	15 ML
2 TBSP.	GRATED PARMESAN CHEESE	30 ML
2 TBSP.	SKIM MILK YOGURT	30 ML
2 TBSP.	LOW-FAT MAYONNAISE	30 ML
2 TBSP.	FINELY CHOPPED GREEN ONION	30 ML
2 TBSP.	CHOPPED PIMIENTO OR RED PEPPER	30 ML
½ TSP.	DRIED DILL	2 ML

PLACE FILLETS IN BAKING DISH AND BRUSH WITH
LEMON JUICE. LET STAND 20 MINUTES. PREHEAT
BROILER. COMBINE REMAINING INGREDIENTS. BROIL
FILLETS 6-8 MINUTES, UNTIL FLAKY. SPOON PARMESAN
MIXTURE OVER FILLETS AND BROIL ANOTHER
3 MINUTES. SERVE WITH RICE. SERVES 2.

O-SOLE-O-MIO

OR SOLE FOR FOUR!

4	FRESH SOLE FILLETS	4
4 TSP.	BUTTER	20 ML
4 TBSP.	FROZEN ORANGE JUICE CONCENTRATE	60 ML
4	GREEN ONIONS, CHOPPED	4
	SALT & PEPPER TO TASTE	

PREHEAT OVEN TO 450°F (230°C). USING 4, 10"
(25 CM) PIECES OF FOIL, PLACE 1 FILLET IN CENTER
OF EACH. PLACE 1 TSP. (5 ML) BUTTER, 1 TBSP. (15 ML)
ORANGE CONCENTRATE AND CHOPPED GREEN ONION
ON EACH FILLET. WRAP AND SEAL. PLACE ON BAKING
SHEET; BAKE FOR 15 MINUTES. SERVE WITH RICE AND
A GREEN VEGETABLE.

FISH 'N' CHIPS

DUST, DIP & ROLL. VERY HEALTHY. VERY DELICIOUS!

3 LBS.	BAKER POTATOES, UNPEELED	1.5 KG
1 TBSP.	VEGETABLE OIL	15 ML
1/2 TSP.	SALT	2 ML
1/2 TSP.	PEPPER	2 ML
1 1/2 LBS.	ATLANTIC COD	750 G
1/2 CUP	FLOUR	125 ML
2 TSP.	DRY MUSTARD	10 ML
1	EGG, BEATEN	1
1/4 CUP	BREAD CRUMBS	60 ML
3/4 CUP	CORNFLAKE CRUMBS	175 ML
1 TBSP.	VEGETABLE OIL	15 ML

SCRUB POTATOES AND CUT INTO THICK FRENCH FRIES.
PAT DRY AND TOSS WITH OIL, SALT AND PEPPER.
ARRANGE IN A SINGLE LAYER ON A NON-STICK COOKIE
SHEET; BAKE AT 425°F (220°C) FOR 40 MINUTES
TURNING TWICE. CUT FISH INTO SERVING-SIZED
PIECES. PAT DRY. PLACE FLOUR AND MUSTARD IN A
SHALLOW DISH. BEAT EGG IN ANOTHER SHALLOW DISH.
COMBINE CRUMBS AND CORNFLAKES IN YET ANOTHER
DISH! DUST EACH PIECE OF FISH WITH FLOUR. DIP
INTO EGG AND ROLL IN CRUMB MIXTURE. BRUSH
ANOTHER BAKING SHEET WITH OIL AND ARRANGE FISH
IN A SINGLE LAYER. WHEN POTATOES HAVE COOKED FOR
40 MINUTES, PLACE FISH IN OVEN AND BAKE BOTH
FOR 5 MINUTES. TURN AND BAKE ANOTHER 5 MINUTES,
UNTIL FISH IS COOKED THROUGH (SHOULD BE FLAKY).
SERVE WITH REGINA BEACH COLESLAW (PAGE 87).
SERVES 6.

ORANGE STIR-FRIED SHRIMP

ZIPPY GARLIC ORANGE MARINADE

I	GARLIC CLOVE, MINCED	I
I TSP.	GRATED ORANGE RIND	5 ML
1/4 TSP.	HOT RED PEPPER FLAKES	I ML
I TSP.	SOY SAUCE	5 ML
I TSP.	SESAME OIL	5 ML
I LB.	SHRIMP, SHELLED & DEVEINED	500 G

ORANGE SOY SAUCE

1/2 CUP	ORANGE JUICE	125 ML
2 TBSP.	SOY SAUCE	30 ML
I TBSP.	HONEY OR SUGAR	15 ML
2 TSP.	CORNSTARCH	10 ML
I TSP.	SESAME OIL	5 ML

STIR-FRY

I TBSP.	OIL	15 ML
I TBSP.	FINELY CHOPPED FRESH GINGER	15 ML
I	GARLIC CLOVE, MINCED	I
1/2 LB.	GREEN BEANS, SLICED	250 G
1 1/2 CUPS	MUSHROOMS, SLICED	375 ML
I	RED PEPPER, CUT IN STRIPS	I
3	SCALLIONS OR GREEN ONIONS, SLICED DIAGONALLY	3

TO PREPARE MARINADE: IN A LARGE BOWL, BLEND ALL MARINADE INGREDIENTS. ADD SHRIMP; COVER AND REFRIGERATE I HOUR.

CONTINUED ON PAGE 181.

Chicken in Phyllo, page 196
Vegetable Couscous, page 172

Chicken Pot Pie, page 199

ORANGE STIR-FRIED SHRIMP

CONTINUED FROM PAGE 180.

TO MAKE SAUCE: IN A SMALL BOWL, MIX ALL INGREDIENTS UNTIL SMOOTH AND SET ASIDE.

TO STIR-FRY: HEAT WOK OR LARGE FRYING PAN UNTIL HOT. ADD OIL, GINGER AND GARLIC AND STIR-FRY 20 SECONDS. ADD GREEN BEANS, STIR-FRY 3 MINUTES. ADD MUSHROOMS AND RED PEPPER AND STIR-FRY 3 MINUTES MORE. ADD SHRIMP AND MARINADE; STIR-FRY 4 MINUTES, OR JUST UNTIL SHRIMP TURNS PINK. STIR SAUCE. ADD SCALLIONS; STIR INTO SHRIMP UNTIL MIXTURE IS COATED AND SAUCE THICKENS. (AREN'T YOU JUST EXHAUSTED??) SERVES 4.

IF MOST CAR ACCIDENTS OCCUR WITHIN 5 MILES OF HOME, WHY DOESN'T EVERYONE JUST MOVE 10 MILES AWAY?

SHRIMP AND SCALLOP SUPREME

2 TBSP.	OLIVE OIL	30 ML
I	ONION, CHOPPED	I
3	GARLIC CLOVES, MINCED	3
2	28 OZ. (796 ML) CANS TOMATOES, PURÉED WITH JUICE	2
I LB.	SHRIMP, DEVEINED & BUTTERFLIED	500 G
3/4 LB.	SCALLOPS, HALVED IF LARGE	365 G
I CUP	FROZEN PEAS, THAWED	250 ML
1/4 CUP	CHOPPED FRESH PARSLEY	60 ML
I TSP.	SALT	5 ML
1/2 TSP.	PEPPER	2 ML
3 CUPS	COOKED LONG-GRAIN RICE	750 ML

TOPPING

1/3 CUP	BUTTER	75 ML
2	GARLIC CLOVES, MINCED	2
2 CUPS	FRESH BREAD CRUMBS	500 ML
	SALT & PEPPER TO TASTE	

IN DUTCH OVEN HEAT OIL OVER MEDIUM HEAT. COOK ONION AND GARLIC FOR 5 MINUTES. ADD TOMATOES; COOK 15 MINUTES. ADD SEAFOOD; COOK 5 MINUTES. STIR IN PEAS, PARSLEY, SALT AND PEPPER. SEASON RICE WITH SALT AND PEPPER TO TASTE AND SPREAD IN GREASED GLASS 9 X 13" (23 X 33 CM) PAN. SPREAD SEAFOOD MIXTURE OVER RICE.

TO MAKE TOPPING: MELT BUTTER AND SAUTÉ GARLIC. ADD BREAD CRUMBS AND SEASON WITH SALT AND PEPPER. SPRINKLE OVER CASSEROLE. MAY BE REFRIGERATED AT THIS POINT FOR UP

SHRIMP AND SCALLOP SUPREME

CONTINUED FROM PAGE 182.

TO 24 HOURS. REMOVE FROM REFRIGERATOR
1/2 HOUR BEFORE BAKING. BAKE AT 350°F (180°C) FOR
30-40 MINUTES, OR UNTIL BUBBLING AND TOP IS
BROWNED AND CRISP. DO NOT OVERCOOK. SERVE WITH
ASPARAGUS AND WARM ROLLS. SERVES 8-10.

LIME-GRILLED CHICKEN

A LOW-CAL. CREATION TO BROIL OR GRILL. RUB
HERBS BETWEEN YOUR HANDS TO RELEASE FLAVORS.

1/2 CUP	FRESH LIME JUICE (2 LARGE LIMES)	125 ML
1/4 CUP	VEGETABLE OIL	60 ML
2 TBSP.	HONEY	30 ML
1 TSP.	THYME	5 ML
1 TSP.	ROSEMARY	5 ML
1	GARLIC CLOVE, CRUSHED	1
2	WHOLE CHICKEN BREASTS, SKINNED, BONED & HALVED	2

IN A BOWL COMBINE ALL INGREDIENTS, EXCEPT
CHICKEN, WHISKING UNTIL WELL BLENDED.
MARINATE CHICKEN BREASTS IN LIME MIXTURE
1-2 HOURS. BROIL OR GRILL APPROXIMATELY
4 MINUTES PER SIDE, UNTIL CHICKEN IS COOKED
THROUGH. BASTE DURING COOKING. SERVES 4.

ORANGE-ROSEMARY CHICKEN

SPLENDIFEROUS!

2	GARLIC CLOVES	2
1	ROASTING CHICKEN	1
1	ORANGE, QUARTERED	1
4	SPRIGS FRESH ROSEMARY OR	4
	1 TBSP. (15 ML) DRY ROSEMARY	
1 TBSP.	OIL	15 ML
2 TBSP.	ORANGE MARMALADE	30 ML
1 TBSP.	CHOPPED FRESH ROSEMARY OR	15 ML
	1½ TSP. (7 ML) DRY ROSEMARY	

PREHEAT OVEN TO 325°F (160°C). PEEL GARLIC AND PLACE IN CHICKEN CAVITY. STUFF UNPEELED ORANGE WEDGES INTO CAVITY WITH ROSEMARY. CLOSE THE CAVITY AND LOOSELY TIE LEGS TOGETHER. PLACE CHICKEN ON RACK IN ROASTING PAN. BRUSH WITH OIL. ROAST CHICKEN, UNCOVERED, FOR 2 HOURS. BASTE FREQUENTLY WITH PAN JUICES. MIX MARMALADE WITH ROSEMARY. BRUSH OVER CHICKEN AND ROAST, BASTING WITH MIXTURE, ABOUT 10 MORE MINUTES. MAKE GRAVY WITH PAN DRIPPINGS. SERVE WITH MASHED POTATOES.

CLASSIFIED AD: "KITTENS, $1 EACH. CALL ASHLEY."
"KITTENS FREE. CALL ASHLEY'S MOM."

HONEY-MUSTARD CHICKEN

MAKES LOTS OF SAUCE; GREAT WITH RICE.

3 LBS.	CHICKEN PIECES	1.5 KG
½ CUP	LIQUID HONEY	125 ML
¼ CUP	BUTTER OR MARGARINE	60 ML
¼ CUP	DIJON MUSTARD	60 ML
2-4 TSP.	CURRY POWDER	10-20 ML
PINCH	CAYENNE PEPPER	PINCH

PLACE CHICKEN IN SINGLE LAYER IN LARGE
OVENPROOF DISH. COMBINE HONEY, BUTTER, MUSTARD,
CURRY POWDER AND CAYENNE. POUR OVER CHICKEN.
BAKE, UNCOVERED, AT 350°F (180°C) FOR 20 MINUTES,
BASTING ONCE. TURN PIECES OVER, BASTE AGAIN AND
BAKE ANOTHER 20 MINUTES, OR UNTIL PIECES ARE
NO LONGER PINK INSIDE. SERVES 4-6.

THE ONE NICE THING ABOUT STARTING TO FORGET
THINGS IS THAT YOU CAN HIDE YOUR OWN EASTER EGGS.

BARE-NAKED CHICKEN

FAST AND EASY!

4	BONELESS, SKINLESS CHICKEN BREAST HALVES	4
	SALT & PEPPER TO TASTE	
1 TBSP.	BUTTER	15 ML
1/2 CUP	FINELY CHOPPED SHALLOTS	125 ML
1/4 CUP	BALSAMIC VINEGAR	60 ML
1 1/2 CUPS	CHICKEN BROTH	375 ML

SEASON CHICKEN AND BROWN IN BUTTER OVER MEDIUM-HIGH HEAT. REDUCE HEAT AND COOK UNTIL CHICKEN IS NO LONGER PINK IN MIDDLE. DO NOT OVERCOOK! REMOVE TO HEATED DISH AND SET IN WARM OVEN. ADD SHALLOTS TO PAN AND COOK UNTIL TRANSLUCENT. ADD VINEGAR, BOIL AND REDUCE TO GLAZE, STIRRING CONSTANTLY. ADD CHICKEN BROTH AND BOIL UNTIL REDUCED TO 3/4 CUP (175 ML). SPOON OVER CHICKEN AND RETURN DISH TO OVEN UNTIL SERVING TIME. EXCELLENT WITH RICE OR FETTUCCINE. SERVES 4.

TACT IS THE ABILITY TO NOT SAY WHAT YOU REALLY THINK.

GINGER CHICKEN STIR-FRY

DINNER'S READY IN 20 MINUTES.

3 TBSP.	LEMON JUICE, FRESH IS BEST	45 ML
3 TBSP.	SOY SAUCE	45 ML
1 TBSP.	GRATED FRESH GINGER	15 ML
2	GARLIC CLOVES, MINCED	2
1	CHICKEN BREAST, SKINNED & BONED, CUT INTO ½" (1.3 CM) STRIPS	1
2 TSP.	CORNSTARCH	10 ML
⅓ CUP	CHICKEN BROTH	75 ML
1 TBSP.	COOKING OIL	15 ML
1 CUP	SLICED MUSHROOMS	250 ML
1½ CUPS	ASPARAGUS OR GREEN BEANS CUT IN 1½" (4 CM) PIECES	375 ML
3	GREEN ONIONS, SLICED DIAGONALLY INTO 1" (2.5 CM) PIECES	3
	TOASTED SESAME SEEDS	

IN A BOWL COMBINE LEMON JUICE, SOY SAUCE, GINGER AND GARLIC. SPRINKLE 3 TBSP. (45 ML) OF MIXTURE OVER CHICKEN, TOSSING TO COAT. RESERVE REMAINING LIQUID. DISSOLVE CORN-STARCH IN BROTH. HEAT OIL IN FRYING PAN OR WOK. ADD MUSHROOMS AND CHICKEN. STIR OVER HIGH HEAT UNTIL CHICKEN LOSES PINK COLOR. ADD ASPARAGUS AND ONIONS; CONTINUE TO STIR OVER HIGH HEAT UNTIL VEGETABLES ARE TENDER-CRISP. ADD BROTH MIXTURE AND RESERVED LIQUID AND STIR UNTIL THICKENED. SPRINKLE WITH SESAME SEEDS. SERVE HOT OVER RICE OR PASTA. SERVES 4.

SWEET AND SPICY
CASHEW CHICKEN

A DELICIOUS AND COLORFUL STIR-FRY. SERVE OVER RICE ON A LARGE PLATTER OR TAKE THE WOK RIGHT TO THE TABLE.

SAUCE

1/2 CUP	KETCHUP	125 ML
4 TSP.	SOY SAUCE	20 ML
1/2 TSP.	SALT	2 ML
2 TBSP.	WORCESTERSHIRE SAUCE	30 ML
3 TBSP.	SUGAR	45 ML
1 1/2 TSP.	SESAME OIL	7 ML
1/4 TSP.	CAYENNE PEPPER	1 ML
1/2 CUP	CHICKEN BROTH	125 ML

THE REST

2 TBSP.	CORNSTARCH	30 ML
1/2 TSP.	SUGAR	2 ML
1/4 TSP.	SALT	1 ML
3	WHOLE BONELESS, SKINLESS CHICKEN BREASTS, CUT INTO CUBES	3
1/4 CUP	OIL	60 ML
2-3 TBSP.	MINCED FRESH GINGER	30-45 ML
1 TBSP.	MINCED GARLIC	15 ML
1	SMALL ONION, CHOPPED	1
2	RED PEPPERS, CUT IN STRIPS	2
2	CARROTS, THINLY SLICED ON DIAGONAL	2
2 CUPS	SNOW PEAS	500 ML
1 1/2 CUPS	CASHEWS	375 ML
	SPRINKLING OF SESAME SEEDS, TOASTED	

SWEET AND SPICY
CASHEW CHICKEN

CONTINUED FROM PAGE 188.

ARE YOU READY? COMBINE SAUCE INGREDIENTS AND SET ASIDE. IN A BOWL, COMBINE CORNSTARCH, SUGAR AND SALT. ADD CHICKEN AND TOSS. HEAT WOK OR FRYING PAN TO HIGHEST HEAT. ADD OIL. HEAT TO HOT, NOT SMOKING. ADD CHICKEN, GINGER, GARLIC AND ONION. STIR UNTIL CHICKEN IS OPAQUE (ABOUT 1 MINUTE). ADD PEPPERS AND CARROTS. STIR 2-3 MINUTES. ADD PEAS AND SAUCE. COOK UNTIL SAUCE COMES TO A BOIL. ADD CASHEWS AND SPRINKLE WITH SESAME SEEDS. SERVE IMMEDIATELY. SERVES 6. (PICTURED OPPOSITE PAGE 199.)

I HAVE AN AGREEMENT WITH MY WIFE. SHE DOESN'T COMPARE THE MEN IN PLAYGIRL MAGAZINE TO ME - AND I DON'T COMPARE THE MEALS IN GOURMET MAGAZINE TO HERS.

CRUNCHY GARLIC CHICKEN

2 TBSP.	BUTTER, MELTED	30 ML
2 TBSP.	MILK	30 ML
1 TSP.	CHOPPED FRESH CHIVES	5 ML
1/2 TSP.	SALT	2 ML
1	LARGE GARLIC CLOVE, MINCED	1
2 CUPS	CORNFLAKES, CRUSHED	500 ML
3 TBSP.	CHOPPED FRESH PARSLEY	45 ML
1/2 TSP.	PAPRIKA	2 ML
6	CHICKEN BREAST HALVES, BONELESS, SKINLESS	6

HEAT OVEN TO 425°F (220°C). USE NONSTICK SPRAY OR PARCHMENT PAPER ON A BAKING SHEET. IN A DISH, MIX BUTTER, MILK, CHIVES, SALT AND GARLIC TOGETHER. MIX CORNFLAKES, PARSLEY AND PAPRIKA TOGETHER. DIP CHICKEN IN BUTTER MIXTURE, THEN COAT EVENLY IN CORNFLAKE MIXTURE. PLACE ON BAKING SHEET AND SPRAY LIGHTLY WITH COOKING SPRAY. BAKE, UNCOVERED, 20-25 MINUTES. SERVES 4-6.

WHY DO NEWLY MARRIED MEN TWIRL THEIR WEDDING RINGS? THEY'RE LOOKING FOR THE COMBINATION.

OVEN-FRIED CHICKEN

A PERFECT PICNIC "PACK ALONG".

SEASONED FLOUR

1½ CUPS	FLOUR	375 ML
4 TSP.	DRY MUSTARD	20 ML
1 TBSP.	PAPRIKA	15 ML
	SALT & PEPPER TO TASTE	
	CHICKEN PIECES, AS NEEDED	
¼ CUP	BUTTER OR MARGARINE	60 ML

COMBINE SEASONED FLOUR INGREDIENTS AND STORE
IN A JAR. PREHEAT OVEN TO 400°F (200°C). PLACE
REQUIRED AMOUNT OF DRY MIXTURE IN A PAPER
BAG; ADD CHICKEN AND SHAKE DEM BONES. MELT
MARGARINE IN BAKING PAN. PLACE CHICKEN IN PAN
AND BAKE 20 MINUTES. TURN AND BAKE ANOTHER
20 MINUTES, OR UNTIL GOLDEN BROWN.

AEROBIC WORKOUTS AREN'T A NEW INVENTION. BACK ON
THE FARM, WE CALLED THEM CHORES.

LAYERED CHICKEN TORTILLA

FAST, EASY AND DELICIOUS. GARNISH WITH SLICES OF CANTALOUPE AND HONEYDEW - ADD A GREEN SALAD AND OLE! DINNER FOR 6.

3 CUPS	COOKED SHREDDED CHICKEN	750 ML
I CUP	GRATED CHEDDAR CHEESE	250 ML
1/2 CUP	SLICED GREEN ONIONS	125 ML
2 CUPS	FAT-FREE SOUR CREAM	500 ML
4 OZ.	CAN DICED GREEN CHILIES, DRAINED	113 ML
3/4 TSP.	CUMIN	4 ML
12 OZ.	JAR SALSA, MEDIUM HEAT	341 ML
8	8" (20 CM) FLOUR TORTILLAS	8
1/2 CUP	GRATED CHEDDAR CHEESE	125 ML

PREHEAT OVEN TO 400°F (200°C). IN LARGE BOWL STIR TOGETHER CHICKEN, CHEESE, GREEN ONIONS, SOUR CREAM, CHILIES AND CUMIN. POUR I CUP (250 ML) SALSA INTO A 10" (25 CM) PIE PLATE. LAY I TORTILLA IN SALSA, COATING I SIDE. PLACE TORTILLA, SALSA SIDE DOWN, IN A 9" (23 CM) SPRING FORM PAN OR 2-QUART (2 L) ROUND CASSEROLE. SPREAD 1/2 CUP (125 ML) CHICKEN MIXTURE ON TOP OF TORTILLA. REPEAT WITH 3 MORE LAYERS OF TORTILLAS AND CHICKEN. SPREAD WITH 1/2 CUP (125 ML) SALSA. CONTINUE LAYERING TORTILLAS AND CHICKEN MIXTURE, ENDING WITH TORTILLA. TOP WITH THE SALSA LEFT OVER FROM DIPPING THE TORTILLAS. SPRINKLE ON THE CHEESE. BAKE FOR 35-40 MINUTES. LET STAND IO MINUTES AND CUT INTO WEDGES. SERVE WITH ADDITIONAL SALSA.

EL GRANDO CHICKEN QUESADILLAS

NOT YOUR ORDINARY QUESADILLA, IT'S A KNIFE AND FORKER!

1		MILD GREEN CHILI	1
1/2		RED PEPPER	1/2
1/2		YELLOW PEPPER	1/2
1		WHOLE CHICKEN BREAST, BONED & SKINNED	1
1/2 TSP.		CHILI POWDER	2 ML
1/2 TSP.		CUMIN	2 ML
		SALT & FRESHLY GROUND PEPPER TO TASTE	
2		10" (25 CM) FLOUR TORTILLAS	2
1/3 CUP		GRATED MONTEREY JACK CHEESE	75 ML
1/3 CUP		GRATED JALAPEÑO JACK CHEESE	75 ML
1/4 CUP		DICED RIPE PAPAYA	60 ML

FOR GARNISH

1/4 CUP		GUACAMOLE	60 ML
1/4 CUP		SOUR CREAM	60 ML
1/4 CUP		CHUNKY SALSA	60 ML

ROAST THE CHILI AND PEPPERS UNDER THE BROILER UNTIL CHARRED. PUT IN A PLASTIC BAG AND LET STAND 10 MINUTES TO STEAM. COOL, PEEL AND DICE. SEASON CHICKEN WITH CHILI POWDER, CUMIN, SALT AND PEPPER. GRILL CHICKEN UNTIL JUST OPAQUE THROUGHOUT. CUT INTO THIN STRIPS. PLACE TORTILLA ON MEDIUM HOT GRILL OR IN FRYING PAN OVER MEDIUM-HIGH HEAT. SPRINKLE WITH HALF OF THE CHEESES, DICED CHILI PEPPERS, PAPAYAS AND WARM CHICKEN. WHEN CHEESE IS MELTED AND TORTILLA IS LIGHTLY BROWNED, FOLD TORTILLA IN HALF AND PLACE IN OVEN TO KEEP WARM. REPEAT WITH SECOND TORTILLA. CUT EACH QUESADILLA INTO 4 WEDGES. GARNISH WITH GUACAMOLE, SOUR CREAM AND SALSA. SERVE IMMEDIATELY.

SOUTHWESTERN CHICKEN CHILI

CHILI, LIKE MEN, IMPROVES WITH AGE!

2½ LBS.	SKINLESS, BONELESS CHICKEN BREASTS	1.25 KG
2 TBSP.	VEGETABLE OIL	30 ML
2	ONIONS, CHOPPED	
2	GARLIC CLOVES, MINCED	
3 TBSP.	CHILI POWDER (USE ALL OF IT!)	45 ML
2 TSP.	CUMIN	10 ML
1 TSP.	OREGANO	5 ML
3 TBSP.	CORIANDER	45 ML
	SALT & PEPPER TO TASTE	
4	CARROTS, SLICED	
3	STALKS CELERY, CHOPPED	
28 OZ.	CAN TOMATOES	796 ML
3 TBSP.	TOMATO PASTE	45 ML
2 TBSP.	LIME JUICE	30 ML
1 TSP.	SUGAR	5 ML
12 OZ.	CAN KERNEL CORN	341 ML
14 OZ.	CAN KIDNEY BEANS	398 ML
14 OZ.	CAN GARBANZO BEANS	398 ML
1	GREEN PEPPER, SEEDED & CHOPPED	

CUT CHICKEN INTO BITE-SIZED PIECES. IN A DUTCH OVEN, BROWN CHICKEN IN OIL. ADD ONIONS AND GARLIC AND SAUTÉ UNTIL ONIONS ARE SOFT. ADD CHILI, CUMIN, OREGANO, CORIANDER, SALT AND PEPPER. COOK AND STIR FOR 3 MINUTES. ADD CARROTS, CELERY, TOMATOES, TOMATO PASTE, LIME JUICE AND SUGAR TO CHICKEN MIXTURE. BRING TO BOIL, REDUCE TO SIMMER, COVER AND COOK FOR 1 HOUR. ADD CORN, KIDNEY BEANS, GARBANZO BEANS AND GREEN PEPPER.

SOUTHWESTERN CHICKEN CHILI

CONTINUED FROM PAGE 194.

SIMMER 30 MINUTES MORE. SERVES MORE THAN 8 GOOD FRIENDS (OR 9 RELATIVES AND 1 AMAZED MOTHER-IN-LAW!). SERVE WITH A SALAD AND CRUSTY ROLLS.

CHICKEN ENCHILADA CASSEROLE

THIS IS A MUST!

6	SMALL CORN OR 3 LARGE FLOUR TORTILLAS	6
1	LARGE ONION, DICED	1
2 TBSP.	OIL	30 ML
4 OZ.	CAN GREEN CHILIES, SEEDED & FINELY CHOPPED	114 ML
10 OZ.	CAN CREAM OF MUSHROOM SOUP	284 ML
2 CUPS	GRATED CHEDDAR CHEESE	500 ML
2 CUPS	GRATED MOZZARELLA CHEESE	500 ML
1 CUP	SALSA	250 ML
3-4 CUPS	COOKED CHICKEN, CUT INTO LARGE BITE-SIZED PIECES	750 ML-1 L

CUT EACH TORTILLA INTO 6 PIECES. SAUTÉ ONION IN OIL. ADD CHILIES, SOUP AND HALF THE GRATED CHEESES. COOK SLOWLY UNTIL CHEESE MELTS. LINE A BUTTERED 1½-QUART (1.5 L) CASSEROLE WITH HALF THE TORTILLA PIECES. COVER WITH ½ CUP (125 ML) SALSA. LAYER WITH HALF THE CHICKEN, THEN HALF THE CHEESE SAUCE. REPEAT LAYERS. TOP WITH THE REMAINING GRATED CHEESES. BAKE AT 325°F (160°C) FOR 50-60 MINUTES. LET STAND (OR SIT IF YOUR PREFER!) FOR 10 MINUTES. SERVES 6.

CHICKEN FOR COMPANY!

8	PHYLLO PASTRY SHEETS	8
¼ CUP	BUTTER, MELTED	60 ML
4	BONELESS, SKINLESS CHICKEN BREASTS, HALVED	4
1	BUNCH OF FRESH SPINACH LEAVES, STEMS REMOVED	1
1	BUNCH FRESH BASIL LEAVES, CHOPPED	1
1	LARGE RED PEPPER, CUT IN STRIPS	1
¾ CUP	FETA CHEESE, CRUMBLED	175 ML

LAY 1 SHEET OF PHYLLO ON COUNTER AND FOLD IN HALF (NOT LENGTH-WISE). BRUSH MELTED BUTTER ON EDGES. PLACE ONE-HALF CHICKEN BREAST IN THE MIDDLE, NEAR THE BOTTOM OF PHYLLO. LAYER SPINACH LEAVES, A SPRINKLING OF BASIL, A FEW PEPPER STRIPS AND SOME FETA CHEESE ON TOP OF CHICKEN. ROLL CHICKEN AND PHYLLO OVER ONCE. FOLD EDGES TOWARD THE MIDDLE AND CONTINUE ROLLING TO FORM A SMALL RECTANGULAR PACKAGE. BRUSH WITH A LITTLE BUTTER. PLACE ON A COOKIE SHEET AND COVER WITH A SLIGHTLY DAMP CLOTH WHILE MAKING THE OTHERS. THESE CAN BE WRAPPED IN PLASTIC WRAP AND REFRIGERATED OVERNIGHT. PREHEAT OVEN TO 375°F (190°C) AND PLACE RACK IN MIDDLE OF OVEN. BAKE FOR 25-30 MINUTES. SERVE WITH VEGETABLE COUSCOUS (PAGE 172). (PICTURED OPPOSITE PAGE 180.)

WHY DOES DIANE ALWAYS GET THE CREDIT?

4	BONELESS, SKINLESS CHICKEN BREAST HALVES	4
1/2 TSP.	SALT	2 ML
1/2 TSP.	FRESHLY GROUND PEPPER	2 ML
1 TBSP.	BUTTER OR VEGETABLE OIL	15 ML
1 TBSP.	BUTTER OR MARGARINE	15 ML
3 TBSP.	CHOPPED GREEN ONION	45 ML
	JUICE OF 1/2 LIME OR LEMON	
2 TBSP.	BRANDY, OPTIONAL (ZELDA LOVES THIS)	30 ML
3 TBSP.	CHOPPED FRESH PARSLEY	45 ML
2 TSP.	DIJON MUSTARD	10 ML
1/4 CUP	CHICKEN BROTH	60 ML

PLACE CHICKEN BREAST HALVES BETWEEN SHEETS OF WAXED PAPER AND POUND SLIGHTLY WITH FLAT SIDE OF MALLET. SPRINKLE WITH SALT AND PEPPER. HEAT OIL AND BUTTER TOGETHER IN LARGE FRYING PAN. COOK CHICKEN OVER MEDIUM-HIGH HEAT 4 MINUTES EACH SIDE. PLACE IN SERVING DISH AND SET IN WARM OVEN. ADD ONIONS, LIME JUICE, BRANDY, PARSLEY AND MUSTARD TO PAN. COOK 15 SECONDS, WHISKING CONSTANTLY. WHISK IN BROTH, STIRRING UNTIL SAUCE IS SMOOTH. POUR OVER WARM CHICKEN AND SERVE WITH NOODLES OR NEW POTATOES AND A SALAD. SERVES 4.

CHICKEN BREASTS STUFFED WITH ASPARAGUS

CELEBRATE THE RITES OF SPRING!

4	WHOLE CHICKEN BREASTS, HALVED, BONED & POUNDED	4
24	MEDIUM ASPARAGUS SPEARS, LIGHTLY BLANCHED	24
1/4 CUP	BUTTER, MELTED	60 ML
1/4 CUP	DIJON MUSTARD	60 ML
2	GARLIC CLOVES, FINELY CHOPPED	2
1/4 CUP	WHITE WINE	60 ML
1 1/2 CUPS	BREAD CRUMBS	375 ML
1 TBSP.	GRATED PARMESAN CHEESE	15 ML
2 TBSP.	FINELY CHOPPED PARSLEY	30 ML

PREPARE CHICKEN AND ASPARAGUS. COMBINE THE BUTTER, MUSTARD, GARLIC AND WINE. DIP THE CHICKEN BREASTS IN THIS MIXTURE TO COAT THEM. PLACE 3 ASPARAGUS SPEARS ON EACH BREAST AND ROLL, SECURING WITH A TOOTHPICK. MIX BREAD CRUMBS, PARMESAN AND PARSLEY TOGETHER AND ROLL THE BREASTS IN THIS MIXTURE. BAKE 30 MINUTES AT 350°F (180°C). SERVES 4-6. PASS THE BLENDER HOLLANDAISE SAUCE (PAGE 38) AND HEAR THE RAVES.

A MAN GETTING A DIVORCE: GOING THROUGH THE CHANGE OF WIFE.

Satay, page 208

Sweet and Spicy Cashew Chicken, page 188

CHICKEN POT PIE

1/4 CUP	BUTTER	60	ML
1/4 CUP	FLOUR	60	ML
	SALT & PEPPER TO TASTE		
2 TBSP.	FINELY CHOPPED ONION	30	ML
3 CUPS	CHICKEN BROTH	750	ML
2	CARROTS, CHOPPED IN SMALL PIECES	2	
2	CELERY STALKS, CHOPPED IN SMALL PIECES	2	
2	POTATOES, CUBED IN SMALL PIECES	2	
3 CUPS	SLICED MUSHROOMS	750	ML
2 TBSP.	BUTTER	30	ML
1/2 CUP	PEAS	125	ML
3 CUPS	COOKED & DICED CHICKEN	750	ML
	PASTRY TO COVER 3-QT. (3 L) CASSEROLE OR FROZEN PUFF PASTRY DOUGH		

MELT BUTTER IN LARGE SAUCEPAN OVER MEDIUM HEAT. BLEND IN FLOUR, SALT, PEPPER AND ONION. GRADUALLY STIR IN CHICKEN BROTH. COOK, STIRRING CONSTANTLY, UNTIL SMOOTH AND THICKENED. ADD CARROTS, CELERY AND POTATOES. COOK UNTIL FORK TENDER. IN A SMALL FRYING PAN, COOK THE MUSHROOMS IN BUTTER. ADD MUSHROOMS, PEAS AND CHICKEN TO VEGETABLE MIXTURE. MIX WELL AND POUR INTO LARGE CASSEROLE. COVER WITH ROLLED PASTRY AND SLASH (WATCH IT!) TO ALLOW STEAM TO ESCAPE. BAKE IN PREHEATED 400°F (200°C) OVEN FOR ABOUT 45 MINUTES, OR UNTIL PASTRY IS GOLDEN. IF PASTRY BECOMES TOO BROWN, COVER LOOSELY WITH FOIL. (PICTURED OPPOSITE PAGE 181.)

CHICKEN IN WINE

VERY QUICK – AND VERY GOOD!

3 LBS.	CUT-UP CHICKEN PIECES	1.5 KG
1/2 CUP	SEASONED FLOUR	125 ML
6 TBSP.	OIL	90 ML
2 CUPS	SLICED FRESH MUSHROOMS	500 ML
1 TBSP.	BUTTER	15 ML
10 OZ.	CAN MUSHROOM SOUP	284 ML
1/2 CUP	CHICKEN BROTH	125 ML
1/2 CUP	ORANGE JUICE	125 ML
1/2 CUP	DRY WHITE WINE (VERMOUTH IS FINE)	125 ML
1 TBSP.	BROWN SUGAR	15 ML
1/2 TSP.	SALT	2 ML
4	CARROTS, SLICED	4

WASH AND PAT DRY CHICKEN PIECES. PUT FLOUR IN PLASTIC BAG AND SHAKE CHICKEN IN IT. IN FRYING PAN, HEAT OIL AND BROWN CHICKEN. REMOVE CHICKEN TO LARGE CASSEROLE. COOK MUSHROOMS IN BUTTER AND ADD TO CASSEROLE. COMBINE REMAINING INGREDIENTS; POUR OVER CHICKEN AND MUSHROOMS AND BAKE AT 350°F (180°C) FOR 1 HOUR. SERVE OVER RICE WITH A FRESH GREEN SALAD.

THERE'S A NEW RESTAURANT THAT FEATURES HOMESTYLE BREAKFAST. THE WAITER WEARS A BATHROBE AND ASKS YOU TO LET THE DOG IN.

CLASSY CHICKEN

THIS IS REALLY EASY AND YOUR COMPANY WILL LOVE IT.

3	CHICKEN BREASTS, SKINNED & BONED	3
1/4 TSP.	PEPPER	1 ML
3 TBSP.	OIL	45 ML
10 OZ.	PKG. FROZEN ASPARAGUS OR BROCCOLI (FRESH IS EVEN BETTER)	280 G
10 OZ.	CAN CREAM OF CHICKEN SOUP	284 ML
1/2 CUP	MAYONNAISE	125 ML
1 TSP.	CURRY POWDER	5 ML
1 TSP.	LEMON JUICE	5 ML
1 CUP	GRATED CHEDDAR CHEESE	250 ML

CUT CHICKEN INTO BITE-SIZED PIECES AND SPRINKLE WITH PEPPER. SAUTÉ IN OIL OVER MEDIUM HEAT UNTIL OPAQUE, ABOUT 6 MINUTES. DRAIN. COOK ASPARAGUS OR BROCCOLI UNTIL TENDER CRISP; DRAIN AND ARRANGE IN BOTTOM OF BUTTERED CASSEROLE. PLACE CHICKEN ON TOP. MIX TOGETHER SOUP, MAYONNAISE, CURRY AND LEMON JUICE AND POUR OVER CHICKEN. SPRINKLE WITH CHEDDAR CHEESE AND BAKE, UNCOVERED, AT 350°F (180°C) FOR 30-35 MINUTES. SERVES 6.

IT MAKES NO SENSE TO WALK TO THE CARWASH!

JAPANESE CHICKEN WINGS

GREAT FOR CROWDS AND KIDS! TASTES GOOD WARMED UP IF THERE'S ANY LEFT.

3 LBS.	CHICKEN WINGS, TIPS REMOVED	1.5 KG
1	EGG	1
1/3 CUP	FLOUR	75 ML
1 CUP	BUTTER	250 ML

SAUCE

3 TBSP.	SOY SAUCE	45 ML
3 TBSP.	WATER	45 ML
1 CUP	WHITE SUGAR	250 ML
1/2 CUP	VINEGAR	125 ML

CUT WINGS IN HALF. DIP IN SLIGHTLY BEATEN EGG AND THEN IN FLOUR. FRY IN BUTTER UNTIL DEEP BROWN AND CRISP. PLACE IN SHALLOW ROASTING PAN. MIX ALL SAUCE INGREDIENTS TOGETHER AND POUR OVER CHICKEN WINGS. BAKE AT 350°F (180°C) FOR 1/2 HOUR. BASTE WINGS WITH SAUCE DURING COOKING.

THE RACE TRACK IS WHERE ONE FILLY CAN BE ANOTHER MAN'S FOLLY.

LAMB

Marinated Bar-B-Qued Lamb
Greek Lamb Stew

PORK

Greek Ribs
Pork Loin Roast
Satay

VEAL

Veal Scallopini and Mushrooms
Osso Buco Milanese

BEEF

Beef Extraordinaire with Sauce Diane
Baked Steak with Mustard Sauce
Marinated Flank Steak
Cabbage Roll Casserole
Ginger-Fried Beef
Burritos
Shepherd's Pie
Family Favorite Meatloaf
Stroganoff Meatballs
Casserole for a Cold Night
Spaghetti Skillet Dinner
Bean Stuff

MARINATED BAR-B-QUED LAMB

USE THIS MARINADE ON LAMB CHOPS OR A BUTTERFLIED LEG OF LAMB (ONLY YOUR BUTCHER KNOWS FOR SURE).

GARLIC AND HERB MARINADE

I CUP	DRY RED WINE	250 ML
½ CUP	OLIVE OIL	125 ML
2-3	GARLIC CLOVES, MINCED	2-3
I TSP.	DRIED OREGANO	5 ML
I TSP.	DRIED THYME	5 ML
I TSP.	DRIED PARSLEY	5 ML
	SALT & PEPPER TO TASTE	
	JUICE OF I LEMON	
	BONED LEG OF LAMB	

MIX ALL MARINADE INGREDIENTS TOGETHER. POUR OVER LAMB, COVER AND MARINATE FOR 24 HOURS IN REFRIGERATOR. TURN OCCASIONALLY.

PREHEAT BAR-B-QUE TO HIGH. SEAR LAMB OVER HIGH HEAT FOR 5 MINUTES ON EACH SIDE. REDUCE TO MEDIUM HEAT AND FINISH COOKING UNTIL DESIRED DONENESS, BASTING FREQUENTLY WITH REMAINING MARINADE. LAMB CAN BE SLIGHTLY PINK.

A SMITH AND WESSON BEATS 4 ACES.

GREEK LAMB STEW

MOUTH-WATERING AROMAS FROM YOUR KITCHEN AND KUDOS FROM YOUR COMPANY.

3 LBS.	BONELESS LAMB (LEG OR SHOULDER)	1.5 KG
3 TBSP.	OLIVE OIL	45 ML
4	MEDIUM ONIONS, CHOPPED	4
4	GARLIC CLOVES, MINCED	4
28 OZ.	CAN TOMATOES	796 ML
5½ OZ.	CAN TOMATO PASTE	156 ML
1 CUP	DRY RED WINE	250 ML
½ CUP	CURRANTS, RINSED IN WARM WATER	125 ML
2 TBSP.	BROWN SUGAR	30 ML
1½ TSP.	CUMIN	7 ML
1 TSP.	GRATED ORANGE RIND	5 ML
2	BAY LEAVES	2
1	CINNAMON STICK	1
½ CUP	CHOPPED FRESH PARSLEY	125 ML
1-2 TSP.	SALT	5-10 ML
1 TSP.	FRESHLY GROUND PEPPER	5 ML

TRIM LAMB AND CUT INTO BITE-SIZED PIECES. IN DUTCH OVEN, BROWN LAMB IN 3 BATCHES USING 1 TBSP. (15 ML) OIL WITH EACH BATCH. RETURN LAMB (AND ALL THOSE ACCUMULATED JUICES) TO THE POT. ADD ONIONS AND GARLIC AND COOK, COVERED, UNTIL ONIONS ARE SOFTENED. PURÉE TOMATOES AND ADD TO POT. ADD REMAINING INGREDIENTS AND BRING TO BOIL. REDUCE HEAT AND SIMMER, COVERED, AT LEAST 1 HOUR. DISCARD BAY LEAVES AND CINNAMON. SERVES 8. SERVE OVER RICE. THE FLAVOR IMPROVES IF YOU MAKE THIS DELICIOUS STEW THE DAY BEFORE.

GREEK RIBS

DON'T ASK! JUST MAKE THEM.

> SPARERIBS
> FRESH LEMON JUICE
> SEASONING SALT
> GARLIC SALT
> DRIED TARRAGON OR OREGANO

COVER RIBS WITH WATER; BRING TO A BOIL. REDUCE HEAT AND SIMMER FOR 20 MINUTES. DRAIN RIBS AND PLACE ON BROILER PAN. SQUEEZE LEMON JUICE LIBERALLY OVER RIBS AND THEN SPRINKLE THE SEASONINGS TO YOUR HEART'S CONTENT. BAKE AT 350°F (180°C) FOR 30-40 MINUTES. SERVE WITH RICE AND PAPAYA AVOCADO SALAD (PAGE 74). YOUR COMPANY WILL BE THRILLED.

BEFORE I GOT MARRIED, I HAD THREE THEORIES ABOUT RAISING CHILDREN. NOW I HAVE THREE CHILDREN AND NO THEORIES.

PORK LOIN ROAST

YOU NEED A ZINGER - THIS IS IT!! SURE TO BECOME A FAVORITE.

| 4-6 LB. | BONELESS PORK LOIN ROAST | 2-2.5 KG |

PLUM SAUCE:

1 CUP	PLUM JAM	250 ML
1/3 CUP	ORANGE JUICE CONCENTRATE	75 ML
1/3 CUP	PINEAPPLE JUICE	75 ML
1/4 CUP	SOY SAUCE	60 ML
1 TSP.	ONION POWDER	5 ML
1/4 TSP.	GARLIC POWDER	1 ML

PREHEAT OVEN TO 350°F (180°C). LINE ROASTING PAN WITH FOIL. COOK ROAST UNTIL TEMPERATURE ON MEAT THERMOMETER REACHES 170°F (77°C) (30 MINUTES PER POUND). COMBINE SAUCE INGREDIENTS IN A SMALL SAUCEPAN AND SIMMER FOR 5 MINUTES. AFTER ROAST REACHES 170°F (77°C), BRUSH FREQUENTLY WITH SAUCE WHILE CONTINUING TO ROAST FOR A FURTHER 30 MINUTES. PASS REMAINING SAUCE WITH ROAST. SERVE WITH ROASTED NEW POTATOES WITH ROSEMARY (PAGE 161) AND A VEGETABLE. SERVES 6.

NOWADAYS TWO CAN LIVE AS CHEAPLY AS ONE - IF BOTH ARE WORKING.

RAVE NOTICES: A BAR-B-QUED INDONESIAN DISH WE HIGHLY RECOMMEND FOR YOUR NEXT DINNER PARTY OR SUMMER COOKOUT. THERE WON'T BE A SPECK LEFT OVER.

1½ LBS.	PORK TENDERLOIN (OR CHICKEN BREAST), IN 1" (2.5 CM) CUBES	750 G
2 TBSP.	BUTTER	30 ML
1 TBSP.	LEMON JUICE	15 ML
	GRATED RIND OF 1 LEMON	
½ TSP.	TABASCO	2 ML
3 TBSP.	GRATED ONION	45 ML
1 TBSP.	BROWN SUGAR	15 ML
1 TSP.	CORIANDER	5 ML
½ TSP.	GROUND CUMIN	2 ML
¼ TSP.	GINGER	1 ML
1	GARLIC CLOVE, CRUSHED	1
½ CUP	INDONESIAN SOY SAUCE	125 ML
	OR TERIYAKI SAUCE	
	SALT & PEPPER TO TASTE	
	WOODEN SKEWERS	

PLACE PORK TENDERLOIN IN SHALLOW DISH. MELT BUTTER IN SAUCEPAN AND ADD REMAINING INGREDIENTS. BRING TO A BOIL AND SIMMER 5 MINUTES. POUR OVER MEAT, COVER AND REFRIGERATE OVERNIGHT. TURN MEAT PERIODICALLY (BUTTER WILL CONGEAL BUT DON'T WORRY). REMOVE MEAT FROM MARINADE (RESERVE) AND PUT 5-6 PIECES ON EACH SKEWER. GRILL ON BAR-B-QUE, TURNING FREQUENTLY, FOR 15 MINUTES (DON'T OVERCOOK).

SATAY

CONTINUED FROM PAGE 208.

REHEAT MARINADE AND DRIZZLE OVER MEAT. SET ON A PLATTER ON A BED OF RICE. SERVE WITH FRESH SPINACH SALAD (PAGE 80). SERVES 6-8. (PICTURED OPPOSITE PAGE 198.)

VEAL SCALLOPINI AND MUSHROOMS

1½ LBS.	VEAL SCALLOPINI	750 G
¼ CUP	FLOUR	60 ML
½ TSP.	SALT	2 ML
¼ CUP	BUTTER	60 ML
1	GARLIC CLOVE, MINCED	1
3 CUPS	SLICED MUSHROOMS	750 ML
3 TBSP.	LEMON JUICE	45 ML
¼ CUP	CHICKEN BROTH	60 ML
¼ CUP	DRY WHITE WINE (VERMOUTH IS FINE)	60 ML

CUT VEAL INTO SERVING-SIZE PIECES. MIX FLOUR AND SALT TOGETHER IN A BAG AND SHAKE WITH VEAL TO COAT. SAUTÉ IN BUTTER. REMOVE MEAT AND SET ASIDE. SAUTÉ GARLIC AND MUSHROOMS; ADD LEMON JUICE, CHICKEN BROTH AND WINE. ADD VEAL, COVER AND SIMMER OVER MEDIUM HEAT FOR 20 MINUTES. SERVE WITH BUTTERED NOODLES AND PAPAYA AVOCADO SALAD (PAGE 74). SERVES 4-6.

OSSO BUCO MILANESE

CLASSIC ITALIAN FARE - A FLAVORFUL STEW MADE WITH VEAL SHANKS.

1/4 CUP	FLOUR	60 ML
	SALT & FRESHLY GROUND PEPPER	
6	PIECES VEAL SHANK, 1/2 LB. (250 G) EACH	6
1/3 CUP	OLIVE OIL	75 ML
3 TBSP.	BUTTER	45 ML
2	LARGE CARROTS, PEELED & SLICED	2
1	LARGE ONION, DICED	1
2	CELERY STALKS, SLICED	2
1 TBSP.	CHOPPED GARLIC	15 ML
2	BAY LEAVES, CRUSHED	2
3 TBSP.	CHOPPED FRESH MARJORAM OR 1 TBSP. (15 ML) DRIED MARJORAM	45 ML
3 TBSP.	CHOPPED FRESH BASIL OR 1 TBSP. (15 ML) DRIED BASIL	45 ML
1 CUP	CHOPPED FRESH PARSLEY	250 ML
	GRATED RIND OF 1 LEMON	
1 1/2 CUPS	DRY WHITE WINE	375 ML
19 OZ.	CAN ITALIAN PLUM TOMATOES, DRAINED & COARSELY CHOPPED	540 ML
1 1/2 CUPS	CHICKEN BROTH	375 ML

GREMOLATA*

4 TSP.	CHOPPED FRESH PARSLEY	20 ML
2 TSP.	GRATED LEMON RIND	10 ML
1	GARLIC CLOVE, FINELY CHOPPED	1

COMBINE FLOUR, SALT AND PEPPER IN A PLASTIC BAG. ADD VEAL SHANKS AND COAT WITH FLOUR MIXTURE. HEAT OIL IN A LARGE FRYING PAN AND

OSSO BUCO MILANESE

CONTINUED FROM PAGE 210.

BROWN VEAL ON BOTH SIDES. REMOVE VEAL AND REDUCE HEAT. ADD BUTTER, CARROTS, ONION, CELERY, GARLIC, BAY LEAVES, MARJORAM, BASIL, PARSLEY AND LEMON RIND. SAUTÉ FOR 5 MINUTES. ADD WINE AND CONTINUE COOKING FOR 5 MINUTES MORE. STIR IN TOMATOES AND BROTH. PLACE VEAL IN A CASSEROLE WITH THE SAUCE AND BAKE, COVERED, AT 325°F (160°C) FOR 2 HOURS. SERVE WITH RISOTTO, (PAGE 168.) AND GARNISH WITH GREMOLATA. SERVES 6.

* GREMOLATA, ADDS A FRESH INTENSE FLAVOR TO OSSO BUCO AND OTHER DISHES. FOR MINT GREMOLATA, MINT CAN BE SUBSTITUTED FOR PARSLEY AND FOR ORANGE GREMOLATA, SUBSTITUTE ORANGE RIND FOR LEMON. ALL 3 VERSIONS ARE DELICIOUS WITH OSSO BUCO.

NEVER TRUST A MAN WHO SAYS HE'S THE BOSS AT HOME - HE PROBABLY LIES ABOUT OTHER THINGS TOO.

BEEF EXTRAORDINAIRE
WITH SAUCE DIANE

WHEN THE BOSS COMES TO DINNER . . .

4 LBS.	BEEF TENDERLOIN	2 KG
³⁄₄ LB.	MUSHROOMS, SLICED	365 G
1½ CUPS	SLICED GREEN ONIONS	375 ML
½ CUP	BUTTER, MELTED	125 ML
2 TSP.	DRY MUSTARD	10 ML
1 TBSP.	LEMON JUICE	15 ML
1 TBSP.	WORCESTERSHIRE SAUCE	15 ML
1 TSP.	SALT	5 ML

PREHEAT OVEN TO 500°F (260°C). PLACE TENDERLOIN ON RACK IN PAN AND ROAST FOR 30 MINUTES. ADD ¼ CUP (60 ML) WATER TO PAN TO STOP ANY SMOKING. USE MEAT THERMOMETER – 30 MINUTES WILL COOK BEEF TO MEDIUM-RARE STAGE. WHILE MEAT IS COOKING, SAUTÉ THE MUSHROOMS AND GREEN ONIONS IN THE MELTED BUTTER WITH MUSTARD FOR 5 MINUTES. ADD REMAINING INGREDIENTS AND COOK AN ADDITIONAL 5 MINUTES. KEEP WARM. PLACE MEAT ON PLATTER. SERVE WITH SAUCE, ROASTED NEW POTATOES WITH ROSEMARY (PAGE 161) AND ASPARAGUS VINAIGRETTE (PAGE 151). SERVES 8. SO, DID YOU GET THE RAISE?

BACHELOR PAD: A PLACE WHERE ALL THE HOUSEPLANTS ARE DEAD, BUT SOMETHING'S GROWING IN THE FRIDGE.

BAKED STEAK WITH MUSTARD SAUCE

2½"	THICK SIRLOIN STEAK	6 CM
	FRESHLY GROUND PEPPER, TO TASTE	
1	MEDIUM ONION, FINELY CHOPPED	1
1 CUP	KETCHUP	250 ML
3 TBSP.	BUTTER, MELTED	45 ML
1 TBSP.	LEMON JUICE	15 ML
1	SMALL GREEN PEPPER, SEEDED & SLICED	1
	FEW DROPS WORCESTERSHIRE SAUCE	
	CHOPPED FRESH PARSLEY (1 SMALL BUNCH)	

MUSTARD SAUCE

2 TBSP.	BUTTER	30 ML
2 TBSP.	BAR-B-QUE SAUCE	30 ML
2 TSP.	WORCESTERSHIRE SAUCE	10 ML
2 TSP.	DRY MUSTARD	10 ML
2 TBSP.	CREAM	30 ML

PREHEAT BROILER. PLACE STEAK IN BROILER PAN 4" (10 CM) BELOW HEAT. SEAR BOTH SIDES. REMOVE MEAT AND DRAIN OFF FAT. SEASON WITH PEPPER. MIX ALL INGREDIENTS AND POUR OVER STEAK IN PAN. BAKE AT 425°F (220°C) FOR 30 MINUTES. REMOVE TO A WARM PLATTER.

TO MAKE MUSTARD SAUCE: MELT BUTTER AND MIX ALL INGREDIENTS EXCEPT CREAM. HEAT OVER MEDIUM HEAT. REMOVE FROM HEAT; STIR IN CREAM. HEAT AGAIN. POUR OVER COOKED STEAK AND SPRINKLE WITH PARSLEY. SERVE WITH BAKED POTATOES AND CAESAR SALAD (PAGE 77).

MARINATED FLANK STEAK

THIS TENDER, TASTY STEAK MAY BE SERVED HOT ON FRENCH BREAD OR COLD THE NEXT DAY FOR SANDWICHES. EXCELLENT BAR-B-QUE FARE.

2 LB.	FLANK STEAK	1 KG

DIJON MARINADE

3 TBSP.	DIJON MUSTARD	45 ML
1 TBSP.	SOY SAUCE	15 ML
1 TBSP.	GRATED FRESH GINGER OR	15 ML
	1 TSP. (5 ML) GROUND GINGER	
1/2 TSP.	DRIED THYME	2 ML
1/2 TSP.	FRESHLY GROUND PEPPER	2 ML

OR

SUPER TENDER MARINADE

1/3 CUP	VEGETABLE OIL	75 ML
1/3 CUP	RED WINE VINEGAR	75 ML
1/3 CUP	DARK SOY SAUCE	75 ML

COMBINE MARINADE INGREDIENTS. SLASH EDGES OF STEAK SO THEY WON'T CURL UP DURING COOKING. PLACE STEAK IN MARINADE, COVER AND REFRIGERATE SEVERAL HOURS OR OVERNIGHT, TURNING ONCE OR TWICE. REMOVE FROM MARINADE AND BAR-B-QUE OR BROIL 4 MINUTES EACH SIDE – MEAT MUST BE PINK ON INSIDE. SLICE THINLY ACROSS THE GRAIN. DON'T DISCARD THE DELICIOUS DRIPPINGS – SPOON OVER BEEF. SERVES 4.

CABBAGE ROLL CASSEROLE

A FAST ALTERNATIVE FOR CABBAGE ROLLS!

1 1/2 LBS.	GROUND BEEF	750 G
2	MEDIUM ONIONS, CHOPPED	2
1	GARLIC CLOVE, MINCED	1
1 TSP.	SALT	5 ML
1/4 TSP.	PEPPER	1 ML
14 OZ.	CAN TOMATO SAUCE	398 ML
14 OZ.	CAN WATER	398 ML
1/2 CUP	UNCOOKED LONG-GRAIN RICE	125 ML
4 CUPS	SHREDDED CABBAGE	1 L
	SOUR CREAM	

BROWN BEEF WITH ONIONS. ADD GARLIC, SALT, PEPPER, TOMATO SAUCE AND WATER. BRING TO A BOIL AND STIR IN RICE. COVER AND SIMMER FOR 20 MINUTES. PLACE 1/2 OF THE CABBAGE IN A GREASED BAKING DISH; COVER WITH 1/2 THE RICE MIXTURE. REPEAT LAYERS. COVER AND BAKE IN 350°F (180°C) OVEN FOR 1 HOUR. SERVE WITH SOUR CREAM. MAY BE REFRIGERATED BEFORE BAKING. SERVES 6.

EVERYBODY SHOULD PAY THEIR INCOME TAX WITH A SMILE. I TRIED - BUT THEY WANTED CASH.

GINGER-FRIED BEEF

1 LB.	FLANK OR SIRLOIN STEAK	500 G
2	EGGS, BEATEN	2
3/4 CUP	CORNSTARCH	175 ML
1/2 CUP	WATER	125 ML
	VEGETABLE OIL	
2/3 CUP	SHREDDED CARROTS	150 ML
2 TBSP.	CHOPPED GREEN ONIONS	30 ML
1/4 CUP	FINELY CHOPPED FRESH GINGER	60 ML
4	GARLIC CLOVES, CHOPPED	4
3 TBSP.	SOY SAUCE	45 ML
2 TBSP.	WINE, RED OR WHITE	30 ML
2 TBSP.	WHITE VINEGAR	30 ML
1 TBSP.	SESAME OIL	15 ML
1/2 CUP	SUGAR	125 ML
	DASH CRUSHED CHILI FLAKES	

SLICE PARTIALLY FROZEN STEAK ACROSS THE GRAIN
INTO NARROW STRIPS. MIX BEEF AND EGGS. DISSOLVE
CORNSTARCH IN WATER AND MIX WITH BEEF-EGG
MIXTURE. POUR 1" (2.5 CM) OF OIL INTO WOK, HEAT
TO BOILING HOT, BUT NOT SMOKING. ADD BEEF TO
OIL, 1/4 AT A TIME. SEPARATE WITH A FORK (OR
CHOPSTICKS IF YOU'RE TALENTED) AND COOK,
STIRRING FREQUENTLY UNTIL CRISPY. REMOVE,
DRAIN AND SET ASIDE. (THIS MUCH CAN BE DONE
IN ADVANCE.) PUT 1 TBSP. (15 ML) OIL IN WOK.
ADD CARROTS, ONION, GINGER AND GARLIC AND
STIR BRIEFLY OVER HIGH HEAT. ADD REMAINING
INGREDIENTS AND BRING TO A BOIL. ADD BEEF;
MIX WELL. SERVE WITH STEAMED RICE OF COURSE.
SERVES 4.

BURRITOS

GREAT FOR HUNGRY KIDS! NUKE 'EM WHEN YOU NEED 'EM. MAKES 20.

2 LBS.	LEAN GROUND BEEF	1 KG
1	MEDIUM ONION, CHOPPED	1
2 TBSP.	TACO SEASONING (1 PKG.)	30 ML
1/4 TSP.	PEPPER	1 ML
1/4 TSP.	OREGANO	1 ML
2 TBSP.	CHOPPED FRESH PARSLEY	30 ML
1 CUP	SOUR CREAM (FAT-FREE IS FINE)	250 ML
2 LBS.	MONTEREY JACK CHEESE, GRATED	1 KG
1 CUP	MEDIUM TACO SAUCE	250 ML
20	FLOUR TORTILLA SHELLS	20

IN A LARGE FRYING PAN, BROWN GROUND BEEF AND ONIONS. ADD TACO SEASONING, PEPPER, OREGANO, PARSLEY AND SOUR CREAM. ADD 1/2 THE CHEESE AND 1/2 THE TACO SAUCE, MIXING WELL. PLACE 2 TBSP. (30 ML) OR MORE OF BEEF MIXTURE ON EACH TORTILLA SHELL AND ROLL UP. PLACE SEAM SIDE DOWN IN 9 X 13" (23 X 33 CM) CASSEROLE. TOP WITH REMAINING CHEESE AND TACO SAUCE. BAKE AT 350°F. (180°C) FOR 15 MINUTES, OR UNTIL CHEESE MELTS AND IS HEATED THROUGH. IF YOU WANT TO MAKE INDIVIDUAL BURRITOS, USE ALL THE CHEESE AND TACO SAUCE, THEN WRAP EACH BURRITO IN PLASTIC AND FREEZE.

THE TROUBLE WITH JOGGING IS THAT BY THE TIME YOU REALIZE YOU'RE NOT IN SHAPE FOR IT, IT'S TOO FAR TO WALK BACK!

SHEPHERD'S PIE

THIS COMFORT-FOOD FAVORITE TASTES EVEN BETTER TOPPED WITH GARLIC MASHED POTATOES.

1½ LBS.	LEAN GROUND BEEF OR GROUND LEFT-OVER ROAST	750 G
1 CUP	CHOPPED ONIONS	250 ML
2	GARLIC CLOVES, MINCED	2
¼ CUP	FLOUR	60 ML
	SALT & PEPPER TO TASTE	
¼ TSP.	DRIED THYME	1 ML
¼ TSP.	DRIED SAVORY	1 ML
10 OZ.	CAN BEEF BROTH	284 ML
½	CAN WATER	½
2 TSP.	WORCESTERSHIRE SAUCE	10 ML
1	BAY LEAF	1
½ CUP	FINELY DICED CARROTS	125 ML
½ CUP	FROZEN CORN	125 ML

GARLIC MASHED POTATOES

2 LBS.	POTATOES (5-6 MEDIUM), PEELED AND CUBED	1 KG
6	GARLIC CLOVES, PEELED & LIGHTLY CRUSHED	6
¾ CUP	BUTTERMILK OR 2% MILK	175 ML
	SALT & PEPPER TO TASTE	
1	EGG, LIGHTLY BEATEN	1

USING A LARGE NONSTICK FRYING PAN, COOK GROUND BEEF OVER MEDIUM HEAT UNTIL NO LONGER PINK. BREAK MEAT UP AS IT COOKS. ADD ONIONS AND GARLIC; COOK UNTIL SOFTENED. STIR IN FLOUR, SALT, PEPPER, THYME AND SAVORY. ADD BROTH, WATER, WORCESTERSHIRE,

CONTINUED FROM PAGE 218.

BAY LEAF AND CARROTS. SIMMER, STIRRING OCCASIONALLY, FOR ABOUT 20 MINUTES, OR UNTIL QUITE THICK AND CARROTS ARE TENDER. STIR IN CORN. REMOVE BAY LEAF. SPREAD MIXTURE IN A DEEP CASSEROLE. LET COOL SLIGHTLY.

TO MAKE GARLIC MASHED POTATOES: PLACE POTATOES IN A SAUCEPAN WITH GARLIC AND COVER WITH WATER. ADD SALT, BRING TO BOIL AND SIMMER GENTLY UNTIL TENDER. DRAIN WELL AND MASH. BEAT IN BUTTERMILK, SALT AND PEPPER. RESERVE 1 TBSP. (15 ML) OF BEATEN EGG AND ADD REMAINDER TO MIXTURE. SPREAD POTATO MIXTURE OVER MEAT AND BRUSH WITH RESERVED EGG. BAKE AT 350°F (180°C) FOR 40-45 MINUTES. SERVES 6.

A WOMAN'S WORK THAT IS NEVER DONE IS THE STUFF SHE ASKED HER HUSBAND TO DO.

FAMILY FAVORITE MEATLOAF

WE ARE AMAZED AT HOW OFTEN WE ARE ASKED FOR GOOD OLD MEAT LOAF - HERE'S OUR FAVORITE.

I LB.	LEAN GROUND BEEF	500 G
I	MEDIUM ONION, CHOPPED	I
1/2 CUP	MILK	125 ML
I	EGG, BEATEN	I
8	CRUSHED SODA CRACKERS	8
	SALT & PEPPER TO TASTE	

SAUCE

1/4 CUP	KETCHUP	60 ML
1/4 CUP	WATER	60 ML
I TSP.	DRY MUSTARD	5 ML
1/2 CUP	BROWN SUGAR	125 ML

COMBINE GROUND BEEF, ONION, MILK, EGG, CRACKERS, SALT AND PEPPER AND MIX WELL. PLACE IN A LARGE LOAF PAN AND MAKE A GROOVE DOWN THE CENTER OF LOAF. IN A BOWL COMBINE KETCHUP, WATER, MUSTARD AND BROWN SUGAR. POUR OVER MEAT AND BAKE AT 350°F (180°C) FOR I HOUR; DRAIN. SERVE WITH BAKED POTATOES AND A GREEN VEGETABLE. SERVES 4-6.

IF A BOOK ABOUT FAILURES DOESN'T SELL, IS IT A SUCCESS?

STROGANOFF MEATBALLS

A GUARANTEED FAMILY HIT!

MEATBALLS

2 LBS.	LEAN GROUND BEEF	1 KG
1½ CUPS	BREAD CRUMBS	375 ML
¼ CUP	MILK	60 ML
¼ CUP	FINELY CHOPPED ONION	60 ML
2	EGGS, BEATEN	2
	SALT & PEPPER TO TASTE	

SOUR-CREAM SAUCE

1 CUP	CHOPPED ONION	250 ML
¼ CUP	BUTTER	60 ML
¼ CUP	FLOUR	60 ML
¼ CUP	KETCHUP	60 ML
2	10 OZ. (284 ML) CANS CONSOMMÉ (UNDILUTED)	2
2 CUPS	FAT-FREE SOUR CREAM	500 ML

TO MAKE MEATBALLS: COMBINE ALL INGREDIENTS IN LARGE BOWL. MIX WELL AND ROLL IN BALLS OF DESIRED SIZE. PLACE ON EDGED COOKIE SHEET AND BAKE AT 375°F (190°C) FOR 25-30 MINUTES. REMOVE FROM OVEN, DRAIN AND SET ASIDE.

TO MAKE SAUCE: BROWN ONION IN BUTTER. ADD FLOUR AND MIX WELL. ADD KETCHUP AND CONSOMMÉ, COOKING SLOWLY UNTIL THICKENED. ADD SOUR CREAM, THEN MEATBALLS. PLACE IN CASSEROLE AND KEEP WARM IN 250°F (120°C) UNTIL SERVING TIME. SERVE OVER BROAD EGG NOODLES. SERVES 6.

CASSEROLE FOR A COLD NIGHT

1 LB.	LEAN GROUND BEEF	500 G
7½ OZ.	CAN TOMATO SAUCE	213 G
1	GARLIC CLOVE, MINCED	1
	SALT AND PEPPER TO TASTE	
2 TSP.	SUGAR	10 ML
14 OZ.	CAN TOMATOES	398 ML
3 CUPS	BROAD EGG NOODLES, COOKED AND DRAINED	750 ML
4 OZ.	LIGHT CREAM CHEESE, CUBED	115 G
1 CUP	SOUR CREAM (FAT-FREE IS FINE)	250 ML
6	GREEN ONIONS, CHOPPED	6
1½ CUPS	GRATED LIGHT CHEDDAR CHEESE	375 ML

BROWN MEAT AND DRAIN. ADD TOMATO SAUCE, GARLIC, SALT, PEPPER, SUGAR AND TOMATOES. COVER AND SIMMER OVER LOW HEAT FOR 45 MINUTES. PREHEAT OVEN TO 350°F (180°C). COMBINE HOT NOODLES WITH CUBED CREAM CHEESE. STIR TO MELT CHEESE. ADD SOUR CREAM AND GREEN ONIONS. IN A GREASED 3-QUART (3 L) BAKING DISH, LAYER MEAT SAUCE, NOODLE MIXTURE AND CHEDDAR CHEESE ALTERNATELY. BAKE, UNCOVERED, FOR 30 MINUTES. SERVES 6.

WHY ISN'T PHONETICS SPELLED THE WAY IT SOUNDS?

SPAGHETTI SKILLET DINNER

FIXIN'S FOR YOUR FAMILY IN ONE PAN.

1 LB.	LEAN HAMBURGER	500 G
1 CUP	CHOPPED ONION	250 ML
1/2 CUP	CHOPPED GREEN PEPPER	125 ML
1 CUP	SLICED MUSHROOMS	250 ML
28 OZ.	CAN TOMATOES	796 ML
1	HANDFUL SPAGHETTI, BROKEN	1
1 CUP	WATER	250 ML
1 1/2 TSP.	ITALIAN SEASONING	7 ML
	SALT & PEPPER TO TASTE	
1 CUP	GRATED MOZZARELLA CHEESE	250 ML

BROWN HAMBURGER AND ONIONS. MIX IN GREEN
PEPPER AND MUSHROOMS AND COOK FOR A FEW
MINUTES. ADD TOMATOES WITH JUICE, BROKEN
SPAGHETTI AND WATER. STIR. ADD SPICES. COVER
AND COOK ABOUT 15 MINUTES, OR UNTIL SPAGHETTI
IS TENDER, STIRRING OCCASIONALLY. ADD CHEESE AND
STIR UNTIL MELTED. SERVES 4-6.

EAGLES MAY SOAR, BUT WEASELS DON'T GET SUCKED INTO
JET ENGINES.

A TASTY VARIATION OF CHILI!

6	SLICES BACON	6
1 LB.	LEAN GROUND BEEF	500 G
1	ONION, CHOPPED	1
1	GREEN PEPPER, CHOPPED	1
1	GARLIC CLOVE, MINCED	1
2 TBSP.	MOLASSES	30 ML
2 TBSP.	BROWN SUGAR	30 ML
1 TSP.	DRY MUSTARD	5 ML
1/3 CUP	VINEGAR	75 ML
19 OZ.	CAN TOMATOES	540 ML
14 OZ.	CAN KIDNEY BEANS	398 ML
14 OZ.	CAN LIMA BEANS, DRAINED	398 ML
14 OZ.	CAN PORK & BEANS	398 ML
1 TSP.	WORCESTERSHIRE SAUCE	5 ML
	SALT, PEPPER & TABASCO SAUCE, TO TASTE	

FRY BACON UNTIL CRISP. CRUMBLE. BROWN BEEF AND ONION. COMBINE WITH REMAINING INGREDIENTS IN A LARGE CASSEROLE. BAKE AT 300°F (150°C) OVEN FOR 2 HOURS. SERVE WITH CAESAR SALAD (PAGE 77) AND BAGUETTE STICKS (PAGE 20). SERVES 4-6.

IF BARBIE IS SO POPULAR, WHY DO YOU HAVE TO BUY HER FRIENDS.

COOKIES

Whipped Shortbread
Jewish Shortbread
Ginger Snaps
Fresh Apple Cookies
Tutti-Frutti Cookies
B.L.'s Cookies
Mona's Mother's Mother's Best Friend's Favorite
Cookie of the Month
After Angel Food Cookies
Peanut Butter Cookies
Chocolate Whammy Cookies
Chocolate-Chocolate Chip Cookies
Chocolate Rum Cookies
Chocolate Espresso Cookies

SQUARES

Fantastic Fudge Brownies
Decadent Caramel-Pecan Brownies
Apple Brownies
Pecan Shortbread Squares
Butter Tart Slice
Cranberry Squares
Nanaimo Bars
Matrimonial Bars
Lemon Bars
Puffed Wheat Squares

CANDIES & NUTS

Cranberry Pistachio Bark
Shortcut Almond Roca
Turtles
Xmas Toffee
Nutchos
Spiced Pecans
Magic Mixed Nuts

WHIPPED SHORTBREAD

THESE MELT IN YOUR MOUTH. THE SECRET IS IN THE BEATING.

1 CUP	BUTTER (DO NOT USE MARGARINE)	250 ML
1/2 CUP	ICING SUGAR	125 ML
1 1/2 CUPS	FLOUR	375 ML

CREAM BUTTER AND SUGAR; ADD FLOUR AND BEAT FOR 10 MINUTES. DROP FROM SMALL SPOON ONTO COOKIE SHEET. DECORATE WITH MARASCHINO CHERRY PIECES, IF YOU WISH. BAKE AT 350°F (180°C) FOR ABOUT 10-12 MINUTES, UNTIL BOTTOMS ARE LIGHTLY BROWNED. MAKES ABOUT 3 DOZEN SMALL COOKIES. THIS RECIPE DOUBLES WELL.

JEWISH SHORTBREAD

1 CUP	BUTTER, ROOM TEMPERATURE (NEVER USE MARGARINE)	250 ML
1/3 CUP	WHITE SUGAR	75 ML
1 TSP.	VANILLA	5 ML
1/2 CUP	FINELY GROUND WALNUTS OR PECANS	125 ML
1 2/3 CUPS	FLOUR	400 ML
PINCH	SALT	PINCH
1/2 CUP	WHITE SUGAR	125 ML
4 TSP.	CINNAMON	20 ML

CREAM TOGETHER BUTTER AND SUGAR. ADD VANILLA, NUTS, FLOUR AND SALT AND BEAT WELL. SHAPE INTO CRESCENTS AND PLACE 1" (2.5 CM) APART ON AN UNGREASED COOKIE SHEET. BAKE AT 325°F (160°C) FOR 15-20 MINUTES. WHILE STILL WARM, COAT WITH SUGAR AND CINNAMON OR FOR VARIETY COAT WITH ICING SUGAR. MAKES 2-3 DOZEN COOKIES.

GINGER SNAPS

ALSO PERFECT FOR GINGERBREAD MEN.

³/₄ CUP	BUTTER OR MARGARINE	175 ML
I CUP	SUGAR	250 ML
¼ CUP	MOLASSES	60 ML
I	EGG, BEATEN	I
2 CUPS	FLOUR	500 ML
¼ TSP.	SALT	I ML
2 TSP.	BAKING SODA	10 ML
I-2 TSP.	CINNAMON	5-10 ML
I-2 TSP.	GROUND CLOVES	5-10 ML
I-2 TSP.	GROUND GINGER	5-10 ML
	WHITE SUGAR	

CREAM TOGETHER BUTTER AND SUGAR. ADD MOLASSES
AND EGG. BEAT TOGETHER. COMBINE FLOUR, SALT,
BAKING SODA AND SPICES. ADD TO CREAMED MIXTURE
AND MIX WELL. ROLL INTO BALLS, THEN IN SUGAR.
PRESS FLAT WITH A FORK. BAKE AT 375°F (190°C) FOR
15 MINUTES. MAKES 4 DOZEN COOKIES. (DEPENDING ON
THE SIZE OF YOUR BALLS)

THERE ARE THREE KINDS OF PEOPLE: THOSE WHO CAN
COUNT AND THOSE WHO CAN'T.

FRESH APPLE COOKIES

TEACHER'S CHOICE.

2 CUPS	FLOUR	500 ML
1 TSP.	BAKING SODA	5 ML
1/2 CUP	BUTTER, SOFTENED	125 ML
1 1/3 CUPS	PACKED BROWN SUGAR	325 ML
1/2 TSP.	SALT	2 ML
1 TSP.	CINNAMON	5 ML
1 TSP.	GROUND CLOVES	5 ML
1/2 TSP.	NUTMEG	2 ML
1	EGG, BEATEN	1
1/4 CUP	APPLE JUICE OR MILK	60 ML
1 CUP	CHOPPED PEELED APPLES	250 ML
1/2 CUP	CHOPPED NUTS	125 ML
1 CUP	RAISINS	250 ML

VANILLA GLAZE

1 CUP	ICING SUGAR	250 ML
1 TBSP.	BUTTER, SOFTENED	15 ML
1/4 TSP.	VANILLA	1 ML
1/4 TSP.	SALT	1 ML
1 1/2 TBSP.	MILK	22 ML

TO MAKE COOKIES: PREHEAT OVEN TO 375°F (190°C). COMBINE FLOUR AND BAKING SODA IN MEDIUM BOWL. IN A LARGE BOWL, CREAM TOGETHER BUTTER, BROWN SUGAR, SALT, CINNAMON, CLOVES, NUTMEG AND EGG. ADD HALF THE FLOUR TO THE BUTTER MIXTURE AND BLEND WELL. MIX IN JUICE OR MILK. ADD THE APPLES, NUTS AND RAISINS TO THE REMAINING FLOUR. ADD THIS APPLE MIXTURE TO THE BUTTER MIXTURE. DROP BY SPOONFULS ON GREASED COOKIE SHEETS AND BAKE FOR 10 MINUTES OR UNTIL COOKIES ARE FIRM.

TO MAKE GLAZE: BLEND ALL INGREDIENTS TOGETHER UNTIL SMOOTH. WHILE COOKIES ARE HOT, SPREAD WITH VANILLA GLAZE. MAKES 3 DOZEN.

TUTTI-FRUTTI COOKIES

A BOP BOPPA LOOMA A BOP, BAM BOOM!

1½ CUPS	FLOUR	375 ML
2 TSP.	BAKING POWDER	10 ML
½ TSP.	SALT	2 ML
½ CUP	BUTTER, SOFTENED	125 ML
1 CUP	SUGAR	250 ML
¼ CUP	SOUR CREAM (FAT-FREE IS FINE)	60 ML
1	LARGE EGG	1
2 CUPS	SWEETENED FLAKED COCONUT, TOASTED GOLDEN, COOLED	500 ML
1 CUP	PACKED DRIED APRICOTS, QUARTERED	250 ML
1 CUP	DRIED CRANBERRIES	250 ML

IN A BOWL, MIX TOGETHER FLOUR, BAKING POWDER AND SALT. IN ANOTHER BOWL BEAT TOGETHER BUTTER AND SUGAR UNTIL LIGHT AND FLUFFY. ADD FLOUR MIXTURE, SOUR CREAM AND EGG AND MIX WELL. STIR IN COCONUT, APRICOTS AND CRANBERRIES. HALVE DOUGH. ON A SHEET OF WAXED PAPER, FORM EACH HALF INTO A 10" (25 CM) LOG. WRAP IN WAXED PAPER AND CHILL FOR 4 HOURS, OR UNTIL FIRM. PREHEAT OVEN TO 350°F (180°C). SPRAY BAKING SHEETS. CUT LOGS INTO ⅓" (1 CM) THICK SLICES AND ARRANGE ON BAKING SHEETS. BAKE IN MIDDLE OF OVEN UNTIL GOLDEN, ABOUT 10 MINUTES. TRANSFER TO RACKS TO COOL. MAKES ABOUT 4 DOZEN COOKIES.

TO TOAST COCONUT: SPREAD ON BAKING SHEET, PLACE ON TOP OVEN RACK, TURN ON BROILER AND WATCH CAREFULLY. STIR FREQUENTLY.

GUESS WHAT! – YOU'RE ABOUT TO MAKE DAD'S COOKIES!

1 CUP	BUTTER OR MARGARINE	250	ML
1 CUP	WHITE SUGAR	250	ML
1/2 CUP	BROWN SUGAR	125	ML
1	EGG		1
1 TSP.	VANILLA	5	ML
1 1/2 CUPS	ROLLED OATS	375	ML
1 1/2 CUPS	FLOUR	375	ML
1 CUP	COCONUT	250	ML
1 TSP.	BAKING SODA	5	ML
1 TSP.	BAKING POWDER	5	ML
2 TBSP.	MOLASSES	30	ML
1 1/2 TSP.	CINNAMON	7	ML
1 TSP.	ALLSPICE	5	ML
1 TSP.	NUTMEG	5	ML

CREAM TOGETHER BUTTER AND SUGARS. ADD EGG AND VANILLA. STIR IN REMAINING INGREDIENTS. MIX WELL. ROLL IN SMALL BALLS AND PLACE ON COOKIE SHEET. DO NOT PRESS DOWN. BAKE AT 350°F (180°C) FOR 10-12 MINUTES. MAKES 4 DOZEN.

A CONCLUSION IS THE PLACE WHERE YOU GOT TIRED OF THINKING.

MONA'S MOTHER'S MOTHER'S BEST FRIEND'S FAVORITE

THIS IS A VERRRY OLD RECIPE!

1 CUP	BUTTER	250 ML
1 CUP	WHITE SUGAR	250 ML
1/2 CUP	BROWN SUGAR	125 ML
1	EGG	1
1 1/2 CUPS	FLOUR	375 ML
1 TSP.	BAKING POWDER	5 ML
1 TSP.	BAKING SODA	5 ML
1 1/4 CUPS	ROLLED OATS	300 ML
3/4 CUP	COCONUT	175 ML

CREAM BUTTER AND SUGARS. ADD EGG AND BEAT WELL. MIX IN FLOUR, BAKING POWDER AND SODA UNTIL JUST BLENDED. STIR IN OATS AND COCONUT. ROLL INTO 1" (2.5 CM) BALLS AND PRESS WITH A FORK DIPPED IN WATER. BAKE AT 350°F (180°C) FOR 12-15 MINUTES. MAKES 3 DOZEN COOKIES.

WHAT HAPPENS IF YOU GET SCARED HALF TO DEATH TWICE?

COOKIE OF THE MONTH

THESE WILL FILL UP EVERY COOKIE JAR YOU OWN - THEY FREEZE WELL!

I CUP	BUTTER	250 ML
I CUP	SUGAR	250 ML
I CUP	BROWN SUGAR	250 ML
I	EGG	I
I CUP	VEGETABLE OIL	250 ML
I TSP.	VANILLA	5 ML
I CUP	ROLLED OATS	250 ML
I CUP	CRUSHED CORNFLAKES	250 ML
1/2 CUP	SHREDDED COCONUT	125 ML
1/2 CUP	CHOPPED WALNUTS OR PECANS	125 ML
3 1/2 CUPS	FLOUR	825 ML
I TSP.	BAKING SODA	5 ML
I TSP.	SALT	5 ML

PREHEAT OVEN TO 325°F (160°C). CREAM TOGETHER BUTTER AND SUGARS UNTIL LIGHT AND FLUFFY. ADD EGG, OIL AND VANILLA. MIX WELL. ADD OATS, CORNFLAKES, COCONUT AND NUTS. STIR WELL. ADD FLOUR, SODA AND SALT. STIR UNTIL WELL BLENDED. DROP BY TEASPOONFULS ON GREASED COOKIE SHEETS AND FLATTEN WITH FORK DIPPED IN WATER. BAKE 10-15 MINUTES. MAKES 8 DOZEN.

HOW DO YOU GET RID OF A GARBAGE CAN?

AFTER ANGEL FOOD COOKIES

THE VERY THING FOR LEFTOVER EGG YOLKS. SOFT AND CHEWY; ALSO KNOWN AS AFTER MERINGUE COOKIES.

2/3 CUP	BUTTER	150 ML
1/2 CUP	BROWN SUGAR	125 ML
1/2 CUP	WHITE SUGAR	125 ML
1/2 TSP.	VANILLA	2 ML
5	EGG YOLKS	5
1 1/2 CUPS	FLOUR	375 ML
1/2 TSP.	BAKING SODA	2 ML
1 TSP.	BAKING POWDER	5 ML
1/4 TSP.	SALT	1 ML
1/2 TSP.	CINNAMON	2 ML
1/2 CUP	CHOPPED WALNUTS	125 ML
1/2 CUP	CHOPPED DATES	125 ML
1/2 CUP	RAISINS	125 ML

CREAM BUTTER AND SUGARS. ADD VANILLA AND EGG YOLKS. MIX FLOUR, BAKING SODA, BAKING POWDER, SALT AND CINNAMON. ADD TO CREAMED MIXTURE AND MIX UNTIL SMOOTH. ADD WALNUTS, DATES AND RAISINS AND BLEND WELL. PLACE MEDIUM SPOONFULS OF DOUGH ON A GREASED COOKIE SHEET. BAKE AT 350°F (180°C) FOR 15 MINUTES. MAKES 4 DOZEN COOKIES.

I DRIVE WAY TOO FAST TO WORRY ABOUT CHOLESTEROL.

PEANUT BUTTER COOKIES

YOU ASKED FOR IT! YOU GOT IT!

1/3 CUP	BUTTER OR MARGARINE	75 ML
1/2 CUP	BROWN SUGAR	125 ML
1/2 CUP	WHITE SUGAR	125 ML
1/2 CUP	PEANUT BUTTER	125 ML
1	EGG, LIGHTLY BEATEN	1
1 CUP	FLOUR	250 ML
1 TSP.	BAKING SODA	5 ML
1/2 TSP.	SALT	2 ML
	SUGAR FOR COATING	

CREAM TOGETHER BUTTER AND SUGARS. ADD PEANUT BUTTER AND MIX WELL. ADD EGG AND THEN THE DRY INGREDIENTS. ROLL INTO BALLS AND THEN IN SUGAR. PLACE ON GREASED COOKIE SHEET. PRESS FLAT WITH A FORK. BAKE AT 350°F (180°C) FOR 10 MINUTES. MAKES 3 DOZEN COOKIES.

I CAN ONLY PLEASE ONE PERSON EACH DAY. TODAY ISN'T YOUR DAY. TOMORROW ISN'T LOOKING TOO GOOD EITHER.

CHOCOLATE WHAMMY COOKIES

THESE ARE A KNOCK-OUT!

2½ CUPS	OATMEAL	625 ML
1 CUP	BUTTER	250 ML
1 CUP	WHITE SUGAR	250 ML
1 CUP	BROWN SUGAR	250 ML
2	EGGS	2
1 TSP.	VANILLA	5 ML
2 CUPS	FLOUR	500 ML
½ TSP.	SALT	2 ML
1 TSP.	BAKING POWDER	5 ML
1 TSP.	BAKING SODA	5 ML
2 CUPS	CHOCOLATE CHIPS	500 ML
4 OZ.	HERSHEY BAR, GRATED	115 G
1½ CUPS	CHOPPED NUTS (YOUR CHOICE)	375 ML

PLACE OATMEAL IN A FOOD PROCESSOR AND BLEND TO A FINE POWDER. CREAM TOGETHER BUTTER AND SUGARS. ADD EGGS AND VANILLA. ADD FLOUR, OATMEAL, SALT, BAKING POWDER AND BAKING SODA. MIX WELL. ADD CHOCOLATE CHIPS, HERSHEY BAR AND NUTS. (YOU MAY HAVE TO USE YOUR HANDS TO GET THIS WELL COMBINED). ROLL INTO BALLS AND PLACE 2" (5 CM) APART ON A COOKIE SHEET. DON'T PRESS DOWN. BAKE FOR 10-12 MINUTES AT 375°F (190°C). MAKES 4-5 DOZEN COOKIES.

LAUGHING STOCK: CATTLE WITH A SENSE OF HUMOR.

CHOCOLATE-CHOCOLATE CHIP COOKIES

YUMMY - TASTES LIKE A BROWNIE!

1 3/4 CUPS	FLOUR	425 ML
3/4 TSP.	BAKING SODA	3 ML
1 CUP	BUTTER OR MARGARINE	250 ML
1 TSP.	VANILLA	5 ML
1 CUP	SUGAR	250 ML
1/2 CUP	PACKED BROWN SUGAR	125 ML
1	EGG	1
1/3 CUP	COCOA POWDER	75 ML
2 TBSP.	MILK	30 ML
1 CUP	CHOPPED PECANS OR WALNUTS	250 ML
3/4 CUP	SEMISWEET CHOCOLATE CHIPS	175 ML

PREHEAT OVEN TO 350°F (180°C). STIR TOGETHER FLOUR AND BAKING SODA. SET ASIDE. IN A LARGE BOWL, CREAM TOGETHER BUTTER, VANILLA AND SUGARS. BEAT UNTIL FLUFFY. BEAT IN EGG, THEN COCOA, THEN MILK. MIX IN FLOUR UNTIL JUST BLENDED. STIR IN NUTS AND CHOCOLATE CHIPS. DROP BY SPOONFULS ON GREASED COOKIE SHEETS AND BAKE FOR 12 MINUTES. COOL SLIGHTLY BEFORE REMOVING FROM COOKIE SHEET. MAKES 3 DOZEN COOKIES.

WHEN IT RAINS, WHY DON'T SHEEP SHRINK?

CHOCOLATE RUM COOKIES

NO SUGAR IN THESE COOKIES! CHOCOLATEY AND SLIGHTLY BITTER - VERY ADDICTIVE!

1 1/4 CUPS	FLOUR	300 ML
1 1/2 TSP.	BAKING POWDER	7 ML
1/2 TSP.	SALT	2 ML
1/2 CUP	GROUND HAZELNUTS	125 ML
12 OZ.	BITTERSWEET CHOCOLATE	340 G
1/4 CUP	BUTTER	60 ML
1/4 CUP	DARK RUM	60 ML
2	LARGE EGGS	2
1/4 CUP	ICING SUGAR (FOR SPRINKLING)	60 ML

IN A BOWL, MIX FLOUR, BAKING POWDER, SALT AND HAZELNUTS TOGETHER. IN A DOUBLE-BOILER WITH BARELY SIMMERING WATER, MELT CHOCOLATE AND BUTTER, STIRRING OCCASIONALLY. STIR IN RUM AND COOL. WHISK IN EGGS AND STIR IN FLOUR MIXTURE. COVER AND CHILL DOUGH ABOUT 1 HOUR, OR UNTIL FIRM ENOUGH TO HANDLE.

HALVE DOUGH AND FORM INTO TWO 10" (25 CM) LOGS ON WAXED PAPER. WRAP IN PAPER AND CHILL 4 HOURS, OR UNTIL FIRM. PREHEAT OVEN TO 350°F (180°C). SPRAY 2 BAKING SHEETS. CUT LOGS INTO 1/2" (1.3 CM) ROUNDS AND ARRANGE ABOUT 1" (2.5 CM) APART ON BAKING SHEETS. BAKE COOKIES IN BATCHES FOR 8 MINUTES AND TRANSFER TO RACK. COOKIES SHOULD BE THICK AND CAKE-LIKE. COOL COOKIES COMPLETELY AND SPRINKLE WITH ICING SUGAR. MAKES ABOUT 3 DOZEN COOKIES.

CHOCOLATE ESPRESSO COOKIES

SPECIAL ENOUGH TO SERVE AT A DINNER PARTY
WITH A DISH OF FRESH STRAWBERRIES.

1 CUP	FLOUR	250 ML
1/2 CUP	COCOA POWDER	125 ML
1/2 TSP.	SALT	2 ML
1/4 TSP.	BAKING SODA	1 ML
3 TBSP.	BUTTER	45 ML
3 TBSP.	MARGARINE	45 ML
1/2 CUP	PLUS 2 TBSP. (30 ML) SUGAR	155 ML
1/2 CUP	BROWN SUGAR	125 ML
1 1/2 TBSP.	INSTANT ESPRESSO POWDER	22 ML
	OR INSTANT COFFEE POWDER	
1 TSP.	VANILLA	5 ML
1	EGG WHITE	1

SIFT FLOUR, COCOA POWDER, SALT AND BAKING SODA
IN A SMALL BOWL. IN ANOTHER BOWL, BEAT BUTTER
AND MARGARINE UNTIL CREAMY. ADD SUGARS, ESPRESSO
POWDER AND VANILLA AND BEAT UNTIL BLENDED. MIX IN
EGG WHITE. ADD DRY INGREDIENTS AND BEAT JUST
UNTIL BLENDED. KNEAD UNTIL DOUGH IS SMOOTH. WRAP
DOUGH IN WAXED PAPER AND REFRIGERATE FOR 1 HOUR.
PREHEAT OVEN TO 350°F (180°C). ROLL DOUGH TO 1/8"
(3 MM) THICKNESS ON BOARD SPRINKLED WITH ICING
SUGAR AND CUT WITH COOKIE CUTTER. TRANSFER
TO COOKIE SHEET AND BAKE 10-12 MINUTES. MAKES
2 1/2 DOZEN CRISP COOKIES.

NEVER EAT PRUNES WHEN YOU'RE FAMISHED.

FANTASTIC FUDGE BROWNIES

MEN LOVE THEM - SO DO CHILDREN, (AND MOMS NOT ON DIETS!).

BROWNIES

1 CUP	BUTTER	250 ML
2 CUPS	SUGAR	500 ML
1/4 CUP	COCOA POWDER	60 ML
4	EGGS, BEATEN	4
1 TSP.	VANILLA	5 ML
1 CUP	FLOUR	250 ML
1 CUP	CHOPPED WALNUTS OR PECANS	250 ML

ICING

2 CUPS	ICING SUGAR	500 ML
2 TBSP.	BUTTER	30 ML
2 TBSP.	COCOA POWDER	30 ML
2 TBSP.	BOILING WATER	30 ML
2 TSP.	VANILLA	10 ML

TO MAKE BROWNIES: CREAM TOGETHER BUTTER, SUGAR AND COCOA POWDER. MIX IN BEATEN EGGS AND VANILLA. ADD FLOUR AND STIR. FOLD IN NUTS. BAKE IN A GREASED 9 X 13" (23 X 33 CM) PAN AT 350°F (180°C) FOR 40-45 MINUTES. TOP WILL APPEAR TO BE UNDERDONE (FALLS IN MIDDLE) BUT DON'T OVERCOOK. SHOULD BE MOIST AND CHEWY.

TO MAKE ICING: BEAT ALL INGREDIENTS TOGETHER WHILE BROWNIES ARE BAKING. POUR ON TOP AS SOON AS BROWNIES COME OUT OF THE OVEN. IT WILL MELT INTO A SHINY GLAZE.

DECADENT CARAMEL-
PECAN BROWNIES

BROWNIES WITH A CARAMEL SURPRISE!

1 CUP	PECANS	250 ML
4 OZ.	UNSWEETENED CHOCOLATE	115 G
	(4 SQUARES)	
2/3 CUP	BUTTER	150 ML
1 1/4 CUPS	SUGAR	300 ML
3	EGGS, BEATEN	3
1 TSP.	VANILLA	5 ML
1 CUP	FLOUR	250 ML
4	1 3/4 OZ. (52 G) CARAMILK BARS	4

ICING

2 CUPS	SEMISWEET CHOCOLATE CHIPS	500 ML
1/2 CUP	HALF & HALF CREAM	125 ML

PREHEAT OVEN TO 325°F (160°C). ON A COOKIE SHEET, TOAST WHOLE PECANS FOR 10 MINUTES. COOL AND COARSELY CHOP. GREASE A 9 X 13" (23 X 33 CM) GLASS PAN. COARSELY CHOP CHOCOLATE AND COMBINE WITH BUTTER IN SAUCEPAN. STIR OVER LOW HEAT UNTIL MELTED. (DON'T BURN THE CHOCOLATE!) COOL UNTIL LUKEWARM. STIR IN SUGAR, EGGS AND VANILLA. GRADUALLY ADD FLOUR TO MIXTURE. ADD PECANS AND CARAMILK SECTIONS. SPREAD INTO PAN AND BAKE IN CENTER OF OVEN 20-25 MINUTES. DO NOT OVER BAKE.

TO MAKE ICING: MELT CHOCOLATE CHIPS AND CREAM OVER LOW HEAT, STIRRING UNTIL MIXTURE IS SMOOTH. SPREAD OVER WARM BROWNIE. "ON-REAL"!

APPLE BROWNIES

THIS IS IT - EVERYONE'S NEXT FAVORITE.

1 CUP	BUTTER OR MARGARINE	250 ML
1/2 TSP.	SALT	2 ML
2 CUPS	SUGAR	500 ML
2	EGGS, BEATEN	2
2 CUPS	FLOUR	500 ML
1 TSP.	BAKING POWDER	5 ML
1 TSP.	BAKING SODA	5 ML
1 TSP.	CINNAMON	5 ML
2 CUPS	PEELED, SLICED GRANNY SMITH APPLES	500 ML
1/2 CUP	CHOPPED PECANS OR WALNUTS	125 ML

PREHEAT OVEN TO 325°F (160°C). GREASE A 9 X 13" (23 X 33 CM) PAN. CREAM TOGETHER BUTTER, SALT AND SUGAR. BEAT IN EGGS. ADD FLOUR, BAKING POWDER, BAKING SODA AND CINNAMON; MIX WELL. ADD APPLE SLICES AND NUTS. MIXTURE IS QUITE THICK - DON'T BE SNITCHING ANY DOUGH! SPREAD EVENLY IN PAN AND BAKE FOR 35-40 MINUTES. SERVE WARM WITH VANILLA ICE CREAM OR FROZEN YOGURT.

DID YOU HEAR ABOUT THE NEW DOLL, DIVORCE BARBIE!? IT COMES WITH ALL OF KEN'S STUFF.

PECAN SHORTBREAD SQUARES

CRUST

I CUP	BUTTER	250 ML
1/3 CUP	FIRMLY PACKED BROWN SUGAR	75 ML
I	EGG	I
I TSP.	LEMON JUICE	5 ML
3 CUPS	FLOUR	750 ML
2 1/2 CUPS	PECAN HALVES	625 ML

HONEY BUTTER FILLING

3/4 CUP	BUTTER	175 ML
1/2 CUP	HONEY	125 ML
3/4 CUP	BROWN SUGAR	175 ML
3 TBSP.	CREAM	45 ML

TO MAKE CRUST: PREHEAT OVEN TO 350°F (180°C). THOROUGHLY MIX BUTTER, SUGAR, EGG, LEMON JUICE AND FLOUR AND PRESS INTO A 10 X 15" (25 X 38 CM) EDGED COOKIE SHEET. PRICK WITH A FORK AND BAKE FOR 20 MINUTES. COVER CRUST WITH PECAN HALVES.

TO MAKE FILLING: IN A HEAVY SAUCEPAN, MELT BUTTER AND HONEY. ADD BROWN SUGAR AND BRING TO A BOIL, WHISKING CONTINUOUSLY, UNTIL DARK BROWN, 5-7 MINUTES. REMOVE FROM HEAT AND ADD CREAM. MIX AND POUR OVER CRUST. RETURN TO OVEN FOR 20 MINUTES. COOL BEFORE CUTTING.

A KNIFE THAT CUTS FOUR LOAVES OF BREAD SIMULTANEOUSLY - A FOUR LOAF CLEAVER.

BUTTER TART SLICE

A SLICE OF LIFE - ALL TARTS SHOULD TASTE SO GOOD!

CRUST

1 CUP	BUTTER	250 ML
2 CUPS	FLOUR	500 ML
1/4 CUP	SUGAR	60 ML
PINCH	SALT	PINCH

BUTTER TART FILLING

1/4 CUP	BUTTER	60 ML
3	EGGS, BEATEN	3
2 CUPS	BROWN SUGAR	500 ML
1 TBSP.	BAKING POWDER	15 ML
PINCH	SALT	PINCH
3/4 CUP	COCONUT	175 ML
1 TSP.	VANILLA	5 ML
1 CUP	RAISINS	250 ML
1 TBSP.	FLOUR	15 ML
1 CUP	CHOPPED PECANS (OPTIONAL)	250 ML

TO MAKE CRUST: CUT BUTTER INTO DRY INGREDIENTS WITH PASTRY BLENDER UNTIL CRUMBLY. PRESS INTO AN UNGREASED 9 X 13" (23 X 33 CM) PAN.

TO MAKE FILLING: MELT BUTTER; ADD EGGS AND REMAINING INGREDIENTS. MIX AND POUR OVER CRUST. BAKE AT 350°F (180°C) FOR 35 MINUTES. CUT WHEN COOL.

CRANBERRY SQUARES

ADD THIS GOODIE TO YOUR HOLIDAY BAKING LIST.

CRUST

½ CUP	COLD BUTTER	125 ML
¼ CUP	SUGAR	60 ML
1 CUP	FLOUR	250 ML

CRANBERRY FILLING

1½ CUPS	FRESH OR FROZEN CRANBERRIES	375 ML
¼ CUP	PACKED BROWN SUGAR	60 ML
2	EGGS	2
1 CUP	FIRMLY PACKED BROWN SUGAR	250 ML
1 TSP.	VANILLA	5 ML
⅓ CUP	FLOUR	75 ML
½ TSP.	BAKING POWDER	2 ML
¼ TSP.	SALT	1 ML

TO MAKE CRUST: CUT BUTTER INTO SUGAR AND FLOUR UNTIL CRUMBLY. PAT INTO AN 8" (20 CM) SQUARE PAN. BAKE AT 350°F (180°C) FOR 15-20 MINUTES, OR UNTIL GOLDEN.

TO MAKE FILLING: IN A SAUCEPAN, COOK CRANBERRIES AND ¼ CUP (60 ML) BROWN SUGAR OVER MEDIUM-LOW HEAT UNTIL BERRIES ARE SOFTENED AND THE SKINS POP (ABOUT 10 MINUTES). COOL. IN A LARGE BOWL, BEAT EGGS AND GRADUALLY ADD 1 CUP (250 ML) OF BROWN SUGAR. BEAT UNTIL THICKENED. BEAT IN VANILLA. COMBINE DRY INGREDIENTS AND ADD TO EGG MIXTURE. STIR IN COOLED CRANBERRIES AND SPREAD MIXTURE OVER CRUST. BAKE AT 350°F (180°C) FOR 35-40 MINUTES. DON'T OVERBAKE.

NANAIMO BARS

THIS RECIPE IS OLDER THAN WE ARE!
A.K.A. "GEORGE!"

FIRST LAYER

1/2 CUP	BUTTER, MELTED	125 ML
1/4 CUP	BROWN SUGAR	60 ML
3 TBSP.	COCOA POWDER	45 ML
1	EGG, BEATEN	1
2 CUPS	GRAHAM WAFER CRUMBS	500 ML
1 CUP	FLAKED COCONUT	250 ML
1/2 CUP	CHOPPED WALNUTS	125 ML

SECOND LAYER

2 CUPS	ICING SUGAR	500 ML
1/4 CUP	BUTTER, SOFTENED	60 ML
1/4 CUP	CREAM OR MILK	60 ML
2 TBSP.	CUSTARD POWDER	30 ML

THIRD LAYER

3	1 OZ. (30 G) CHOCOLATE SQUARES (SWEET OR SEMISWEET)	3
1/4 CUP	BUTTER	60 ML

TO MAKE FIRST LAYER: COMBINE INGREDIENTS AND PAT INTO A 9" (23 CM) SQUARE UNGREASED PAN. CHILL FOR 1/2 HOUR.

TO MAKE SECOND LAYER: BEAT ALL INGREDIENTS UNTIL SMOOTH AND FLUFFY. SPREAD CAREFULLY ON TOP OF FIRST LAYER.

TO MAKE THIRD LAYER: MELT CHOCOLATE AND BUTTER TOGETHER. SPREAD OVER SECOND LAYER AND CHILL. CUT IN SMALL BARS - VERY RICH AND VERY DELICIOUS!

AT LAST - THE VERY THING FOR ALL THAT RHUBARB YOU FROZE LAST FALL, OR USE THE TRADITIONAL DATE FILLING.

RHUBARB FILLING

3 CUPS	CHOPPED RHUBARB	750 ML
1½ CUPS	SUGAR	375 ML
2 TBSP.	CORNSTARCH	30 ML
1 TSP.	VANILLA	5 ML

OR

DATE FILLING

½ LB.	CHOPPED DATES	250 G
½ CUP	WATER	125 ML
2 TBSP.	BROWN SUGAR	30 ML
1 TSP.	GRATED ORANGE RIND	5 ML
2 TBSP.	ORANGE JUICE	30 ML
1 TSP.	LEMON JUICE	5 ML

CRUST

1½ CUPS	ROLLED OATS	375 ML
1½ CUPS	FLOUR	375 ML
½ TSP.	BAKING SODA	2 ML
1 TSP.	BAKING POWDER	5 ML
¼ TSP.	SALT	1 ML
1 CUP	BROWN SUGAR	250 ML
1 CUP	BUTTER	250 ML

TO MAKE FILLING: COMBINE FILLING INGREDIENTS AND COOK UNTIL THICK. IF MAKING DATE FILLING, ADD FRUIT JUICES AFTER COOKING. COOL COMPLETELY.

TO MAKE CRUST: PREHEAT OVEN TO 350°F (180°C). COMBINE INGREDIENTS AND PAT ⅔ OF MIXTURE INTO

MATRIMONIAL BARS

CONTINUED FROM PAGE 246.

A GREASED 9" (23 CM) SQUARE PAN. SPREAD FILLING AND SPRINKLE WITH REMAINING CRUMBS. BAKE FOR 30-35 MINUTES. CHILL BEFORE CUTTING.

LEMON BARS

ANOTHER CLASSIC!

CRUST

1 CUP	FLOUR	250 ML
1/2 CUP	BUTTER	125 ML
1/4 CUP	SUGAR	60 ML
PINCH	SALT	PINCH

LEMON CUSTARD

1 CUP	SUGAR	250 ML
2 TBSP.	FLOUR	30 ML
1/4 TSP.	BAKING POWDER	1 ML
	RIND OF 1 LEMON, FINELY GRATED	
	JUICE OF 1 LEMON, 3 TBSP. (45 ML)	
2	EGGS, BEATEN	2
	SPRINKLING OF ICING SUGAR	

TO MAKE CRUST: CUT BUTTER INTO DRY INGREDIENTS AND PRESS INTO UNGREASED 9" (23 CM) SQUARE PAN. BAKE AT 350°F (180°C) FOR 20 MINUTES.

TO MAKE CUSTARD: BEAT ALL INGREDIENTS TOGETHER AND POUR OVER CRUST. BAKE AT 350°F (180°C) FOR 25 MINUTES. COOL AND SPRINKLE WITH ICING SUGAR. CUT INTO SQUARES.

PUFFED WHEAT SQUARES

AUNT EDITH'S PUFFED WHEAT SQUARES HELPED PUT LONGVIEW ON THE MAP!

1/2 CUP	BUTTER OR MARGARINE	125 ML
1 CUP	CORN SYRUP	250 ML
1 CUP	WHITE SUGAR	250 ML
1/4 CUP	BROWN SUGAR	60 ML
6 HEAPING TBSP.	COCOA POWDER	90 ML
1 TSP.	VANILLA	5 ML
10 CUPS	PUFFED WHEAT	2.5 L

COMBINE BUTTER, CORN SYRUP, SUGARS AND COCOA POWDER IN A HEAVY SAUCEPAN. BRING TO BOIL. REMOVE FROM HEAT AND ADD VANILLA. POUR OVER PUFFED WHEAT. MIX WELL AND PRESS INTO A GREASED 9 X 13" (23 X 33 CM) PAN. MAKES 24 SQUARES.

AN APPLE A DAY WILL KEEP THE DOCTOR AWAY - ASSUMING OF COURSE THAT IT HASN'T BEEN GROWN IN CHEMICAL SOIL, SPRAYED WITH PESTICIDES AND THEN COVERED WITH WAX.

CRANBERRY PISTACHIO BARK

A FOOLPROOF CANDY FOR CHRISTMAS GIFT-GIVING.

I LB.	GOOD QUALITY WHITE CHOCOLATE	500 G
I CUP	DRIED CRANBERRIES	250 ML
I CUP	SHELLED PISTACHIOS	250 ML

BE SURE AND BUY EXTRA – YOU'LL
HAVE TO BRIBE THE PISTACHIO SHELLER!

MELT CHOCOLATE IN THE TOP OF A DOUBLE BOILER. LET COOL TO ROOM TEMPERATURE. ROAST PISTACHIOS AT 350°F (180°C) FOR 5-7 MINUTES. SET ASIDE TO COOL.

STIR CRANBERRIES AND PISTACHIOS INTO MELTED CHOCOLATE. POUR ONTO FOIL-LINED 10 X 15" (25 X 38 CM) EDGED COOKIE SHEET. REFRIGERATE FOR AT LEAST I HOUR, THEN BREAK INTO PIECES. MAKES ABOUT 1½ POUNDS (750 G). (PICTURED OPPOSITE PAGE 252.)

SANTA'S ELVES ARE JUST A BUNCH OF SUBORDINATE CLAUSES.

SHORTCUT ALMOND ROCA

THE SECRET TO THIS POPULAR TREAT IS OWNING A CANDY THERMOMETER.

1 TBSP.	CORN SYRUP	15 ML
1¼ CUPS	WHITE SUGAR	300 ML
1 CUP	BUTTER	250 ML
¼ CUP	WATER	60 ML
1¼ CUPS	TOASTED SLIVERED ALMONDS	300 ML
¾ CUP	CHOCOLATE CHIPS	175 ML

IN A LARGE HEAVY SAUCEPAN, GENTLY BOIL SYRUP, SUGAR, BUTTER AND WATER UNTIL "HARD CRACK" APPEARS ON CANDY THERMOMETER, 300°F (150°C). DO NOT STIR. THIS STEP TAKES AT LEAST 20 MINUTES. REMOVE FROM HEAT, ADD ALMONDS AND STIR WELL. SPREAD ON AN UNGREASED COOKIE SHEET AND, BEFORE CANDY IS ALLOWED TO COOL, SPRINKLE WITH CHOCOLATE CHIPS. AS THEY MELT, SPREAD THE CHOCOLATE CHIPS EVENLY OVER THE CANDY. COOL IN REFRIGERATOR OR FREEZER. BREAK INTO BITE-SIZED PIECES AND HIDE SOME. WHATEVER YOU LEAVE OUT DISAPPEARS! (THIS DOES NOT DOUBLE WELL.)
(PICTURED OPPOSITE PAGE 252.)

ESCHEW OBFUSCATION

TURTLES

THESE ARE BETTER THAN STORE BOUGHT!

50	CARAMELS, UNWRAPPED	50
2 TBSP.	HALF & HALF CREAM	30 ML
1½ LBS.	GOOD-QUALITY MILK CHOCOLATE	750 G
¾ LB.	PECAN HALVES	365 G

PLACE CARAMELS IN FREEZER FOR ½ HOUR – WRAPPERS COME OFF IN A FLASH! MELT CARAMELS OVER LOW HEAT AND ADD CREAM. IN A DOUBLE BOILER, MELT CHOCOLATE TO A SMOOTH CONSISTENCY. TO MAKE EACH TURTLE PLACE 3 PECANS ON THE COOKIE SHEET, LAYING 2 PECANS BESIDE EACH OTHER AND THE OTHER ON TOP. TURTLES SHOULD BE 1" (2.5 CM) APART. DIP A SPOON INTO MELTED CARAMEL AND DIP THE BOTTOM OF THE TOP PECAN INTO IT. PLACE IT ON TOP OF THE OTHER 2. (THIS HOLDS THEM TOGETHER). SPOON MORE CARAMEL OVER THE NUTS. WHEN COOKIE SHEET IS FULL, PLACE IN FREEZER UNTIL CARAMEL IS SET. WHEN READY TO "DIP", PUT A TURTLE ON A FORK AND POUR CHOCOLATE FROM A LARGE SPOON OVER THE NUTS AND CARAMEL. IT SHOULD COVER THE TURTLE COMPLETELY. PLACE TURTLE ON COOKIE SHEET AND CONTINUE UNTIL ALL TURTLES ARE DIPPED. REFRIGERATE UNTIL COMPLETELY SET. STORE IN AN AIRTIGHT CONTAINER AND KEEP IN A COOL PLACE. MAKES 50 TURTLES.

XMAS TOFFEE

YOUR KIDS WILL LOVE HELPING YOU - FOR THE FIRST 3 MINUTES! SOFT CHEWY CANDIES.

1 LB.	BUTTER	500 G
4 CUPS	WHITE SUGAR	1 L
10 OZ.	CAN SWEETENED CONDENSED MILK	300 ML
2 CUPS	GOLDEN CORN SYRUP	500 ML

MIX ALL INGREDIENTS IN LARGE SAUCEPAN. GRADUALLY BRING TO BOIL. REDUCE HEAT AND COOK GENTLY 20-30 MINUTES, UNTIL MIXTURE REACHES THE SOFT BALL STAGE, 250°F (120°C) (USE CANDY THERMOMETER). POUR ONTO 2 WELL-BUTTERED COOKIE SHEETS. WHEN SET, CUT INTO SMALL PIECES AND WRAP IN WAXED PAPER, TWISTING BOTH ENDS CLOSED. MAKES 20 DOZEN.

FAVORITE OXYMORONS:
PRETTY UGLY, WORKING VACATION, RAP MUSIC.

NUTCHOS

CALL THEM COOKIES - CALL THEM CANDIES - CALL THEM DELICIOUS!

2	10 OZ. (300 G) PKGS. SEMISWEET CHOCOLATE CHIPS	2
10 OZ.	PKG. PEANUT BUTTER CHIPS	300 G
2 CUPS	SALTED PEANUTS	500 ML
7 OZ.	BAG RIPPLE POTATO CHIPS, COARSELY CRUMBLED	200 G

Shortcut Almond Roca, page 250
Cranberry Pistachio Bark, page 249

A "Grand" Cake, page 286

NUTCHOS

CONTINUED FROM PAGE 252.

IN A DOUBLE BOILER, MELT CHOCOLATE AND PEANUT BUTTER CHIPS. STIR IN PEANUTS AND CRUMBLED CHIPS. DROP ON COOKIE SHEET AND LEAVE TO COOL. STORE IN REFRIGERATOR. YOU CAN ALSO FREEZE THESE AND EAT THEM WHEN YOU'RE DOING THE LAUNDRY! MAKES ABOUT 48.

HOW DO THEY GET THE DEER TO CROSS AT THE YELLOW ROAD SIGN?

SPICED PECANS

A GREAT GIFTABLE.

2 CUPS	PECAN HALVES	500 ML
1 1/2 TBSP.	BUTTER	22 ML
1 TSP.	SALT	5 ML
2 TSP.	SOY SAUCE	10 ML
1/4 TSP.	TABASCO SAUCE	1 ML

PREHEAT OVEN TO 300°F (150°C). PLACE PECANS ON A BAKING SHEET. MELT BUTTER AND ADD REMAINING INGREDIENTS. POUR OVER PECANS. BAKE 15 MINUTES. STIR AND TOSS DURING COOKING TIME. COOL AND DIG IN - YUMMY!

MAGIC MIXED NUTS

THESE SWEET AND SPICY NUTS JUST PLAIN DISAPPEAR!

2	EGG WHITES	2
4 CUPS	UNSALTED NUTS: CASHEWS, ALMONDS, PECANS & HAZELNUTS	1 L
1/2 CUP	SUGAR	125 ML
1 TSP.	CINNAMON	5 ML
1 TSP.	CAYENNE PEPPER	5 ML
1/2 TSP.	SALT	2 ML

PREHEAT OVEN TO 325°F (160°C). PLACE EGG WHITES IN A LARGE BOWL. WHISK JUST UNTIL FOAMY. STIR IN NUTS UNTIL COATED. COMBINE SUGAR WITH CINNAMON, CAYENNE PEPPER AND SALT. POUR OVER NUTS AND TOSS UNTIL COATED. SPREAD EVENLY ON GREASED COOKIE SHEETS AND BAKE 20-25 MINUTES, STIRRING FREQUENTLY. COOL AND STORE IN SEALED CONTAINERS. MAKES 4 CUPS (1 L).

THREE RABBITS IN A ROW HOPPING BACKWARDS SIMULTANEOUSLY - A RECEDING HARELINE.

DESSERTS

Chilled Lemon Soufflé
Frozen Lemon Puff
Fruit 'N' Booze
Brandy Mint Cream
Crème Brûlée
Shortbread Tarts with Cheese 'N' Fruit
Shortbread Tarts with Lemon Filling
Pavlova
Rhubarb & Strawberry Crumble
Social Apple Betty
Apple Pecan Phyllo Crisps
Tiramisu
Grand Slam Finale
Blueberry Bonanza
Chocolate Mocha Cheesecake
Best of Bridge Classic Cheesecake
Pumpkin Cheesecake
Aces
Upside-Down Chocolate Fudge Pudding
Country Spice Pudding Cake
Fruit Cocktail Cake
Good Old-Fashioned Gingerbread
Lemon Sauce
Victorian Orange 'Peel' Cake
Poppy Seed Cake
Sensational Lemon Roll
Chocolate Roll
A "Grand" Cake
Chocolate Raspberry Torte
Super Chocolate Cake
Chocolate Zucchini Cake
Chocolate Angel Food Cake
Karrot's Cake

CHILLED LEMON SOUFFLÉ

THIS SIMPLE CITRUS SOUFFLÉ HITS THE SPOT AFTER A SPICY MEAL. SERVES 6-8.

1 TBSP.	UNFLAVORED GELATIN (1 PKG.)	15 ML
1/4 CUP	COLD WATER	60 ML
4	EGGS, SEPARATED	4
1 CUP	SUGAR	250 ML
1/2 CUP	FRESH LEMON JUICE	125 ML
1 1/2 TBSP.	GRATED LEMON ZEST	22 ML
1 CUP	WHIPPING CREAM	250 ML

PLACE GELATIN IN WATER AND SET ASIDE TO SOFTEN. IN A HEAVY SAUCEPAN, OVER LOW HEAT, WHISK THE EGG YOLKS UNTIL SMOOTH. WHISK IN THE SUGAR, LEMON JUICE AND ZEST. COOK, STIRRING, UNTIL SLIGHTLY THICKENED, ABOUT 10 MINUTES. STIR IN SOFTENED GELATIN AND COOK UNTIL DISSOLVED, 1-2 MINUTES. POUR INTO LARGE MIXING BOWL AND ALLOW TO COOL. WHIP CREAM UNTIL SOFT PEAKS FORM, DO NOT OVERBEAT. FOLD WHIPPED CREAM INTO CHILLED LEMON MIXTURE UNTIL BLENDED. BEAT EGG WHITES UNTIL STIFF BUT NOT DRY. FOLD INTO LEMON-CREAM MIXTURE. SPOON MIXTURE INTO A GLASS DISH AND REFRIGERATE UNTIL SET - ABOUT 2 HOURS.

CHANGE IS INEVITABLE - EXCEPT FROM A VENDING MACHINE.

FROZEN LEMON PUFF

GUARANTEED RAVES AND A GREAT MAKE AHEAD.

5	EGGS (SEPARATE 3 AND RESERVE WHITES)	5
3/4 CUP	FRESH LEMON JUICE	175 ML
1 CUP	SUGAR	250 ML
2 CUPS	WHIPPING CREAM	500 ML
	VANILLA WAFERS TO COVER BOTTOM AND SIDES OF PAN	
DASH	CREAM OF TARTAR	DASH
1/4 CUP	ICING SUGAR	60 ML

WHISK 2 EGGS AND 3 EGG YOLKS, LEMON JUICE AND SUGAR TOGETHER IN THE TOP OF A DOUBLE BOILER AND COOK UNTIL THICK, STIRRING CONSTANTLY. COOL. WHIP THE CREAM AND FOLD INTO LEMON MIXTURE. LINE SIDES AND BOTTOM OF A 9" (23 CM) SPRINGFORM PAN WITH VANILLA WAFERS. POUR LEMON MIXTURE INTO THE PAN. BEAT THE 3 EGG WHITES UNTIL FOAMY. ADD CREAM OF TARTAR AND ICING SUGAR AND BEAT UNTIL PEAKS ARE STIFF. SPREAD ON THE LEMON MIXTURE AND BROWN UNDER THE BROILER. (WATCH CAREFULLY!) COVER WITH FOIL MAKING SURE IT DOESN'T TOUCH THE MERINGUE. FREEZE 8 HOURS OR MORE. REMOVE FROM FREEZER (TAKING FOIL OFF IMMEDIATELY) AT LEAST 1 1/2 HOURS BEFORE SERVING. SERVES 10-12.

THE PEOPLE WHO ASSURE YOU THAT MONEY ISN'T EVERYTHING USUALLY HAVE EVERYTHING.

FRUIT 'N' BOOZE

CAP'N MORGAN WAS NO FUN TIL HE HAD HIS FRUIT WITH RUM.

FRUIT

1	CANTALOUPE	1
1	HONEY DEW MELON	1
	1/4 OF A SMALL WATERMELON	
1 CUP	FRESH OR FROZEN BLUEBERRIES	250 ML

SAUCE

2/3 CUP	SUGAR	150 ML
1/3 CUP	WATER	75 ML
1 TSP.	LIME RIND	5 ML
6 TBSP.	LIME JUICE	90 ML
1/2 CUP	LIGHT RUM	125 ML

FRUIT: SCOOP MELON INTO BALLS AND ADD BERRIES. CHILL.

SAUCE: MIX SUGAR WITH WATER IN SAUCEPAN, BRING TO BOIL, REDUCE HEAT AND SIMMER FOR 5 MINUTES. ADD LIME RIND AND LET COOL TO ROOM TEMPERATURE. STIR IN LIME JUICE AND RUM. POUR OVER FRUIT AND CHILL SEVERAL HOURS. SERVES 6-8.

BRANDY MINT CREAM

THIS IS A TERRIFIC DRINK TO SERVE AS A DESSERT.

2 QTS.	FRENCH VANILLA ICE CREAM	2 L
1/2 CUP	CRÈME DE MENTHE	125 ML
1 CUP	BRANDY	250 ML

LET ICE CREAM SIT AT ROOM TEMPERATURE TO SOFTEN. WHIRL ALL INGREDIENTS TOGETHER IN A BLENDER. POUR INTO STEM GLASSES. SERVES 6.

CRÈME BRÛLÉE

AN OLDE ENGLISH TRADITION . . . PIP PIP STIFF
UPPER CRUST AND ALL THAT.

2 CUPS	WHIPPING CREAM	500 ML
1/3 CUP	WHITE SUGAR	75 ML
5	EGG YOLKS	5
	BROWN SUGAR	

SCALD CREAM (BRING IT JUST TO A BOIL). ADD
SUGAR AND STIR TO DISSOLVE. REMOVE FROM HEAT.
IN A LARGE BOWL, BEAT EGG YOLKS. WHISK CREAM
VERY SLOWLY INTO YOLKS. POUR MIXTURE INTO AN
8" (20 CM) SHALLOW BOWL OR 6-8 RAMEKINS. BAKE
IN A LARGE PAN WITH 1" (2.5 CM) OF WATER AT
325°F (160°C) FOR 30-40 MINUTES. AT THE END OF
30 MINUTES GIVE A "SHAKE" TEST AND CONTINUE
TO COOK IF THE CUSTARD DOESN'T LOOK FIRM. COOL.
REFRIGERATE 12 HOURS. SPRINKLE 1/4" (1 CM) BROWN
SUGAR ON TOP. BROIL UNTIL IT MELTS AND IS
GOLDEN BROWN.

NOTE: EGG WHITES MAY BE FROZEN IN SEALED
CONTAINERS FOR USE LATER.

KINDRED: FEAR OF RELATIVES

SHORTBREAD TARTS WITH CHEESE 'N' FRUIT OR LEMON FILLING

SO PRETTY TO LOOK AT - MORE FUN TO EAT!

SHORTBREAD TARTS

1 CUP	BUTTER	250 ML
1/2 CUP	ICING SUGAR	125 ML
1 1/2 CUPS	FLOUR	375 ML
1 TBSP.	CORNSTARCH	15 ML

MIX INGREDIENTS IN MIXMASTER. DON'T ROLL BUT PAT INTO TINY TART TINS, 1 1/2" (4 CM), WITH YOUR FINGERS TO FORM SHELLS. PRICK THE BOTTOMS WITH A FORK AND BAKE 20 MINUTES AT 300°F-325°F (150-160°C). AFTER 10 MINUTES, PRICK BOTTOMS AGAIN AS SHELLS PUFF UP. THIS RECIPE DOUBLES WELL AND THEY FREEZE BEAUTIFULLY.

CHEESE 'N' FRUIT FILLING

8 OZ.	CREAM CHEESE, SOFTENED	250 G
10 OZ.	CAN SWEETENED CONDENSED MILK (EAGLE BRAND)	300 ML
1/3 CUP	LEMON JUICE	75 ML
1 TSP.	VANILLA	5 ML

IN A LARGE BOWL BEAT CHEESE UNTIL FLUFFY. GRADUALLY BEAT IN MILK. STIR IN LEMON JUICE AND VANILLA. CHILL SEVERAL HOURS. KEEPS WELL IN REFRIGERATOR. FILL TARTS AND DECORATE WITH SMALL PIECES OF KIWI AND STRAWBERRIES.

SHORTBREAD TARTS

CONTINUED FROM PAGE 260.

<u>LEMON FILLING</u>

½ CUP	FRESH LEMON JUICE	125 ML
1 TBSP.	GRATED LEMON RIND	15 ML
1 CUP	SUGAR	250 ML
3	EGGS, WELL BEATEN	3
½ CUP	BUTTER, ROOM TEMPERATURE	125 ML

PUT JUICE AND RIND IN DOUBLE-BOILER. WHISK IN SUGAR, EGGS AND BUTTER AND BLEND WELL. PLACE OVER GENTLY BOILING WATER AND WHISK CONSTANTLY UNTIL MIXTURE BECOMES CLEAR AND THICKENS. COOL. KEEPS WELL IN THE REFRIGERATOR.

FAVORITE OXYMORONS: FOUND MISSING, ALONE TOGETHER, LIVING DEAD

PAVLOVA

NEW ZEALAND'S NATIONAL DESSERT.

4	EGG WHITES	4
1 CUP	WHITE SUGAR	250 ML
1/2 TSP.	VANILLA	2 ML
1 TSP.	VINEGAR	5 ML
2 CUPS	WHIPPING CREAM	500 ML
	FRESH FRUIT: KIWI, BLUEBERRIES	
	& STRAWBERRIES ARE PERFECT	
1/2 CUP	TOASTED SLIVERED ALMONDS	125 ML

BEAT EGG WHITES UNTIL SOFT PEAKS FORM.
CONTINUE BEATING WHILE ADDING SUGAR SLOWLY,
1 TBSP. (15 ML) AT A TIME. ADD VANILLA AND VINEGAR.
BEAT UNTIL VERY STIFF. PLACE WAXED OR BROWN
PAPER ON A COOKIE SHEET AND SPREAD MIXTURE IN
A CIRCLE, SLIGHTLY SMALLER THAN DESIRED SIZE.
BAKE 1 HOUR AT 275°F (140°C). TURN OVEN OFF AND
LEAVE MERINGUE IN OVEN OVERNIGHT TO DRY. PEEL
OFF PAPER. TOP WITH WHIPPED CREAM, FRESH FRUIT,
AND TOASTED ALMONDS.

HOW DO YOU KEEP A DUMMY IN SUSPENSE? . . . I'LL LET
YOU KNOW TOMORROW.

RHUBARB AND
STRAWBERRY CRUMBLE

A CLASSIC PAIR IN A CLASSIC DESSERT.

TOPPING

¾ CUP	PECAN HALVES, TOASTED	175 ML
1½ CUPS	FLOUR	375 ML
½ CUP	FIRMLY PACKED BROWN SUGAR	125 ML
1½ TSP.	GRATED ORANGE ZEST	7 ML
¼ TSP.	NUTMEG	1 ML
½ CUP	BUTTER, SOFTENED	125 ML

FILLING

4 CUPS	1" (2.5 CM) PIECES OF RHUBARB	1 L
2 CUPS	SLICED STRAWBERRIES	500 ML
3 TBSP.	FLOUR	45 ML
½ CUP	SUGAR	125 ML

TO MAKE TOPPING: PREHEAT OVEN TO 350°F (180°C). SPREAD PECANS ON A BAKING SHEET AND PLACE IN OVEN FOR 5-7 MINUTES, OR UNTIL LIGHTLY TOASTED. REMOVE AND LET COOL. COARSELY CHOP NUTS AND SET ASIDE. STIR TOGETHER FLOUR, BROWN SUGAR, ORANGE ZEST AND NUTMEG. ADD THE FLOUR MIXTURE TO THE SOFTENED BUTTER AND MIX WITH A FORK TO FORM A CRUMBLY MIXTURE; ADD PECANS AND STIR INTO MIXTURE UNTIL EVENLY DISTRIBUTED.

TO MAKE FILLING: PLACE CUT FRUIT IN AN 8 X 11" (20 X 28 CM) CASSEROLE OR SHALLOW BAKING DISH, ADD FLOUR AND SUGAR AND TOSS UNTIL WELL MIXED. SPRINKLE WITH TOPPING AND BAKE AT 375°F (180°C) FOR 35-40 MINUTES, UNTIL TOP IS GOLDEN. COOL FOR 10 MINUTES AND SERVE WITH VANILLA ICE CREAM. SERVES 8. (PICTURED OPPOSITE PAGE 271.)

SOCIAL APPLE BETTY

EVERYONE LOVES THIS OLD ENGLISH RECIPE. BE SURE TO SERVE IT WARM WITH WHIPPING CREAM OR ICE CREAM.

| 6 | APPLES, PEELED, SLICED | 6 |
| | CINNAMON - TO TASTE | |

CRUST

½ CUP	BUTTER, ROOM TEMPERATURE	125 ML
1 CUP	BROWN SUGAR	250 ML
¾ CUP	FLOUR	175 ML

FILL A SMALL CASSEROLE ⅔ FULL WITH SLICED APPLES, ADDING THE CINNAMON TO TASTE. IF THE APPLES ARE TART, YOU MAY WANT TO ADD SOME SUGAR.

TO MAKE CRUST: CREAM BUTTER AND BROWN SUGAR. ADD FLOUR AND MIX TO A CRUMBLY MIXTURE. SPRINKLE MIXTURE OVER APPLES AND PAT FIRMLY INTO A CRUST. BAKE AT 350°F (180°C) FOR 40 MINUTES. SERVES 6.

OK - SO WHAT'S THE SPEED OF DARK?

APPLE PECAN PHYLLO CRISPS

YES! - A YUMMY SKINNY DESSERT!

SHELLS

2	SHEETS PHYLLO PASTRY	2
2 TSP.	BUTTER, MELTED	10 ML

FILLING

1/3 CUP	BROWN SUGAR	75 ML
1 TSP.	GRATED LEMON RIND	5 ML
1 TBSP.	LEMON JUICE	15 ML
1/2 TSP.	CINNAMON	2 ML
3 CUPS	PEELED, SLICED APPLES	750 ML
2 TBSP.	CHOPPED TOASTED PECANS	30 ML
	ICING SUGAR TO SPRINKLE	

TO PREPARE SHELLS: PREHEAT OVEN TO 400°F (200°C). LAY PHYLLO SHEET ON WORK SURFACE AND BRUSH WITH HALF THE BUTTER. USING SCISSORS, CUT INTO 3, 5" (13 CM) WIDE STRIPS. FOLD ENDS IN TO MAKE A RECTANGLE OF 3 LAYERS AND GENTLY MOLD INTO MUFFIN CUPS. REPEAT WITH REMAINING PHYLLO AND BUTTER - MAKES 6 SHELLS. BAKE 5 MINUTES, OR UNTIL GOLDEN. THESE CAN BE STORED IN AN AIRTIGHT CONTAINER FOR UP TO 3 DAYS.

TO PREPARE FILLING: IN A HEAVY SKILLET, HEAT SUGAR, LEMON RIND, LEMON JUICE AND CINNAMON UNTIL BUBBLY. ADD APPLES AND COOK, STIRRING FREQUENTLY, FOR 5 MINUTES, OR UNTIL TENDER. LET COOL SLIGHTLY. SPOON INTO PREPARED SHELLS. SPRINKLE WITH TOASTED PECANS, THEN ICING SUGAR. SERVES 6.

TIRAMISU

THIS MEANS "IT LIFTS ME UP".

4	EGGS, SEPARATED	4
3/4 CUP	SUGAR	175 ML
2	8 OZ. (250 G) PKGS. CREAM CHEESE, ROOM TEMPERATURE	2
1/2 CUP	STRONG COFFEE	125 ML
1/4 CUP	KAHLUA OR RUM	60 ML
8 OZ.	PKG. LADY FINGERS OR VANILLA WAFERS	250 G
2	1 OZ. (30 G) SQUARES SEMISWEET CHOCOLATE, FINELY GRATED	2

BEAT EGG YOLKS IN MEDIUM-SIZED BOWL. ADD SUGAR GRADUALLY UNTIL WELL MIXED. ADD CREAM CHEESE AND MIX WELL. IN A DEEP BOWL, BEAT EGG WHITES UNTIL SOFT PEAKS FORM. FOLD INTO CHEESE MIXTURE. SPREAD 1/4 OF CHEESE MIXTURE INTO A LARGE GLASS SERVING BOWL. DIP LADY FINGERS IN MIXTURE OF KAHLUA AND COFFEE AND COVER CHEESE LAYER. REPEAT 3 TIMES, SPRINKLING CHOCOLATE ON EACH AND ENDING WITH CHEESE AND CHOCOLATE. REFRIGERATE 6 HOURS OR OVERNIGHT. SERVE CHILLED TO 8-10 UPLIFTED GUESTS.

HOW IS IT POSSIBLE TO HAVE A CIVIL WAR?

A BEST OF BRIDGE TRADITION!

1 CUP	VANILLA WAFER COOKIE CRUMBS (30 WAFERS)	250 ML
1/2 CUP	TOASTED ALMONDS, FINELY CHOPPED	125 ML
1/4 CUP	BUTTER, MELTED	60 ML
4 CUPS	FRESH STRAWBERRIES	1 L
12 OZ.	GOOD QUALITY WHITE CHOCOLATE	340 G
4 OZ.	CREAM CHEESE	115 G
1/4 CUP	SUGAR	60 ML
1/4 CUP	ORANGE LIQUEUR OR FROZEN ORANGE JUICE CONCENTRATE	60 ML
1 TSP.	VANILLA	5 ML
2 CUPS	WHIPPING CREAM	500 ML
	COCOA POWDER	

COMBINE WAFER CRUMBS, ALMONDS AND BUTTER. PRESS INTO BOTTOM OF A 9" (23 CM) SPRINGFORM PAN. WASH, DRY AND HULL BERRIES. RESERVE A COUPLE FOR GARNISH. CUT A FEW STRAWBERRIES IN HALF, LENGTHWISE, AND PRESS FLAT SIDES ALL AROUND SIDE OF SPRINGFORM PAN. ARRANGE WHOLE BERRIES, POINTS UP, ON CRUST. CHOP CHOCOLATE AND MELT IN DOUBLE BOILER OR MICROWAVE. COOL SLIGHTLY. BEAT CHEESE UNTIL SMOOTH, THEN BEAT IN SUGAR. MIX IN LIQUEUR (OR JUICE) AND VANILLA. SLOWLY BEAT IN CHOCOLATE. WHIP THE CREAM. STIR ABOUT 1/3 OF CREAM INTO CHOCOLATE MIXTURE AND FOLD IN THE REMAINDER. POUR OVER BERRIES, SHAKING PAN GENTLY TO FILL IN BETWEEN BERRIES. REFRIGERATE AT LEAST 3 HOURS (OVERNIGHT IS FINE). REMOVE SIDES AND BOTTOM OF SPRINGFORM PAN. DUST WITH COCOA AND GARNISH WITH RESERVED STRAWBERRIES.
(PICTURED OPPOSITE PAGE 270.)

BLUEBERRY BONANZA

YOU'VE GOT IT - ANOTHER EASY DESSERT GUARANTEED TO PLEASE.

CRUST

3 CUPS	DIGESTIVE BISCUIT CRUMBS (27 BISCUITS)	750 ML
1 TSP.	SUGAR	5 ML
1/4 TSP.	CINNAMON	1 ML
1/2 CUP	BUTTER, MELTED	125 ML

CHEESE LAYER

8 OZ.	PKG. CREAM CHEESE	250 G
1/2 CUP	SUGAR	125 ML
2	EGGS	2
1 TSP.	VANILLA	5 ML

BLUEBERRY LAYER

3 CUPS	FROZEN BLUEBERRIES	750 ML
1/2 CUP	SUGAR	125 ML
1/2 CUP	WATER	125 ML
1 TBSP.	LEMON JUICE	15 ML
4 TSP.	CORNSTARCH	20 ML
1/2 CUP	COLD WATER	125 ML

TOPPING

2 CUPS	WHIPPING CREAM	500 ML
2 TBSP.	SUGAR	30 ML
3	DIGESTIVE BISCUITS, CRUSHED	3

THE REASON ADULTS ARE ALWAYS ASKING LITTLE KIDS WHAT THEY WANT TO BE WHEN THEY GROW UP IS BECAUSE THEY'RE LOOKING FOR IDEAS.

CONTINUED FROM PAGE 268.

TO MAKE CRUST: MIX INGREDIENTS TOGETHER AND PAT LIGHTLY INTO A 9 X 13" (23 X 33 CM) PAN AND BAKE AT 325°F (160°C) FOR 10 MINUTES.

TO MAKE CHEESE LAYER: MIX INGREDIENTS TOGETHER AND SPREAD OVER CRUST. BAKE AT 325°F (160°C) FOR 20 MINUTES.

TO MAKE BLUEBERRY LAYER: COMBINE BLUEBERRIES, SUGAR, WATER AND LEMON JUICE IN A SAUCEPAN AND BRING TO A BOIL. DISSOLVE CORNSTARCH IN THE COLD WATER AND ADD TO THE BLUEBERRY MIXTURE. STIR UNTIL THICKENED AND POUR OVER BAKED CHEESE LAYER. COOL COMPLETELY.

TO MAKE TOPPING: WHIP CREAM WITH SUGAR AND SPREAD ON TOP OF BLUEBERRY LAYER. SPRINKLE WITH DIGESTIVE BISCUIT CRUMBS AND REFRIGERATE UNTIL SERVING TIME. IF YOU MAKE THIS THE NIGHT BEFORE, DON'T WHIP THE CREAM UNTIL JUST BEFORE SERVING. SERVES 10-12.

IF THE NUMBER 2 PENCIL IS THE MOST POPULAR, WHY IS IT STILL NUMBER 2?

CHOCOLATE-MOCHA CHEESECAKE

WHO'D BELIEVE THIS IS LOW FAT?

16 OZ.	LOW-FAT SMALL-CURD COTTAGE CHEESE	500 G
8 OZ.	FAT-REDUCED CREAM CHEESE, ROOM TEMPERATURE	250 G
1 CUP	SUGAR	250 ML
1 TBSP.	VANILLA	15 ML
2 TSP.	INSTANT ESPRESSO POWDER OR INSTANT COFFEE POWDER	10 ML
1/4 TSP	SALT	1 ML
3	LARGE EGGS, ROOM TEMPERATURE	3
5-6 TBSP.	UNSWEETENED COCOA POWDER	75-90 ML
1/4 CUP	SUGAR	60 ML

PREHEAT OVEN TO 350°F (180°C). LINE BOTTOM OF 8" (20 CM) CIRCULAR CAKE PAN OR PIE PLATE AND BUILD SIDES UP TO 2" (5 CM) WITH PARCHMENT OR BROWN PAPER. SPRAY SIDES WITH VEGETABLE OIL SPRAY.

BLEND COTTAGE CHEESE IN PROCESSOR UNTIL SMOOTH. ADD CHEESE AND MIX WELL. ADD 1 CUP (250 ML) SUGAR, VANILLA, ESPRESSO POWDER AND SALT; BLEND. ADD EGGS AND PROCESS JUST UNTIL SMOOTH. POUR 2 CUPS (500 ML) OF BATTER INTO MEASURING CUP. ADD COCOA POWDER AND 1/4 CUP (60 ML) SUGAR TO BATTER IN PROCESSOR AND BLEND WELL. POUR COCOA BATTER INTO PREPARED PAN. POUR COFFEE BATTER DIRECTLY INTO CENTER OF COCOA

CONTINUED ON PAGE 271.

Grand Slam Finale, page 267

Rhubarb and Strawberry Crumble, page 263

CHOCOLATE-MOCHA CHEESECAKE

CONTINUED FROM PAGE 270.

BATTER (COFFEE BATTER WILL PUSH COCOA BATTER TO EDGE). RUN A SMALL KNIFE THROUGH BATTERS TO CREATE A MARBLED PATTERN. SET CAKE PAN INTO 9 X 13" (23 X 33 CM) PAN. POUR ENOUGH BOILING WATER INTO BAKING PAN TO COME HALFWAY UP SIDES OF CAKE PAN. SET PAN IN OVEN. BAKE CAKE UNTIL EDGES JUST BEGIN TO PUFF AND CRACK AND CENTER IS JUST SET, ABOUT 50 MINUTES. REMOVE CAKE PAN FROM WATER AND SET ON RACK TO COOL. COVER CAKE IN PAN WITH PLASTIC WRAP AND REFRIGERATE FOR ABOUT 6 HOURS. REMOVE WRAP; PUT PLATE ON TOP OF CAKE PAN AND INVERT. TAP BOTTOM LIGHTLY TO LOOSEN CAKE FROM PAN. COVER AND REFRIGERATE. THIS CAN BE MADE AHEAD. SERVES 10-12.

WHATEVER A MAN SEWS, HE RIPS.

BEST OF BRIDGE CLASSIC CHEESECAKE

CRUST

1 3/4 CUPS	GRAHAM WAFER CRUMBS	425 ML
1/4 CUP	FINELY CHOPPED WALNUTS	60 ML
1/2 TSP.	CINNAMON	2 ML
1/2 CUP	BUTTER, MELTED	125 ML

FILLING

2	8 OZ. (250 G) PKGS. CREAM CHEESE	2
1 CUP	SUGAR	250 ML
3	EGGS	3
2 1/2 CUPS	SOUR CREAM	625 ML
2 TSP.	VANILLA	10 ML

TOPPING

15 OZ.	PKG. FROZEN SLICED STRAWBERRIES WITH JUICE, THAWED	425 G

TO MAKE CRUST: COMBINE INGREDIENTS AND PRESS INTO A LIGHTLY GREASED 10" (25 CM) SPRINGFORM PAN.

TO MAKE FILLING: PREHEAT OVEN TO 325°F (160°C). BLEND CHEESE, SUGAR AND EGGS. ADD SOUR CREAM AND VANILLA. MIX WELL AND POUR ONTO CRUST. BAKE FOR 1 1/2 HOURS.

SERVE WEDGES WITH STRAWBERRY TOPPING.

BUFFET: A FRENCH WORD THAT MEANS "GET UP AND GET IT YOURSELF".

PUMPKIN CHEESECAKE

A GRAND FINALE FOR THANKSGIVING DINNER.

GINGER SNAP CRUST

1 CUP	CRUSHED GINGER SNAPS	250 ML
3 TBSP.	BUTTER, MELTED	45 ML
1 TSP.	CINNAMON	5 ML
2 TBSP.	BROWN SUGAR	30 ML

FILLING

4	8 OZ. (250 G) PKGS. CREAM CHEESE, SOFTENED	4
1½ CUPS	SUGAR	375 ML
5	EGGS	5
¼ CUP	FLOUR	60 ML
2 TSP.	PUMPKIN PIE SPICE OR EQUAL PARTS GINGER, CINNAMON & NUTMEG	10 ML
14 OZ.	CAN PUMPKIN	398 ML
2 TBSP.	RUM	30 ML
1 CUP	WHIPPING CREAM, WHIPPED	250 ML

CRUST: COMBINE INGREDIENTS. LIGHTLY GREASE A 10" (25 CM) SPRINGFORM PAN AND LINE BOTTOM WITH CRUMB MIXTURE. PAT FIRM AND CHILL.

FILLING: PREHEAT OVEN TO 325°F (160°C). BEAT SOFTENED CREAM CHEESE TILL FLUFFY. SLOWLY BEAT IN SUGAR. ADD EGGS, 1 AT A TIME, BEATING WELL AFTER EACH ADDITION. GRADUALLY BEAT IN FLOUR, SPICES, PUMPKIN AND RUM. POUR BATTER OVER CRUST. BAKE FOR 1½ TO 1¾ HOURS, OR TILL FILLING IS SET. COOL FOR AN HOUR. REFRIGERATE SEVERAL HOURS. GARNISH WITH WHIPPED CREAM AND A SPRINKLE OF CINNAMON. SERVES 10-12.

MAKE IT AHEAD. YOU'LL WANT TO STEAL SPOONFULS BEFORE SERVING TIME.

CHOCOLATE NUT CRUST

1½ CUPS	CRUSHED CHOCOLATE WAFERS	375 ML
¼ CUP	BUTTER	60 ML
¾ CUP	CRUSHED PECANS OR ALMONDS	175 ML

CHOCOLATE MOUSSE

¾ CUP	CHOCOLATE CHIPS	175 ML
8 OZ.	CREAM CHEESE	250 G
¼ CUP	SUGAR	60 ML
1 TSP.	VANILLA	5 ML
2	EGGS, SEPARATED	2
¼ CUP	SUGAR	60 ML
1 CUP	WHIPPING CREAM	250 ML
	CHOCOLATE CURLS	

TO MAKE CRUST: PREHEAT OVEN TO 325°F (160°C). COMBINE CHOCOLATE CRUMBS AND BUTTER AND PRESS INTO A 9" (23 CM) SPRINGFORM PAN. SPRINKLE NUTS OVER CRUST. BAKE FOR 10 MINUTES.

TO MAKE MOUSSE: MELT CHOCOLATE CHIPS AND SET ASIDE TO COOL. BLEND CREAM CHEESE, SUGAR AND VANILLA. BEAT EGG YOLKS, ADD AND STIR. MIX IN COOLED CHOCOLATE.

BEAT EGG WHITES UNTIL SOFT PEAKS FORM. ADD SUGAR SLOWLY AND BEAT UNTIL STIFF. FOLD INTO CHOCOLATE MIXTURE. WHIP CREAM AND FOLD INTO THE CHOCOLATE MOUSSE. POUR INTO

CONTINUED FROM PAGE 274.

SPRINGFORM PAN. COVER AND PLACE IN FREEZER OVERNIGHT. REMOVE FROM FREEZER AND REFRIGERATE 5 HOURS BEFORE SERVING. REMOVE FROM PAN AND GARNISH WITH CHOCOLATE CURLS. SERVES 8-10.

── UPSIDE-DOWN CHOCOLATE FUDGE PUDDING ──

A GREAT WINTER DESSERT - THE SAUCE ENDS UP ON THE BOTTOM AND THE CAKE ON TOP!

1 CUP	FLOUR	250 ML
2 TSP.	BAKING POWDER	10 ML
3/4 CUP	SUGAR	175 ML
1/2 TSP.	SALT	2 ML
3 TBSP.	COCOA POWDER	45 ML
1/2 CUP	MILK	125 ML
2 TBSP.	BUTTER OR MARGARINE, MELTED	30 ML
1/4 CUP	CHOPPED PECANS (OPTIONAL)	60 ML
3/4 CUP	BROWN SUGAR	175 ML
1/2 CUP	COCOA POWDER	125 ML
2 CUPS	BOILING WATER	500 ML

PREHEAT OVEN TO 350°F (180°C). MIX FLOUR, BAKING POWDER, SUGAR, SALT AND COCOA TOGETHER. COMBINE MILK AND MELTED BUTTER. ADD TO DRY INGREDIENTS TO FORM A STIFF MIXTURE. ADD NUTS IF DESIRED. PUT INTO A GREASED 8" (20 CM) SQUARE BAKING PAN. COMBINE BROWN SUGAR, COCOA AND BOILING WATER. POUR OVER BATTER AND BAKE FOR 40 MINUTES. SERVE WARM WITH A BIG SCOOP OF VANILLA ICE CREAM. SERVES 4-6.

COUNTRY SPICE
PUDDING CAKE

ANOTHER ONE OF THOSE CAKES WITH BUILT-IN SAUCE - DEELISH!

PUDDING

1 CUP	FLOUR	250 ML
2 TSP.	BAKING POWDER	10 ML
1/2 CUP	BROWN SUGAR	125 ML
1/4 TSP.	CINNAMON	1 ML
1/4 TSP.	SALT	1 ML
3/4 CUP	RAISINS	175 ML
1/2 CUP	MILK	125 ML
1 TSP.	VANILLA	5 ML

SAUCE

1 CUP	BROWN SUGAR	250 ML
1/2 TSP.	NUTMEG	2 ML
1 TSP.	CINNAMON	5 ML
1/3 CUP	BUTTER	75 ML
2 CUPS	BOILING WATER	500 ML
1 TSP.	VANILLA OR 1 TBSP. RUM (15 ML)	5 ML

TO MAKE PUDDING: PREHEAT OVEN TO 375°F (190°C). GREASE AN 8" (20 CM) SQUARE BAKING PAN. COMBINE FLOUR, BAKING POWDER, SUGAR, CINNAMON, SALT AND RAISINS. STIR IN MILK AND VANILLA. SPOON INTO DISH.

TO MAKE SAUCE: COMBINE ALL INGREDIENTS, EXCEPT VANILLA, AND STIR UNTIL BUTTER IS MELTED. NOW, STIR IN THE VANILLA. POUR SAUCE OVER PUDDING AND BAKE, UNCOVERED, FOR 30-35 MINUTES. CAKE IS DONE WHEN A TOOTHPICK INSERTED IN THE CENTER COMES OUT CLEAN. SERVE WARM WITH ICE CREAM OR FROZEN YOGURT. SERVES 6.

FRUIT COCKTAIL CAKE

A GREAT LAST MINUTE DESSERT. ONE FAMILY ALWAYS TAKES THIS SAILING – NOW IT'S CALLED "FRUIT COCKPIT CAKE".

CAKE

2	EGGS	2
1½ CUPS	SUGAR	375 ML
2 TSP.	BAKING SODA	10 ML
½ TSP.	SALT	2 ML
14 OZ.	CAN FRUIT COCKTAIL WITH JUICE OR CRUSHED PINEAPPLE	398 ML
2 CUPS	FLOUR	500 ML

SAUCE

¾ CUP	SUGAR	175 ML
½ CUP	MILK	125 ML
½ CUP	BUTTER	125 ML
1 TSP.	VANILLA OR 2 TBSP. (30 ML) RUM IS A SUPERB SUBSTITUTE!	5 ML

TO MAKE CAKE: BEAT EGGS. ADD ALL INGREDIENTS, EXCEPT FLOUR, AND MIX. ADD FLOUR AND MIX AGAIN. GREASE A 9 X 13" (23 X 33 CM) PAN OR A BUNDT PAN AND POUR IN MIXTURE. BAKE AT 350°F (180°C) FOR 45 MINUTES.

TO MAKE SAUCE: HEAT SUGAR, MILK AND BUTTER IN SAUCEPAN AND BRING TO A BOIL. REMOVE FROM HEAT AND ADD VANILLA. POUR OVER HOT CAKE. (MAKES A LOT, BUT USE ALL OF IT! THE CAKE WILL ABSORB IT.)

SERVE WARM WITH WHIPPED CREAM OR FROZEN VANILLA YOGURT. KEEPS FOR SEVERAL DAYS REFRIGERATED (IF NO ONE KNOWS IT'S THERE).

GOOD OLD-FASHIONED GINGERBREAD

FOUR GENERATIONS CAN'T BE WRONG - IT'S DELICIOUS. SERVE WARM WITH WHIPPED CREAM OR WITH THE FOLLOWING LEMON SAUCE.

1/4 CUP	BUTTER	60	ML
1/4 CUP	SUGAR	60	ML
1 TSP.	CINNAMON	5	ML
1 TSP.	GINGER	5	ML
1 TSP.	CLOVES	5	ML
1 TSP.	SALT	5	ML
1 TSP.	BAKING POWDER	5	ML
1 1/4 CUPS	FLOUR	300	ML
1/2 TSP.	BAKING SODA	2	ML
1/2 CUP	MOLASSES	125	ML
1/4 TSP.	BAKING SODA	1	ML
3/4 CUP	BOILING WATER	175	ML
1	EGG, BEATEN	1	

CREAM TOGETHER BUTTER AND SUGAR. IN A SEPARATE BOWL MIX CINNAMON, GINGER, CLOVES, SALT, BAKING POWDER AND FLOUR. BEAT BAKING SODA INTO MOLASSES UNTIL FOAMY. ADD TO BUTTER MIXTURE. ADD THE 1/4 TSP. (1 ML) OF BAKING SODA TO THE BOILING WATER. ADD THIS ALTERNATELY WITH THE DRY INGREDIENTS TO THE BUTTER-MOLASSES MIXTURE. FOLD IN BEATEN EGG. (THE BATTER WILL BE THIN). POUR INTO GREASED LOAF PAN AND BAKE 30 MINUTES AT 400°F (200°C).

PMS: PARDON MY SCREAMING.

LEMON SAUCE

EXCELLENT ON GINGERBREAD AND CAKES.

1	LEMON, GRATED RIND AND JUICE	1
1¼ CUPS	BOILING WATER	300 ML
2 TBSP.	CORNSTARCH	30 ML
½ CUP	SUGAR	125 ML
PINCH	SALT	PINCH
2 TBSP.	BUTTER	30 ML

ADD LEMON RIND TO BOILING WATER, REDUCE HEAT AND SIMMER FOR 5 MINUTES. IN A SMALL BOWL, MIX CORNSTARCH, SUGAR AND SALT. ADD WATER GRADUALLY, STIRRING CONSTANTLY. RETURN TO SAUCEPAN AND COOK OVER MEDIUM HEAT FOR 10 MINUTES, UNTIL THICKENED. LOWER HEAT AND COOK 5 MINUTES LONGER. REMOVE FROM HEAT, STIR IN LEMON JUICE AND BUTTER. SERVE WARM. MAKES ABOUT 1½ CUPS (375 ML).

YEARS AGO, WHEN SOMEONE WORE SNEAKERS, IT OFTEN MEANT THAT HE COULDN'T AFFORD SHOES. TODAY, IF A PERSON IS WEARING SHOES, HE PROBABLY CAN'T AFFORD SNEAKERS.

VICTORIAN ORANGE 'PEEL' CAKE

ALLOW THE FLAVORS TO MELLOW FOR SEVERAL DAYS. DELICIOUSLY MOIST AND FREEZES WELL.

CAKE

	PEEL OF 3 LARGE ORANGES	
I CUP	RAISINS	250 ML
I CUP	SUGAR	250 ML
1/2 CUP	BUTTER, ROOM TEMPERATURE	125 ML
2	EGGS	2
3/4 CUP	BUTTERMILK	175 ML
2 CUPS	FLOUR	500 ML
I TSP.	BAKING SODA	5 ML
1/2 TSP.	SALT	2 ML
1/2 CUP	CHOPPED WALNUTS	125 ML

ORANGE SYRUP

I CUP	FRESH ORANGE JUICE	250 ML
1/2 CUP	SUGAR	125 ML
2 TBSP.	DARK RUM	30 ML

TO MAKE CAKE: REMOVE WHITE PITH FROM PEEL (IT'S THE BITTER PART). PLACE PEEL AND RAISINS IN PROCESSOR AND MIX UNTIL FINELY CHOPPED. PREHEAT OVEN TO 325°F (160°C). CREAM TOGETHER SUGAR AND BUTTER. ADD EGGS AND BUTTERMILK; MIX THOROUGHLY. MIX FLOUR, BAKING SODA AND SALT; STIR INTO BATTER. MIX IN PEEL, RAISINS AND WALNUTS. POUR INTO A WELL-GREASED 9" OR 10" (23 OR 25 CM) SPRINGFORM PAN AND BAKE 45-50 MINUTES, UNTIL CAKE TESTS DONE.

TO MAKE SYRUP: HEAT ORANGE JUICE, SUGAR AND RUM TOGETHER UNTIL SUGAR IS DISSOLVED.

WHEN CAKE IS DONE, LET STAND 10 MINUTES. REMOVE FROM PAN. RE-INVERT; SLOWLY DRIZZLE SYRUP, A SPOONFUL AT A TIME, OVER CAKE.

POPPY SEED CAKE

THE DAY WE BROUGHT THIS TO THE OFFICE, WE ATE SO MUCH WE HAD TO SKIP LUNCH!

¼ CUP	POPPY SEEDS	60 ML
¼ CUP	MILK	60 ML
18½ OZ.	LEMON CAKE MIX	515 G
4 OZ.	PKG. INSTANT VANILLA PUDDING	115 G
4	EGGS	4
½ CUP	VEGETABLE OIL	125 ML
1 CUP	WARM WATER	250 ML

SPICE MIXTURE

1 TBSP.	COCOA POWDER	15 ML
1 TBSP.	CINNAMON	15 ML
1 TBSP.	WHITE SUGAR	15 ML

GLAZE

3 TBSP.	FRESH LEMON JUICE	45 ML
6 TBSP.	ICING SUGAR	90 ML

SOAK POPPY SEEDS IN MILK FOR AT LEAST 1 HOUR. MIX TOGETHER CAKE MIX, PUDDING, EGGS, OIL AND WATER. ADD POPPY SEED MIXTURE. IN A SMALL BOWL COMBINE SPICE MIXTURE INGREDIENTS. GREASE AND FLOUR A BUNDT PAN. POUR IN A LAYER OF CAKE MIXTURE AND SPRINKLE WITH SPICE MIXTURE, REPEATING UNTIL ALL IS USED. BAKE AT 350°F (180°C) FOR 1 HOUR. COMBINE GLAZE INGREDIENTS. TURN CAKE OUT AND, WHILE STILL WARM, DRIZZLE GLAZE MIXTURE OVER CAKE.

SENSATIONAL LEMON ROLL

THIS IS A WINNER! SERVE WITH STRAWBERRIES AND EXTRA COPIES OF THE RECIPE - EVERYONE WANTS IT!

SPONGE CAKE

3	EGGS	3
I CUP	SUGAR	250 ML
I CUP	FLOUR	250 ML
I TSP.	BAKING POWDER	5 ML
¼ TSP.	SALT	I ML
I TBSP.	GRATED ORANGE RIND	15 ML
⅓ CUP	FRESH ORANGE JUICE	75 ML
I TSP.	VANILLA	5 ML
⅓ CUP	ICING SUGAR	75 ML

LEMON FILLING

2	EGGS	2
I CUP	SUGAR	250 ML
I TBSP.	GRATED LEMON RIND	15 ML
½ CUP	FRESH LEMON JUICE	125 ML
I CUP	WHIPPING CREAM	250 ML
	STRAWBERRIES TO GARNISH	

TO MAKE SPONGE CAKE: PREHEAT OVEN TO 375°F (190°C). LINE 10" X 15" (23 X 38 CM) EDGED COOKIE SHEET WITH PARCHMENT PAPER OR WAXED PAPER. IN LARGE BOWL, BEAT EGGS UNTIL FROTHY. GRADUALLY BEAT IN SUGAR AND CONTINUE BEATING UNTIL THICK AND PALE YELLOW, AT LEAST I MINUTE. MIX TOGETHER FLOUR, BAKING POWDER AND SALT; ADD TO EGG MIXTURE. THEN ADD ORANGE RIND, ORANGE JUICE AND VANILLA. BEAT ON LOW SPEED UNTIL

CONTINUED FROM PAGE 282.

COMBINED. SPOON ONTO PAN (BE SURE AND PUSH BATTER INTO CORNERS); BAKE 15 MINUTES, UNTIL GOLDEN BROWN AND SPRINGY TO TOUCH. DON'T OVERBAKE! PLACE A CLEAN TEA TOWEL ON THE COUNTER. DUST WITH ICING SUGAR. WHEN CAKE IS DONE, LOOSEN FROM EDGES OF PAN WITH A KNIFE AND INVERT OVER TOWEL. REMOVE PAPER AND TRIM OFF CRUSTY EDGES. STARTING FROM THE SHORT END, ROLL UP CAKE AND TOWEL TOGETHER; PLACE ON WIRE RACK TO COOL. (DON'T PANIC IF IT CRACKS OR SPLITS). YOU CAN DO THIS THE NIGHT BEFORE BUT COVER THE COOLED CAKE (STILL ROLLED IN THE TOWEL) WITH PLASTIC WRAP.

TO MAKE LEMON FILLING: IN A DOUBLE BOILER, USE A WHISK TO COMBINE EGGS, SUGAR, LEMON RIND AND JUICE AND COOK UNTIL THICKENED, ABOUT 15 MINUTES. COOL. WHIP CREAM AND FOLD INTO LEMON MIXTURE. COVER AND REFRIGERATE UNTIL READY TO ASSEMBLE.

TO ASSEMBLE: CAREFULLY UNROLL CAKE; REMOVE TOWEL. RESERVE 1/2 CUP (125 ML) OF LEMON MIXTURE FOR DECORATION. SPREAD REMAINING MIXTURE AND GENTLY ROLL UP CAKE. PLACE SEAM SIDE DOWN ON SERVING PLATTER. DECORATE WITH RESERVED FILLING AND STRAWBERRIES. REFRIGERATE AT LEAST 4 HOURS. SERVES 10 GRATEFUL GUESTS.

CHOCOLATE ROLL

5	EGGS	5
1/2 TSP.	CREAM OF TARTAR	2 ML
1 CUP	SUGAR (DIVIDED)	250 ML
1/4 CUP	FLOUR	60 ML
3 TBSP.	COCOA POWDER	45 ML
1 TSP.	VANILLA	5 ML
2 CUPS	WHIPPING CREAM, WHIPPED	500 ML
	ICING SUGAR	

SEPARATE THE EGGS. BEAT WHITES WITH CREAM OF TARTAR UNTIL STIFF. GRADUALLY BEAT IN 1/2 CUP (125 ML) SUGAR. SET ASIDE.

SIFT TOGETHER REMAINING 1/2 CUP (125 ML) SUGAR, FLOUR AND COCOA POWDER. BEAT YOLKS UNTIL THICK. FOLD FLOUR MIXTURE INTO YOLKS AND ADD VANILLA. THIS WILL BE VERY STIFF. CAREFULLY FOLD YOLK MIXTURE INTO BEATEN WHITES. PREHEAT OVEN TO 325°F (160°C). LINE A 10" X 15" (25 X 38 CM) EDGED COOKIE SHEET WITH WAXED PAPER, LEAVING AN OVERLAPPING EDGE. GREASE AND FLOUR PAPER. SPREAD BATTER EVENLY ON PAPER. BAKE FOR 20 MINUTES. PLACE ON A RACK AND COOL FOR 5 MINUTES. PLACE A CLEAN TEA TOWEL ON COUNTER, GENEROUSLY SPRINKLE WITH ICING SUGAR AND TURN CAKE ONTO TOWEL. CAREFULLY PEEL WAXED PAPER OFF THE TOP. CUT OFF ANY DRIED EDGES. ROLL UP CAKE AND TOWEL TOGETHER, BEGINNING AT SHORT END. COOL COMPLETELY - NO MORE THAN A HALF AN HOUR. UNWRAP ROLL AND SPREAD WHIPPED CREAM

CHOCOLATE ROLL

CONTINUED FROM PAGE 284.

OVER SURFACE. ROLL UP CAKE AGAIN BUT THIS TIME - LEAVE OUT THE TOWEL! SPRINKLE WITH ICING SUGAR. SERVE WITH FUDGE SAUCE OR FOAMY BUTTER SAUCE. SERVES 8. FOR COMPANY WHY NOT ADD SOME RUM OR LIQUEUR TO THE WHIPPING CREAM?

FOAMY BUTTER SAUCE

1/2 CUP	BUTTER	125 ML
1	EGG	1
1 CUP	ICING SUGAR	250 ML

COMBINE ALL INGREDIENTS IN TOP OF DOUBLE BOILER. COOK, STIRRING, UNTIL IT FORMS A SMOOTH SAUCE. SERVE WARM OVER CHOCOLATE ROLL.

FUDGE SAUCE

1 TBSP.	BUTTER	15 ML
1	SQUARE UNSWEETENED CHOCOLATE	30 G
1/3 CUP	BOILING WATER	75 ML
1 CUP	SUGAR	250 ML
2 TBSP.	CORN SYRUP	30 ML
1/2 TSP.	VANILLA	2 ML

MELT BUTTER AND CHOCOLATE IN MEDIUM SAUCEPAN. ADD BOILING WATER AND BRING TO A BOIL. ADD SUGAR AND SYRUP. BRING TO BOIL AGAIN AND STIR FOR 5 MINUTES. STIR IN VANILLA. SERVE JUST WARM OVER CHOCOLATE ROLL.

A "GRAND" CAKE

THIS RECIPE CAN BE MADE THE DAY AHEAD IF COVERED AND REFRIGERATED.

CAKE

1¾ CUPS	FLOUR	425 ML
1 TSP.	BAKING SODA	5 ML
½ TSP.	BAKING POWDER	2 ML
1 TSP.	SALT	5 ML
½ CUP	COCOA POWDER	125 ML
½ CUP	BUTTER, ROOM TEMPERATURE	125 ML
1⅔ CUPS	GRANULATED SUGAR	400 ML
3	EGGS	3
1 TSP.	VANILLA	5 ML
1⅓ CUPS	WATER	325 ML
¼ CUP	GRAND MARNIER	60 ML

FILLING

¾ CUP	FROZEN ORANGE JUICE CONCENTRATE	175 ML
¾ CUP	SUGAR	175 ML
1 TBSP.	GELATIN (1 PKG.)	15 ML
	COARSELY GRATED PEEL OF 2 ORANGES	
¼ CUP	GRAND MARNIER	60 ML
2 CUPS	WHIPPING CREAM	500 ML
¾ CUP	ICING SUGAR	175 ML

TO MAKE CAKE: PREHEAT OVEN TO 350°F (180°C). GREASE 2, 8" (20 CM) ROUND CAKE PANS. LINE WITH WAXED PAPER AND GREASE AGAIN. MEASURE FLOUR, BAKING SODA, BAKING POWDER, SALT AND COCOA INTO A BOWL AND SIFT TOGETHER. CREAM BUTTER USING ELECTRIC BEATER. GRADUALLY ADD SUGAR, BEATING UNTIL

A "GRAND" CAKE

CONTINUED FROM PAGE 286.

LIGHT AND FLUFFY. BEAT IN EGGS 1 AT A TIME.
ADD VANILLA. AT LOW SPEED, BEAT IN 1/3 OF FLOUR
MIXTURE, THEN 1/2 OF THE WATER, BEATING ONLY
UNTIL MIXED AFTER EACH ADDITION. BEAT IN
ANOTHER 1/3 FLOUR, REMAINING WATER AND REST
OF FLOUR. POUR INTO PANS AND BAKE FOR
30-35 MINUTES, OR UNTIL CENTER OF CAKE SPRINGS
BACK WHEN LIGHTLY TOUCHED. LET CAKES COOL
5 MINUTES, THEN TURN OUT. REMOVE WAXED PAPER
AND COOL THOROUGHLY ON RACKS.

1-2 HOURS BEFORE ASSEMBLING, SLICE EACH CAKE IN
HALF HORIZONTALLY TO MAKE 4 LAYERS. PLACE LAYERS
CUT SIDE UP AND SPRINKLE EACH WITH 1 TBSP.
(15 ML) GRAND MARNIER.

TO MAKE FILLING: COMBINE JUICE, SUGAR AND
GELATIN IN A SAUCEPAN; COOK OVER MEDIUM HEAT,
STIRRING CONSTANTLY UNTIL SUGAR AND GELATIN
ARE DISSOLVED, ABOUT 5 MINUTES. REMOVE FROM
HEAT AND STIR IN ORANGE PEEL AND GRAND
MARNIER. PRESS A SHEET OF WAXED PAPER ON
SURFACE AND REFRIGERATE UNTIL COOL, ABOUT
20 MINUTES. WHIP CREAM UNTIL SOFT PEAKS FORM.
GRADUALLY BEAT IN ICING SUGAR, THEN FOLD IN
GRAND MARNIER MIXTURE.

TO ASSEMBLE: PLACE 1 LAYER OF CAKE, CUT SIDE UP, ON
SERVING PLATE. SPOON ON 1/4 OF FILLING AND SPREAD.
TOP WITH ANOTHER LAYER AND CONTINUE UNTIL ALL
ARE USED, ENDING WITH FILLING. REFRIGERATE
IMMEDIATELY, LET SET AT LEAST 4 HOURS TO BLEND
FLAVORS. (PICTURED OPPOSITE PAGE 253.)

CHOCOLATE RASPBERRY TORTE

GOD MADE CHOCOLATE AND THE DEVIL THREW THE CALORIES IN!

CAKE

2 CUPS	FLOUR	500 ML
2 TSP.	BAKING SODA	10 ML
1/2 TSP.	SALT	2 ML
1/2 TSP.	BAKING POWDER	2 ML
3	SQUARES UNSWEETENED CHOCOLATE	85 G
1/2 CUP	BUTTER	125 ML
2 CUPS	BROWN SUGAR, PACKED	500 ML
3	EGGS	3
1 1/2 TSP.	VANILLA	7 ML
3/4 CUP	SOUR CREAM	175 ML
1/2 CUP	STRONG COFFEE	125 ML
1/2 CUP	COFFEE-FLAVORED LIQUEUR (KAHLÚA)	125 ML

FILLING

1 CUP	WHIPPING CREAM	250 ML
2 TBSP.	ICING SUGAR	30 ML
12 OZ.	JAR RASPBERRY OR STRAWBERRY JAM	340 ML

FROSTING

1 1/2 CUPS	CHOCOLATE CHIPS	375 ML
3/4 CUP	SOUR CREAM	175 ML
	DASH OF SALT	
	CHOCOLATE CURLS	
	FRESH RASPBERRIES OR STRAWBERRIES	

THE PROBLEM WITH BUCKET SEATS IS THAT NOT EVERYONE HAS THE SAME SIZE BUCKET.

CONTINUED FROM PAGE 288.

NOW TO BUILD IT!

PREHEAT OVEN TO 350°F (180°C). GREASE AND FLOUR 2-9" (23 CM) LAYER CAKE PANS. MIX FLOUR, BAKING SODA, SALT AND BAKING POWDER. MELT CHOCOLATE AND LET COOL. IN A LARGE BOWL BEAT BUTTER, BROWN SUGAR AND EGGS AT A HIGH SPEED UNTIL MIXTURE IS LIGHT AND FLUFFY, ABOUT 5 MINUTES. BEAT IN MELTED CHOCOLATE AND VANILLA. AT LOW SPEED, BEAT IN FLOUR MIXTURE (IN FOURTHS), ALTERNATING WITH SOUR CREAM (IN THIRDS). ADD COFFEE AND LIQUEUR, BLENDING UNTIL SMOOTH. POUR BATTER INTO PANS AND BAKE 30-35 MINUTES, OR UNTIL SURFACE SPRINGS BACK. COOL IN PANS FOR 10 MINUTES, THEN REMOVE FROM PANS AND COOL ON WIRE RACKS.

TO MAKE FILLING: BEAT CREAM UNTIL IT BEGINS TO THICKEN. SPRINKLE IN ICING SUGAR AND BEAT UNTIL STIFF. REFRIGERATE. SLICE CAKE LAYERS IN HALF HORIZONTALLY TO MAKE 4 LAYERS. (CAKE LAYERS CUT MORE EASILY IF FROZEN FIRST). PLACE 1 LAYER, CUT SIDE UP, ON CAKE PLATE. SPREAD WITH ½ CUP (125 ML) RASPBERRY JAM AND ½ CUP (125 ML) WHIPPED CREAM MIXTURE. REPEAT WITH REMAINING LAYERS, ENDING WITH TOP LAYER, CUT SIDE DOWN.

CONTINUED ON PAGE 290

CHOCOLATE RASPBERRY TORTE

CONTINUED FROM PAGE 289.

TO MAKE FROSTING: MELT CHOCOLATE CHIPS IN TOP OF DOUBLE BOILER. ADD SOUR CREAM AND SALT AND BEAT UNTIL FROSTING IS CREAMY AND SMOOTH. FROST TOP AND SIDES OF CAKE. GARNISH WITH CHOCOLATE CURLS AND FRESH BERRIES. (FOR PERFECT CHOCOLATE CURLS, HEAT A CHOCOLATE SQUARE IN MICROWAVE FOR 10 SECONDS AND SHAVE WITH VEGETABLE PEELER.)

SUPER CHOCOLATE CAKE

THIS IS DARN GOOD!

1 CUP	WHITE SUGAR	250 ML
3 TBSP.	BUTTER, ROOM TEMPERATURE	45 ML
1	EGG, BEATEN	1
1/2 CUP	COCOA, FILL WITH BOILING WATER TO MAKE 1 CUP OF (250 ML) LIQUID	125 ML
1/2 TSP.	BAKING SODA	2 ML
1/2 CUP	BOILING WATER	125 ML
1 CUP	FLOUR	250 ML
1 TSP.	BAKING POWDER	5 ML

CREAM TOGETHER SUGAR AND BUTTER; ADD EGG AND COCOA LIQUID. MIX SODA AND BOILING WATER. ADD THIS, FLOUR AND BAKING POWDER, MIX WELL. POUR INTO GREASED 9" (23 CM) SQUARE PAN (THE BATTER WILL BE THIN). BAKE AT 350°F (180°C) FOR 30 MINUTES, OR UNTIL A TOOTHPICK INSERTED IN CENTER COMES OUT CLEAN. (THIS CAKE DOUBLES WELL. BAKE IN A 9 X 13" (23 X 33 CM) PAN OR A BUNDT PAN FOR 40-50 MINUTES.)

CHOCOLATE ZUCCHINI CAKE

A BEST OF BRIDGE FAVORITE.

1/4 CUP	BUTTER	60 ML
1/2 CUP	VEGETABLE OIL	125 ML
1 3/4 CUPS	SUGAR	425 ML
2	EGGS	2
1 TSP.	VANILLA	5 ML
1/2 CUP	BUTTERMILK OR SOUR MILK	125 ML
2 1/2 CUPS	FLOUR	625 ML
1/4 CUP	COCOA POWDER	60 ML
1/2 TSP.	BAKING POWDER	2 ML
1 TSP.	BAKING SODA	5 ML
1/2 TSP.	CINNAMON	2 ML
1/2 TSP.	CLOVES	2 ML
2 CUPS	GRATED ZUCCHINI	500 ML
1/4 CUP	CHOCOLATE CHIPS	60 ML

CREAM TOGETHER BUTTER, OIL, SUGAR, EGGS, VANILLA AND BUTTERMILK. SIFT DRY INGREDIENTS AND ADD TO CREAMED MIXTURE. MIX IN ZUCCHINI AND CHOCOLATE CHIPS. BAKE IN A GREASED AND FLOURED BUNDT PAN OR A 9 X 13" (23 X 33 CM) GREASED PAN AT 325°F (160°C) FOR 45 MINUTES. DELICIOUS!

A DAY WITHOUT SUNSHINE IS LIKE, NIGHT.

CHOCOLATE ANGEL FOOD CAKE

12	EGG WHITES, AT ROOM TEMPERATURE	12
2 TSP.	CREAM OF TARTAR	10 ML
1 CUP	SUGAR	250 ML
2 TSP.	VANILLA	10 ML
3/4 CUP	SUGAR	175 ML
1/4 TSP.	SALT	1 ML
1 CUP	FLOUR	250 ML
1/4 CUP	COCOA POWDER	60 ML
1 1/2 TSP.	BAKING SODA	7 ML
	SPRINKLING OF ICING SUGAR	

PREHEAT OVEN TO 350°F (180°C). IN A LARGE BOWL USING MEDIUM SPEED, BEAT EGG WHITES UNTIL FROTHY. ADD CREAM OF TARTAR; INCREASE MIXER SPEED TO HIGH. GRADUALLY ADD 1 CUP (250 ML) SUGAR AND VANILLA. BEAT UNTIL STIFF, GLOSSY PEAKS FORM. IN ANOTHER BOWL, COMBINE SUGAR, SALT, FLOUR, COCOA AND BAKING SODA. SIFT AND FOLD INTO EGG WHITES 1/3 AT A TIME. SPOON BATTER INTO UNGREASED ANGEL FOOD PAN. BAKE 40 MINUTES, OR UNTIL PICK INSERTED COMES OUT CLEAN. TO COOL CAKE, INVERT PAN. COOL 30 MINUTES. USING KNIFE, RELEASE SIDES AND MIDDLE OF CAKE FROM PAN. INVERT ONTO PLATE. SPRINKLE WITH ICING SUGAR. SERVE WITH FROZEN YOGURT. SERVES 16.

NOTE: TO USE THE EGG YOLKS, MAKE CRÈME BRÛLÉE (PAGE 259) OR AFTER ANGEL FOOD COOKIES (PAGE 233).

I BASE MOST OF MY FASHION TASTE ON WHAT DOESN'T ITCH!

KARROT'S CAKE

SO GOOD FOR YOUR EYESIGHT, NEVER MIND YOUR TASTE BUDS!

CAKE

³/₄ CUP	CORN OIL	175 ML
1 CUP	SUGAR	250 ML
3	EGGS	3
1½ CUPS	FLOUR	375 ML
½ TSP.	SALT	2 ML
1⅓ TSP.	BAKING SODA	6.5 ML
1½ TSP.	CINNAMON	7 ML
2 CUPS	FINELY GRATED CARROTS (4-5)	500 ML

ICING

8 OZ.	PKG. CREAM CHEESE, ROOM TEMPERATURE	250 G
¼ CUP	BUTTER, ROOM TEMPERATURE	60 ML
2½ CUPS	ICING SUGAR	625 ML
2 TSP.	VANILLA	10 ML

TO MAKE CAKE: BEAT TOGETHER OIL AND SUGAR. ADD EGGS, 1 AT A TIME, BEATING WELL AFTER EACH ADDITION. COMBINE DRY INGREDIENTS AND ADD TO EGG MIXTURE. BEAT ALL TOGETHER UNTIL WELL BLENDED. FOLD IN RAW CARROTS. BAKE 1 HOUR AT 300°F (150°C) IN A GREASED 9 X 13" (23 X 33 CM) PAN. (THIS CAN ALSO BE MADE IN A BUNDT PAN).

TO MAKE ICING: SOFTEN CHEESE AND BUTTER; BEAT WELL. ADD SUGAR AND VANILLA AND BEAT AGAIN. SPREAD ON COOLED CAKE.

INDEX

YOUR FAVORITES

YOUR FAVORITES

DB. 250-545-3947